Revelation and the Politics
of Apocalyptic Interpretation

Revelation and the Politics
of Apocalyptic Interpretation

Richard B. Hays
Stefan Alkier
Editors

BAYLOR UNIVERSITY PRESS

Cover design by Dean Bornstein
Cover image: The Four Horsemen of the Apocalypse, from The Apocalypse or the Revelation of St. John, c.1497–98 (woodcut), Durer or Duerer, Albrecht (1471–1528) / Private Collection / Photo © Christie's Images / The Bridgeman Art Library

Library of Congress Cataloging-in-Publication Data

Revelation and the politics of apocalyptic interpretation / Richard B. Hays and Stefan Alkier, editors.
239 p. cm.
  Proceedings of a conference held Oct. 7-10, 2010 at Duke Divinity School.
  Includes bibliographical references (p. 203) and index.
  ISBN 978-1-60258-561-4 (hardback : alk. paper)
  1. Bible. N.T. Revelation--Criticism, interpretation, etc.--Congresses. 2. Bible. N.T. Revelation--Hermeneutics--Congresses. 3. Apocalyptic literature--History and criticism--Congresses. 4. Bible--Hermeneutics--Congresses. I. Hays, Richard B. II. Alkier, Stefan.
  BS2825.52.R48 2012
  228'.06--dc23
                                2011051802

BAYLOR
UNIVERSITY®

Contents

Introduction

Richard B. Hays and Stefan Alkier

The Revelation to John has had a huge impact on western culture and politics. It plays a major role in the religious and political worldview of many Christians, particularly in America. Yet it is sometimes regarded as the joker in the deck of biblical texts: this mysterious visionary text stubbornly refuses to fit into any of the usual theological categories, and it is completely unlike any other book of the New Testament.

Because the book is so difficult to interpret, it has spawned a wide variety of readings, all of which have political consequences. Is it a book that endorses prophetic civil disobedience and resistance to the power of oppressive governments? (John the Seer wrote the book while in exile on the island of Patmos, perhaps because he was regarded as a political threat to imperial authority.)[1] Or, on the other hand, does the book effectively counsel a passive withdrawal from practical political affairs—a withdrawal that has the effect, perhaps unintended, of sanctioning the political status quo? (It is sometimes proposed, for example, that the Apocalypse's visions of cosmic destruction in the endtime make Christians indifferent to ecological concerns: why bother with saving forests if the world will be ending soon?)[2] Does the book prophesy the formation of the modern state of Israel and the current conflicts in the Middle East? If so, should this affect the policies of western governments toward these conflicts? Or is this predictive-prophetic reading a misinterpretation of this ancient first-century text, a misinterpretation that can lead to fanaticism and disastrous political choices?

In any case, Revelation is a strange, visionary book, full of obscure imagery. And this fantastic imagery, drawn from the world of ancient

1

Jewish apocalyptic thought, seems alien to most Christians in mainline Protestant and Catholic churches, where the book is rarely preached on or taught. Indeed, in such churches, it has been de facto shunted to a peripheral status in the canon. One indication of this situation is that the Revised Common Lectionary (the list of Scripture readings prescribed to be read in worship services in ecumenical Protestant churches) includes in its triennial cycle only six passages from the entire book, and even these are carefully edited to screen out strange and violent elements. (The six passages are Rev 1:4-8; 5:11-14; 7:7-19; 21:1-6; 21:10, 21:22–22:5; 22:12-14, 16-17, 20-21.) It is particularly ironic that the framers of the Revised Common Lectionary have carefully deleted from the last of these readings the words of Revelation 22:18-19: "I warn everyone who hears the words of the prophecy of this book: if anyone adds to them, God will add to that person the plagues described in this book; if anyone takes away from the words of the book of this prophecy, God will take away that person's share in the tree of life and in the holy city, which are described in this book." To take another example that is indicative of the church's discomfort with the Apocalypse, none of the material from the letters to the seven churches (Rev 2 and 3) ever shows up in the lectionary. Thus, Christians who hear Revelation read only in public worship in churches that use this lectionary will hear some of its moving words of consolation and promise, but will encounter few of its puzzling visions and strong prophetic words of judgment. And thus the lectionary's sanitized, "G-rated" version of Revelation may itself be a puzzle, for most people, if they know anything at all about Revelation, know it not for its words of comfort but for its prophecies of judgment and doom.

On the other hand, in some evangelical and fundamentalist circles, Revelation seems to stand at the heart of the functional canon: its terrifying images are taken as literal predictions of factual events that must take place very soon in world history. A key text often thought to support such an interpretation is Revelation 22:6: "These words are trustworthy and true, for the Lord, the God of the spirits of the prophets, has sent his angel to show his servants what must soon take place." (Of course, much hinges on what is meant by the word "soon," as well as on the question of the *sense* in which the book's symbolism is "trustworthy and true.") The book of Revelation is a chief source for the story line of the popular *Left Behind* novels, as well as the basis for the widely read writings of Hal Lindsey (*The Late Great Planet Earth*), and for the prophetic warnings of numerous television evangelists.[3] Sadly, such readings of Revelation often seem to justify the judgment of Friedrich Nietzsche that the Apocalypse is "the most rabid outburst of vindictiveness in all recorded history."[4]

In reaction against such readings, modern historical scholarship has often sought to interpret the symbolism of Revelation exclusively in its first-century historical context, reading the book as a Christian outcry against persecution (or perceived persecution) under the Roman Empire.[5] While there is much to be learned from such interpretations, biblical scholars working in this vein have seldom grappled sufficiently with the question of how a work so specifically targeted to first-century historical circumstances might continue to function constructively in Christian theology. The strictly historical approach, complemented by archaeological work, has generated significant new knowledge and insights about the immediate context for the book's composition in the ancient Mediterranean world.[6] But the acquisition of such knowledge merely sets the stage for the hermeneutical task of reflecting on whether or how the Apocalypse might speak to us today.

One aspect of such hermeneutical reflection is the question of Revelation's role within the Christian canon—both in relation to its Old Testament antecedents and in relation to other New Testament texts that seem to describe the salvation offered in Jesus Christ in very different terms. Questions of this kind have a historical dimension, to be sure, but they are also literary and theological in character. To ask about the role of the book of Revelation within the canon, we must consider not only how the author may have been *influenced* by his sources and precursors; we must also consider literary issues about the interplay of images, and we must assess the theological impact of the juxtaposition of diverse ways of conceptualizing God's action in history.

Despite the complexity of these issues, the time is particularly propitious for a reassessment of Revelation. Recent scholarship has opened up several new avenues of inquiry that suggest both the need and the promise of such a fresh assessment. At least five important developments have contributed to this changed hermeneutical situation.

First, during the past generation we have learned a great deal about the diversity of first-century Jewish apocalyptic thought.[7] Some of the Dead Sea Scroll texts give us new insight into the apocalyptic worldview of at least one sectarian Jewish community contemporaneous with the earliest Christian movement—though very different from it.[8] Our increased understanding of apocalyptic traditions in ancient Judaism can contribute to a more nuanced and sympathetic reading of Revelation in a comparative historical context.

Second, at the same time, under the impact of the work of New Testament scholars such as Ernst Käsemann, J. Christiaan Beker, and J. Louis Martyn, we have gained a renewed appreciation for the *theological* importance of apocalyptic thought within the New Testament itself, not just in the book of Revelation, but also particularly in the Synoptic Gospels and Paul. While some theologians have made tentative efforts to engage this new appreciation of the apocalyptic elements in the New Testament,[9] there has been to date no satisfying fresh theological reading of the book of Revelation in light of these developments. Thus, one aim of the present volume is to work toward a constructive *theological* understanding of the Apocalypse that might be of assistance to preachers looking for guidance on how to preach this text and laypeople seeking to understand it more fully.

Third, recent New Testament scholarship has posed important new questions about the relation of the New Testament writings to the Roman imperial order. Several scholars have argued that the early Christian proclamation of Jesus as Lord (*kyrios*) and the announcement of the coming of God's kingdom posed a veiled but profound challenge to the Empire and its claims to sovereignty.[10] It has long been recognized that the Apocalypse represents some sort of confrontation with the power of Rome, but the precise dimensions and practical implications of this challenge require reassessment in light of recent findings. At the same time, ever since the founding of the modern state of Israel, speculative prophetic readings of Revelation have looked to contemporary events in the Middle East as fulfillments of prophecy, and it is sometimes believed that conservative evangelical support for Israel—motivated by heightened endtime expectation—has exercised a significant influence on American foreign policy. The events of recent history have focused attention squarely on the volatile mix of interests in the Middle East as the area of greatest significance for anyone concerned about international peace. We do not suppose that the book of Revelation holds all the keys to solving such problems. Nonetheless, the editors of this volume hope that a careful scholarly study of the politics of the Apocalypse, and of the appropriate hermeneutics for interpreting it, might clarify the ways in which Christians can constructively engage the political challenges of our time, rather than operating out of eschatological "scripts" written by ill-informed interpreters.

Fourth, biblical criticism over the past generation has focused attention on the hermeneutical significance of the biblical *canon*.[11] Rather than attending exclusively to individual books in their original historical setting, some scholarly circles have found it fruitful to focus attention on the literary and theological effects produced by the collection and placement of these writings within a larger composite body of Scriptures. Thus, a working hypothesis of the present volume is that the book of Revelation is best understood within its canonical context in the Christian Bible.

The symbolism of Revelation draws heavily on Old Testament prophetic texts, especially the books of Isaiah, Ezekiel, Daniel, and Zechariah; thus, in order to understand the Apocalypse well, we need to understand the complex way in which the author is reading these books and employing their ideas and images. Further, the book of Revelation must be read also in its relationship to the other witnesses of the New Testament. At issue here is not only the much-discussed problem of the relation of this book to the Johannine tradition found in the Gospel and Epistles of John, but also its connection to the other Gospels and Letters in the New Testament canon. This is not a matter of direct literary dependence, but of the *intertextual* conversation—or, to use a musical metaphor, counterpoint—created by the placement of the Apocalypse within the framework of a body of canonical texts.

Both of these aspects of the interpretation of Revelation—its use of Old Testament sources and its interconnection with other New Testament witnesses—point to a fifth reason why the time is right for a fresh study of the Apocalypse. The field of biblical studies has increasingly moved beyond simple source criticism and developed more refined theoretical models for understanding and practicing *intertextual interpretation*.[12] Consequently, the complex links between the Apocalypse and other biblical texts can be more deeply understood in light of theories of *intertextuality*. Standing in a climactic place of honor at the end of the Christian canon, the book of Revelation is a parade example of intertextual text production, and it demands of its readers sophisticated skills of intertextual reception. Many of the essays in the present volume explore this approach and demonstrate its fruitfulness.

Taken together, these factors led the editors of this volume to propose a collaborative interdisciplinary conference of leading scholars to deliberate about the interpretation of the book of Revelation.[13] We believed that the scholarly developments outlined here could be brought into a fresh conversation to shed new light on this powerful but enigmatic book. Thus, we arranged, with the support and co-sponsorship of the McDonald Agape Foundation, to host a conference entitled "The Book of Revelation: Theology, Politics, and Intertextuality." The conference—organized under the direction of Professor Richard B. Hays of Duke University and Professor Stefan Alkier of the Johann Wolfgang Goethe Universität in Frankfurt am Main, Germany—was held at Duke Divinity School, in Durham, North Carolina, on October 7–10, 2010. The present book assembles the papers delivered on that occasion, subsequently revised by the authors to incorporate new insights that emerged in the course of the conversations within the group of participating scholars.

Nine scholars were invited to deliver major conference papers. Crucial to the design of the conference was the diverse composition of the group. Rather than representing a narrow party line, we sought to encourage a sophisticated consensus interpretation arising out of the conversation of different voices. The group was international in composition, including participants from Canada, England, Germany, Scotland, and the United States. The group was also ecclesially diverse, including representation from the United Methodist, Lutheran, Presbyterian, Anglican, and Roman Catholic churches. Finally, while the majority of the participants were specialists in the study of the New Testament, we also deliberately included experts in the fields of Old Testament and systematic theology. The sequence of papers in this volume reproduces the order in which the papers were presented at the conference.

The first two essays by Michael Gorman and Steve Moyise provide important methodological framing for the papers that will follow. Gorman's essay surveys "the reception/impact history of the book of Revelation." He notes that this strange book presents "a perfect storm for polyvalence" and therefore highlights the need for a "ruled reading" that attends to context, canon, creed, and community, a reading that is hermeneutically grounded by "the central and centering vision" of the slaughtered Lamb. Moyise outlines three models of intertextual interpretation that focus respectively on the rhetorical design of the author, the impact of different intertextual "triggers," and the ideological commitments of communities of interpreters. He suggests that conscious naming of the different intertexts adduced by different interpreters may make the process of interpretation more transparent and lead to greater interpretative humility.

The next five essays in this volume then explore particular intertextual relations and themes of the book of Revelation. Thomas Hieke carefully analyzes the way in which the Apocalypse draws upon Daniel 7 to present a vision of "a reign with a human face" and to provide consolation and hope for a community of Christian readers. Richard Hays focuses on the Christology of Revelation and demonstrates the ways in which the book's intertextual allusions paradoxically portray Jesus as both a sharer in divine identity and as a faithful suffering witness/martyr who models the vocation of his community of followers. Joseph Mangina examines the ecclesiology of Revelation. He observes that in this book "the apocalypsing of Jesus Christ includes the mystery of the church," and that the mystery of the church is bound up with the way in which the church inhabits the scriptural role of Israel. In a wide-ranging essay on the political implications of the Revelation to John, N. T. Wright proposes that the ground of Christian hope lies in the book's vision of "the creator God reclaiming sovereignty over the whole world through the slaughtering of the Lamb, and entrusting to the present worshipping church the responsibility to bear witness to Jesus as the world's true lord." And Stefan Alkier shows how a close reading of Revelation's *intratextual* sign-structure yields a pragmatic interpretation of *Zeugenschaft* (witness) that enables readers to become witnesses rather than warriors. Integral to Alkier's argument is the insight that "[t]he visions do not depict, but rather symbolize, that which will happen and that which happens now."

The final two papers in this volume reflect more broadly on the context in which we now read the book of Revelation. Tobias Nicklas offers a reflective essay that begins from the observation that Revelation serves as a culminating "keystone" of the Christian Bible and asks what would be missing if we did not have this book in the canon. He sketches a number of crucial theological contributions of Revelation, including its critique of comfortable compromise with majority culture, its critical view of the state, its emphasis on the transcendent mystery of God, and its voicing of the cry for justice for those who suffer. But, at the same time, he also explores the ways in which this prophetic book requires supplementation or correction by other voices in the canon. Marianne Meye Thompson concludes this collection of essays with an overview of theological interpretation of the book of Revelation today. After a critical engagement with popular dispensationalist readings, she sets forth five prescriptive theses for theological interpretation, including a final convergence with Nicklas in an appeal that the book of Revelation be read in a canonical context.

Indeed, "convergence" aptly describes the remarkable ways that these independently authored essays point toward a common set of proposals and convictions about the proper interpretation of the Apocalypse for our time. Though the authors come from various cultures and ecclesial contexts, as well as different theological disciplines, they represent broad agreement on certain key points, among which are the following six areas of convergence:

1. Revelation's visions are to be read as poetic symbolism rather than literal description or prediction; literalistic interpretation can lead to disastrous misinterpretation.
2. The book's symbolism must be understood through understanding its intertextual relation to Israel's Scriptures.
3. The book's message is centered christologically on the symbolic depiction of Jesus as crucified and triumphant Lord.

4. The book summons its readers to follow the pattern of Jesus through countercultural, suffering witness to the one God, rather than through acts of violence.
5. In the theological world of the Apocalypse, there can be no separation of the spiritual and political spheres.
6. The book points to the future hope of God's triumphant justice and God's healing of the created world—not its destruction.

When these points of convergence are stated baldly as numbered points, they may seem obvious to some readers, but the nuanced outworking of this hermeneutical approach in the essays collected here is anything but obvious. These essays are filled with luminous, particular insights, and one of the pleasures of reading them together is to see how these nine distinct approaches to the book of Revelation complement and illumine one another.

* * *

At the conference, several faculty members from Duke Divinity School served as respondents to the papers. Though their responses are not included in this volume, we want to record our thanks to the following colleagues for their probing critical responses, which stimulated intense discussion and led to numerous material refinements of the papers in their final published form: Stephen Chapman, Paul J. Griffiths, Willie Jennings, Joel Marcus, David Moffitt, Sujin Pak, Anathea Portier-Young, and C. Kavin Rowe. We are grateful to these scholars for their rich contributions to the conference, as well as to doctoral students who attended the sessions and asked helpful questions.

Marsa McNutt, special assistant to the Dean of Duke Divinity School, labored faithfully for many hours in the administrative work that made the conference come together and flow smoothly. Rachael Wheatley also provided essential logistical support. David Arcus, the Chapel Organist of Duke Divinity School, performed a brilliant concert for the participants on the Goodson Chapel organ—a soul-nourishing interlude in the midst of an intense academic conference. Finally, N. T. Wright provided a splendid conclusion to the proceedings by preaching in Duke University Chapel on Sunday morning, October 10, 2010.

Above all, our particular gratitude goes to Alonzo L. McDonald, who not only provided the necessary funding for this research conference through the McDonald Agape Foundation, but also enriched it by his personal attendance and participation. Al's extensive experience in the world of politics, his theological passion, and his incisive questions opened up many valuable insights for all who were privileged to participate in this event.

In the preparation of the book for publication, skillful editorial work was done by Judith Heyhoe, Faculty Editor at Duke Divinity School. The editors would like to acknowledge her indispensable assistance. Joshua Leim, a doctoral student at Duke, provided research assistance in the editing process and double-checked Hebrew and Greek citations. Thanks are due also to Dr. Carey Newman and his staff at Baylor University Press, who encouraged the publication of this collection of essays and saw it through to production in a timely manner.

* * *

It is impossible for a book such as this to convey adequately the gracious spirit, theological gravitas, good humor, and general joie de vivre that surrounded the whole conference in October of 2010. The participants came to the conclusion of the meetings with a sense—not entirely common in academic conferences—that we had forged new bonds of friendship with one another. Readers of these essays will not find a consensus on all points, but—as noted above—we believe the essays do embody a significant convergence of perspective. They share an appreciation for the symbolic and "theopoetic" power and complexity of the Apocalypse, a resistance to narrowly literalistic predictive readings, a disposition to read the text as calling followers of Jesus to nonviolent resistance of secular power, and a deep engagement with the christocentric message of the book.

The editors dare to hope that readers of these essays will find themselves also drawn into a similar approach to interpretation, and into the conviction that the Spirit may still be speaking to the churches today through the book of Revelation.

Richard B. Hays, Duke Divinity School,
Durham, North Carolina, United States

Stefan Alkier, Johann Wolfgang Goethe-Universität,
Frankfurt am Main, Germany

1

What Has the Spirit Been Saying?
Theological and Hermeneutical Reflections on the Reception/Impact History of the Book of Revelation

Michael J. Gorman

"If you're going to marry the church, you ought to know who she's been with over the years." So begins the study of church history at St. Mary's Seminary, as my Catholic colleague addresses his first-year students, all would-be priests. One might well apply that advice to the study of Revelation, whether or not one is fond enough of the book to marry it, à la Luther and Galatians. If one is going to spend any time with the Apocalypse, and especially if one thinks, as I do, that the church should embrace it enthusiastically,[1] one ought to know something of its story.

For some, Revelation's story, its history of interpretation, is part of the darker side of Christian history. G. K. Chesterton's oft-quoted comment expresses this perspective well: "[T]hough St. John the Evangelist saw many strange monsters in his vision, he saw no creature so wild as one of his own commentators."[2] So also Luther's remark, centuries earlier: "Some have even brewed it [Revelation] into many stupid things out of their own heads."[3] And more recently, Eugene Boring has said that "no other part of the Bible has provided such a happy hunting ground for all sorts of bizarre and dangerous interpretations,"[4] while Luke Johnson laments the book's reception history at some length, saying:

> Few writings in all of literature have been so obsessively read with such generally disastrous results as the Book of Revelation (= the Apocalypse). Its history of interpretation is largely a story of tragic misinterpretation, resulting from a fundamental misapprehension of the work's literary form and purpose. Insofar as its arcane symbols have fed the treasury of prayer and poetry, its influence has been benign. More often, these

same symbols have nurtured delusionary systems, both private and public, to the destruction of their fashioners and to the discredit of the
writing.[5]

Or, in a nutshell: Revelation is "arguably the most dangerous book in the
history of Christendom."[6]

Not everyone shares this sentiment. Judith Kovacs, for instance,
while acknowledging the problems with Revelation and its interpretation, says that "[o]ver time, the book has provided a warrant for protest
against oppressive political and religious systems, a guide for life in the
present, and a resource for worship" and that its "reception history has
some lessons to teach us" for our own day.[7] I would especially emphasize
that the history of interpreting Revelation has not led only to dangerous
and delusionary systems. It has also produced some of the most sublime
music and some of the most penetrating visual art in human history. It
has also expressed the quest for answers to some of humanity's most profound questions about God, the future, and the nature of evil. Witness,
for instance, Bernard McGinn's riveting study *Antichrist: Two Thousand
Years of the Human Fascination with Evil.*[8]

My own fascination with Revelation and its reception history began
thirty years ago in studies with Bruce Metzger at Princeton. Metzger regularly included references to musical, artistic, political, and other interpretations of Revelation over the centuries. When I began teaching Revelation,
first as Metzger's assistant and then on my own, I did the same thing. For
twenty years now, I have offered a course entitled "The Book of Revelation and Its Interpreters." Over the years, my own reading, coupled with
student presentations and papers, has spanned the interpretive gamut
from the church fathers to medieval theologians to the Salvation Army to
contemporary Christian music to graphic novels (what used to be called
"comic books")—and everything in between.

In this essay I reflect theologically and hermeneutically on Revelation's history of interpretation, which I will refer to as both reception
history and impact history, with a slight preference for the latter. After
some general comments about reception/impact history as a theological
discipline, followed by some observations about the various kinds of interpretations of Revelation and some suggestions about the reasons for that
great variety, I will offer seven (naturally) theological and hermeneutical
reflections on the reception/impact history of this last book of the Bible.

Reception/Impact History as Theological and Hermeneutical Discipline

The history of interpretation of biblical books has become something of a cottage industry during the last two decades. Dissertations, monographs, collections of essays, articles, a distinguished commentary series in English (Blackwell Bible Commentaries) as well as one in German (Evangelisch-katholischer Kommentar [EKK]), and sections of professional meetings have all been devoted to the history of interpretation.

The term to describe this phenomenon of studying a text's later interpretation has evolved. "History of interpretation" may wrongly imply, especially for a book like Revelation, that we are limiting ourselves to intellectual history or to written commentary. But "reception history" and "impact history" each suggest a broader range of responses and effects—in and upon music and other arts, politics, liturgy, Christian practices, and so on, as well as on theology. Ulrich Luz, a major advocate of the study of reception history, agrees that it is important to consider these varied aspects of a text's impact. In affirming Gerhad Ebeling's famous remark that "Church history is the history of the exposition of scripture," he claims that Ebeling intended "exposition" to include non-verbal media of interpretation.[9]

Of the two terms I use, by "reception history" I mean to suggest the active response to, and welcome of, a work by its varied audiences, while by "impact history" I wish to suggest the power of the work itself, with a more passive role given to the audience. Theologically, the latter stresses divine initiative and inspiration, the former human response and reaction. As in many other questions of divine initiative and human response, the two can be seen as somewhat distinct but ultimately inseparable.[10]

What I am calling impact history is sometimes also called "effective history." The German word *Wirkungsgeschichte*, borrowed from Gadamer and often translated into English as "effective history," is a much better term in German than in English, since in English "effective history" may imply a narrow focus on that which has been effective or successful according to some arbitrary criteria. If, however, we understand *Wirkungsgeschichte*, as "history of influence and effects,"[11] then "impact history" is a suitable term in English, and better than "effective history."

Reception/impact history, then, is not merely an academic sub-field of historical, liturgical, artistic, or political studies. It is above all a theological discipline that should be taken seriously as such, and it is so in at least three major ways.

First of all, paying attention to impact history (i.e., stressing "impact") is a way of affirming and embodying the theological claim contained in biblical texts such as Isaiah 55:10-11 and Romans 1:16:

> For as the rain and the snow come down from heaven, and do not return there until they have watered the earth, making it bring forth and sprout, giving seed to the sower and bread to the eater, so shall my word be that goes out from my mouth; it shall not return to me empty, but it shall accomplish that which I purpose, and succeed in the thing for which I sent it. (Isa 55:10-11)

> For I am not ashamed of the gospel; it is the power of God for salvation to everyone who has faith, to the Jew first and also to the Greek. (Rom 1:16)

That is to say, the word of the Lord is an effective word, a performative utterance. It makes things happen. Of course this claim does not preclude human involvement (or error!) in the impact history of the text, though it does suggest that studying impact history is not merely an intellectual curiosity but rather a serious theological enterprise.

Second, attending to reception history (i.e., with emphasis on "reception") is a way of affirming and embodying the related theological claim contained in texts such as Romans 15:4a: "For whatever was written in former days was written for our instruction."[12] That is, the word of God speaks beyond its original era and audience to later times and people. Luz bemoans the situation of contemporary New Testament theology, in which reception history does not matter much because, he contends, New Testament theology is seldom seen as a truly theological discipline.[13]

Third, attending to reception/impact history is also a way of affirming and embodying the unity of the church over time that we confess in the creed. Joel Green persuasively argues that a crucial difference between simply reading the Bible and reading it *as Scripture* is that reading it as Scripture entails an assumption that we are part of the one people of God throughout time and space, from the first audience to hear/read the scriptural text, through all later communities of faith, up to our own time.[14] At the same time, we affirm that God speaks through Scripture, not only to the church, but also to the greater world. Musicians and other artists, whether inside the church or not, give expression to the impact of the word of God on humanity. In a certain sense, the ongoing influence of Revelation on various cultures attests both to the power of the Word and to humanity's unity-in-diversity.

These three general theological claims—two about Scripture, one about the church and the world—that argue for the significance of attending to

reception/impact history seriously may be supplemented by other, specifically hermeneutical, reasons to do so. Markus Bockmuehl, in fact, brings
the theological and the hermeneutical together. He claims that "effective
history" helps interpreters see the New Testament

> as not just a historical but also a historic document. Its place in his-
> tory clearly comprises not just an original setting but a history of lived
> responses to the historical and eternal realities to which it testifies. The
> meaning of a text is in practice deeply intertwined with its own tradition
> of hearing and heeding, interpretation and performance.[15]

The specifically hermeneutical reasons for studying reception/impact
history are considered in detail by Luz, who contends that "the study of
reception history is an excellent tool to regain what we might call the
'consciousness of effective history,'"[16] without which we cannot understand "why we have become what we are—spiritually, ecclesiastically, cul-
turally."[17] Luz argues that this consciousness of effective history develops
from the appreciation of a text's reception history (abbreviated here as
RH) in five respects:

1. As with historical study of Scripture's original contexts, but in a
    different way, study of the RH causes us to discover that there is
    no "naïve simultaneity" with the biblical text.[18] Unlike historical
    reconstruction, which creates that infamous "'ugly ditch' of an
    insurmountable distance between past text and present reader,"
    impact history "shows that this historical distance between then
    and now is not an ugly ditch, but a highly diverse landscape."[19]
2. RH helps us recognize the role of the interpreter in interpreta-
    tion, overcome the distance we have found in historical analysis,
    and "de-objectiviz[e]" the process of interpretation.[20] By revealing
    changes and currents in interpretation, it "helps toward a contex-
    tual exegesis."[21]
3. Knowing the text's RH leads to more holistic interpretations
    that consider non-scholarly and non-print interpretations.[22] It
    "reminds theologians that they are not the only, and not the most
    important, persons who interpret the Bible."[23]
4. RH reveals the ecumenical and even universal dimensions of
    interpretation, which may provide us with "different eyes."[24]
5. RH presents us with examples of good and bad interpretations,
    which we can and must judge not only by the theological ideas
    proposed but also by their effects, as Augustine said centuries ago
    in proposing love of God and neighbor as the criterion for evalu-
    ating biblical interpretations.[25]

All of these considerations, I would suggest, apply to Revelation, and there will be echoes of them in my own reflections below.[26] We shall have to return especially to the question of good and bad interpretations (Luz's fifth point) later, but mentioning it now does raise the related questions of why there have been so many interpretations of Revelation and what kinds of interpretations they have been. We begin with the second question.

Revelation and Its Many Interpretations: What

The Apocalypse has given rise to a wonderful, if sometimes bizarre, story of reception and impact. There are the spiritual readings of people like Methodius, Origen, John of the Cross, and John Bunyan; the political readings of the early Anabaptists, Joseph Priestley, Allan Boesak, William Stringfellow, and others; the aesthetic interpretations of artists such as Albrecht Dürer, G. F. Handel, Christina Rossetti, and William Blake; the church-historical interpretations of Joachim of Fiore and his heirs; the millenarian readings of Tim LaHaye, Hal Lindsey, C. I. Scofield, J. N. Darby, and their ancestors, all the way back to Irenaeus; and many others.

The reception/impact history of Revelation has received significant scholarly attention. Perhaps best known in contemporary theological circles are *Mysterious Apocalypse* by Arthur Wainwright and the Blackwell Bible Commentary by Judith Kovacs and Christopher Rowland.[27] Each of these volumes has extensive bibliographies for more detailed studies, while helpful surveys have been written by Kovacs, Rowland, and others.[28]

In their Blackwell commentary, Kovacs and Rowland provide two different ways of organizing the various interpretations of Revelation.[29] They contend that there are two ends of a wide hermeneutical spectrum for Revelation, the "decoding" pole and the "actualizing" pole. Decoding interpreters focus on details and try to make correlations between the text and specific events and people (whether contemporary or future). Actualizing interpreters, on the other hand, seek to "convey the spirit of the text" and to "perform" it in new contexts. Every interpretation, they argue, falls somewhere between these two poles of the spectrum.[30] I refer to these two interpretive poles as representing a hermeneutic of *correspondence* and a hermeneutic of *analogy*.[31]

Additionally, Kovacs and Rowland, like many other students of Revelation's history of interpretation, observe that interpreters of the Apocalypse, while tending to focus on one temporal aspect of the text—the past, present, or future—do not neglect the others. For instance (this is my example, not theirs), even futurist interpreters such as Hal Lindsey and Tim LaHaye view Revelation as a divine word that addressed the first-century church, spoke to and about the church for the last 2,000 years, and speaks to the church today, even as they emphasize its depiction of the future tribulation and associated events.

Combining these two simple systems of classifying approaches to Revelation, we can construct a graphic with an *x*-axis and a *y*-axis where we can plot interpreters' interests between decoding and actualizing strategies and among past, present, and future foci:[32]

DIAGRAM 1
STRATEGIES, GOALS, AND FOCI IN THE INTERPRETATION OF REVELATION

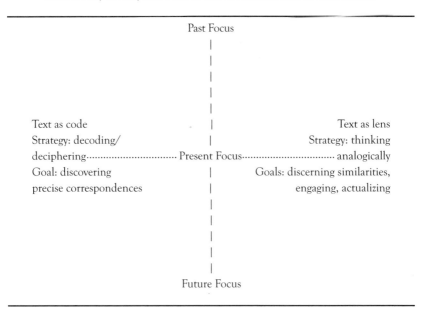

One could plot interpretations at various points on this graphic.

Richard Hays simplifies the whole matter by suggesting that there are three basic approaches to Revelation: predictive, historical, and theopoetic.[33] Of these the first two see the text primarily as code ("a puzzle to be solved"[34]), with one focusing on the future and one on the past. Craig Koester simplifies this schema still further by suggesting that from the earliest interpreters until today, the two primary hermeneutical options have been "futuristic" (like Hays' "predictive") and "timeless" (like Hays' "theopoetic"), that is, "a message about the future of the world" versus "a timeless message about God's relationship to human beings."[35] Why is this the case? Koester implies that it is because there is an "interplay between the futuristic and timeless elements" in Revelation itself, and this interplay has always engaged interpreters.[36] Koester's suggestion raises the even broader question of how we should account for all the various kinds of interpretations of Scripture's final book, to which we now turn.

Revelation and Its Many Interpretations: Why

No less significant than the variety of interpretations of Revelation is the question of the cause of this variety. Why have there been so many differ-ent reading strategies and results? There are at least five dimensions of the book itself that contribute to the incredible multivalence associated with the book of Revelation.

The first dimension is, of course, its *symbolism*. Symbolic language, whether in poetry or apocalyptic texts or elsewhere, is naturally open to multiple interpretations. At times, we may think that precision in the iden-tification and interpretation of a symbol in Revelation is highly important, such as the meaning of the blood on the robe of Jesus in 19:13. Arguments about the cultural referent of this or that detail, or the meaning of a par-ticular symbol, are inevitable, and sometimes critical. But such arguments should not inhibit—and clearly have not inhibited—the experience of the text's poetic, or theopoetic, vision. Indeed, as one critic said about the details of the images in "Ode on a Grecian Urn," the famous poem by John Keats, such disputes "testify to the enigmatic richness of meaning" in the text.[37]

Second, although many people would focus on Revelation's symbolism as the most important factor in its diverse reception history, symbolism alone does not account for all the variety. A second dimension is the *hybrid character* of Revelation. Gregory Linton reminds us that "different generic identities provide the reader with different expectations and therefore different interpretations," that "[d]isagreements about the interpretation of a text are often disagreements about its genre," and that the energy devoted to determining the genre of the Apocalypse is due to the assumed effect of genre on interpretation.[38] Many interpreters would agree with Richard Bauckham that Revelation is a hybrid of three genres, apocalypse, prophecy, and letter,[39] though some would argue that there is not much letter there and that Revelation is an apocalyptic prophecy in an epistolary framework or shell. But numerous interpreters also say that Revelation bears the mark of other genres. Some have called it a drama, a specimen of resistance literature, a manifesto against civil religion, a call to covenant faithfulness, a prediction of the last things, etc. All of these genres "do" different things to readers. If one identifies Revelation as a certain genre, one will interpret it as such, but the hybrid nature of Revelation itself will likely prevent the interpreter from reading it as a pure specimen of that form. The fact that Revelation is a "mixed breed" means that it will have certain features not found in purebreds. That is to say, the hybrid character of Revelation carries with it a kind of creative, generative force.

Linton agrees, arguing that when a text has mixed generic conventions, it offers "multiple possibilities" to the reader.[40] Furthermore, the most sophisticated literary works not only combine genres, they also "deform" genres—they break the rules of the generic game.[41] Drawing on the work of Thomas Ken on genre and interpretation, Linton points to *Moby Dick* as an example of both generic hybridity and generic deformity, and he suggests that this combination normally results not only in a multiplicity of interpretations but also in increased appreciation for the aesthetic value of the literature.[42] The hybrid character means that readers will choose to "foreground" some generic conventions and "background" others,[43] just like people do when they are "bombarded with more sensory stimuli than they can possibly be aware of at one time."[44] They engage in "selective attention."[45] So it is with Revelation.

Third, Linton also notes research indicating that generic hybrids are frequently more intertextual than "purer" forms.[46] This brings us to a third dimension of Revelation that contributes to its multiple interpretations: its *highly intertextual character*. An intertextual work, says Linton, is an "'open work,'" one that "allows readers greater space in which to create their own meaning from the text."[47] "The Apocalypse . . . is highly intertextual, it has mixed conventions of different kinds, and therefore it is open to multiple interpretations."[48] Linton warns—at length—against allowing a predetermined understanding of Revelation's genre, even the genre "apocalypse" (which is itself open to multiple interpretations!) to control or limit its interpretation.[49]

I do not mean to suggest that there are some texts that are non-intertextual. I would suggest, however, that some texts are more intertextual than others, and that a highly intertextual work like Revelation—with links to so many different kinds of texts and extra-textual realities—should also be called an "intertextualizing" or even a "genotextual" work. That is, it creates *extraordinary* quantities of new connections and intertexts (literary, cultural, theological), which in turn combine to create vast numbers of new mosaics and therefore generate an almost limitless supply of interpretations. If we consider this phenomenon theologically, we are driven back to the first of our three general theological claims: the word of God in Revelation is an "open work" that has an inherent performative, creative power. This power of God's word invites not merely objective interpretation of the mosaics it generates, but self-involving participation in the realities to which they testify.[50] We become intimately involved in the interpretive process, as receptive co-participants with others in the impact history of Revelation as divine word.

A fourth dimension of Revelation that contributes to its multiple interpretations is its *symbiosis of otherworldly and this-worldly phenomena*. When the heavenly Christ walks among lampstands (meaning churches) in cities with factual names like Ephesus and Laodicea, when the throne of Satan is identified with a city (Pergamum) having an actual throne-like acropolis, and when the souls of martyrs in heaven can be connected to real people like Antipas, then people's imaginations will be fired up. They will naturally make connections between their realities and hopes, on the one hand, and the realities and hopes expressed in the this-worldly and other-worldly images in Revelation. And since people's contexts will vary immensely from time to time and place to place, those connections will be vary greatly from one another. A contextual interpretation, a contingent theology, will of necessity emerge.

Finally, a fifth dimension of the Apocalypse that results in diverse interpretations is its *canonical position and function*. Like the last act of a play, Revelation is the last act of the canonical drama, the drama of salvation. And as the play's last act often does, it functions as the hermeneutical key to the whole. However, this relationship of the last act to the entire drama is not a one-way street but a relationship of mutual influence, the whole affecting the understanding of the end, and vice versa. This too accounts for diversity in the interpretation of Revelation. What is the story that it brings to its conclusion? What exactly is salvation? These are such weighty questions, with such varied answers, that readings of Revelation, where the story of salvation reaches its goal, are bound to be diverse.

Bringing all these factors together in one book creates a perfect storm for polyvalence. And that is precisely what happens in the case of Revelation. Our task now is to offer several theological and hermeneutical reflections on this reality. We will naturally build, in part, on the more general theological and hermeneutical remarks about impact history and about Revelation made so far.

Seven Theological and Hermeneutical Reflections

By way of a prefatory observation, I would like to make a particular claim about the Apocalypse: it is Scripture writ large, Scripture in high definition, if you will. This final book of the canon is not a subtle text, but one that pops out of the box and lands right in front of your face. This character of Revelation both highlights and exaggerates the theological and hermeneutical issues associated with scriptural interpretation generally and with reception/impact history specifically. If it is true that hard cases make bad law, it is also true that hard cases, or (in this case) hi-def examples of Scripture, may help us see issues more clearly than we otherwise would.

The reception/impact history of Revelation is an exercise in the communion of the saints, which can be an exhilarating but also a frustrating fellowship. It is therefore also an exercise in the spiritual disciplines of tolerance and forgiveness, on the one hand, and of humility and self-criticism, on the other.

If we believe that there is only one church, then the interpretation of Revelation in the church is one of the practices that we share with saints past and present, and the interpretations themselves are part of our common story. Revelation's reception history acts like a meandering path connecting us to its original audience and to all those we find along the way. When Ulrich Luz claims that reception history demonstrates that the "historical distance between then and now is . . . a highly diverse landscape," he also continues by saying that this landscape has "a lot of ups and downs, unexpected views, side-valleys, plains and viewpoints and with a wealth of wonderful and sometimes very strange flowers." Recognizing this wondrous diversity "makes it difficult to condemn and deplore" it, as Protestants in particular have often been wont to do.[51]

We have much to learn from other interpreters, and studying Revelation's reception history has the potential to benefit us immensely. This potential benefit comes not only from past interpreters but also from contemporary readers of Revelation whose theological and cultural perspectives differ from our own. An excellent resource for this is the collection of essays edited by David Rhoads, *From Every People and Nation: The Book of Revelation in Intercultural Perspective.*[52] One example of the impact that reading Revelation with persons from other cultural contexts can have is the experience of American biblical scholars who have taught Revelation in places like South America and India, where they have often found their students unanimously and unhesitatingly connecting the beast of Revelation 13 to the United States.[53]

At the same time, if there is even a grain of truth in G. K. Chesterton's comment cited above—and surely there is—then we will need to learn to tolerate or even forgive interpreters with whom we strongly disagree. Like us, they were and are mostly faithful people partially enlightened and partially blinded by their own personal, ecclesial, and cultural contexts. The reception history of Revelation reveals the need for hermeneutical humility and the corollary need for self-criticism in our scriptural interpretation and in our theology more generally. One scriptural motto for students of Revelation's reception history should surely be, "Let those who are without sin cast the first stone." I for one have yet to find a sinless interpreter, myself included.

This does not mean, however, that we take a laissez-faire attitude toward the interpretation of Revelation, for if scriptural interpretation in general can do harm, interpretations of Revelation can do, and sometimes have done, *enormous* harm.[54] Responsible interpretation requires criticism of bad interpretations, even if we finally forgive the interpreters, however difficult it may be at times to establish criteria for such interpretations. (On this, see further below.) At the same time, Ellen Charry rightly points out that *self*-criticism is especially important for apocalyptic thinkers.[55] I would add that self-criticism is important as well for interpreters of apocalyptic thinkers (such as commentators on Revelation) and for interpreters of interpreters of apocalyptic thinkers (such as historians of Revelation's reception).[56]

The reception/impact history of Revelation demonstrates, in an extreme way, both the almost unlimited polyvalence of Scripture and the corollary need for a ruled reading of Scripture to assess the appropriateness and truthfulness of our interpretations. Elements of such a ruled reading will include context, canon, creed (especially a robust theology of the cross), and community.

As we have already noted, the variety of interpretations of Revelation is stunning, perhaps more varied and, at times, more disconcerting than the interpretation of any other biblical book. As the interpretation of Scripture writ large, the reception history of Revelation shows that almost anything goes.

But of course, at least theologically speaking, it cannot be the case that anything, or even almost anything, goes in the interpretation of Scripture. We speak of "underdetermined" rather than "indeterminate" interpretation (so Stephen Fowl), of "bounded variety" (so Todd Billings), or of "limited polyvalence" (my own term).[57] The reception history of Revelation reveals the need for a ruled reading,[58] for a framework within which Scripture can be interpreted theologically and responsibly. How can we tell a better from a poorer reading of Revelation? A more truthful from a less truthful, or even heretical, reading? To put the issue more starkly, in the words of Todd Billings while considering the relationship between cultural context and interpretive variety: "Some hermeneutical difference is due to human idolatry and sin, a cultural resistance to Scripture's transforming work."[59] Sadly, there have been plenty of very poor readings of Revelation; considering its reception/impact history provides "glimpses of a dark side" that highlight the need for an interpretive framework.[60]

I am not saying anything new for theological interpreters of Scripture by suggesting that four elements of such an interpretive framework are context, canon, creed (or the rule of faith), and community.

- By *context* I mean the original historical and literary contexts of the text, or at least something approximating those slippery entities. Edith Humphrey argues persuasively that the meaning of Revelation's visions, though the accounts of them are very "open" texts, are still in some measure constrained by their social and rhetorical contexts.[61] Therefore, a reading of Revelation that takes no thought of its rhetorical situation and its message to first-century believers in Asia Minor will normally—though not always—be inferior to one that does.[62] I say "not always" because there are certainly inspiring artistic and even textual interpretations of Revelation that manifest no awareness of the original contexts. But I would suggest that these interpretations often do display awareness of other elements of a ruled reading, such as the canon's metanarrative of creation/new creation. That is, they are sensitive to the *canonical* context.

- By *canon*, then, I wish to invoke the larger context of Scripture as a whole and, thereby, the principle of Scripture interpreting Scripture. In particular, with respect to Revelation, I would suggest that two canonical dimensions are particularly critical for good interpretation: the aforementioned metanarrative of creation/new creation and the epistemological criterion of the cross as the self-revelation of God's identity and purposes. Both of these are also central to the book of Revelation itself, as seen in the key images of the slaughtered Lamb and the new heaven and earth, which means that canon and (literary) context reinforce each other.

- By *creed*, I refer to something like the rule of faith, the common Christian convictions that spring forth from the canon and have become central to Christian belief and practice as expressed in the creeds, liturgy, and daily life. Readings of Revelation that explicitly or implicitly contradict fundamental Christian tenets and practices, including the basic demands of Christian discipleship, are *de facto* outside the bounds of appropriate Christian interpretation.[63]

  Of particular importance for interpreting Revelation is Christology—the teaching, ministry, death, and resurrection of Christ. Kovacs and Rowland put it this way: "If one were to expound the Apocalypse in such a way that its images led to a practice at odds with the pattern of Jesus' life, death and resurrection as found in the gospels, there would be an incompatibility with the gospel."[64] There is a special need for a robust theology of the cross when reading Revelation.[65] Like many interpreters, I have argued that the slaughtered Lamb is the central and centering vision in the book of Revelation.[66] *When this image is sidelined or overridden by other images, the interpretation of Revelation will almost certainly become, to one degree or another, anti-Christ.*

- Finally, by *community*, I mean especially the one Christian community, both over time and today, that in its better moments embodies the Augustinian principle of appropriate scriptural interpretation being that which increases love for God and others. With respect to assessing readings of Revelation, this element of ruled reading, in connection with the Christological criterion just noted, may be the most critical of all. Christopher Rowland, for example, has this to say about how to challenge the misguided readings of Revelation in the *Left Behind* series:

> The nature of Revelation's polyvalent imagery means that there is at the end of the day no refuting of readings like this. One can only appeal to consistency with the wider demand of the gospel and its application by generations of men and women in lives of service and involvement with the suffering and the marginalized to counter such world-denying and dehumanizing appropriations of Revelation and other biblical books.[67]

Rowland's comment shows clearly that creed (as I have defined it) and community are inextricably connected in the evaluation of interpretations of Revelation.

The impact history of Revelation vividly illustrates the potential of all of Scripture to excite and even convert the imagination, while revealing also the need for disciplined imagination. The history of Revelation's interpretation reminds us of the theopoetic character of all Scripture and, at its best, of Christian theology.

I allude here, of course, to Richard Hays' book *The Conversion of the Imagination*, a work on Paul's interpretation of Scripture, but a title with broader theological and hermeneutical import.[68] I refer as well to the comment of my teacher Bruce Metzger that Revelation appeals "primarily to our *imagination*—not, however, a freewheeling imagination, but a disciplined imagination."[69] The impact history of Revelation suggests that one of the primary effects of scriptural interpretation has been, and ought to be, the conversion of our imaginations. Richard Bauckham's comment about Revelation, that its intent is "to purge and to refurbish the Christian imagination,"[70] is both correct and applicable to Scripture more broadly, too. Revelation is a visionary book, the adjective referring not only to its contents but also to its power to "get us to view things differently."[71]

So-called "scientific" exegesis seldom accomplishes this as powerfully as other forms of interpretation do. In spite of the excesses and misinterpretations, Revelation also has had its share of inspired and inspiring interpreters, lovers of the book whose imaginations were captured by its visions, and whose converted imaginations have, in turn, ignited those of others. Without eschewing historical-critical pursuits, Kovacs and Rowland argue that any interpretation of biblical visionary texts like Revelation that "stimulates a later reader to 'see again' what the biblical prophet saw in his vision might in fact offer an understanding of the text that is more faithful to the text than the results of patient historical exposition."[72]

Artistic interpreters, such as G. F. Handel and William Blake, to name just two, have been especially tuned to Revelation's aesthetic and liturgical dimensions, and thus its ability to excite the imagination in the contemplation and worship of God, and in the consideration of divine mysteries. Others have had their political imaginations converted by Revelation's offer of hope to the oppressed, whether we think of certain Negro spirituals or Allan Boesak's *Comfort and Protest*, once again to offer just two examples.[73] The influence of these aspects of Revelation through the centuries has been not merely benign, as Luke Johnson claims in the text cited early in this essay, but transformative.[74] We will return to political interpretations momentarily; for now, I want to consider briefly the significance of artistic interpretations.

Probably more than any other biblical book, Revelation has been interpreted by musical and visual artists. Many contemporary interpreters of Scripture, especially biblical scholars, are "bounded by the captivity of our interpretive imagination to the representation of meaning in *words*," as A. K. M. Adam puts it.[75] He contends that, because human communication is often nonverbal, our theological hermeneutics must take interpretations that are not verbal, or not exclusively verbal, much more seriously. Adam writes: "Indeed, the more one attends to the ways we encounter and reason through meaning in non-verbal understanding, the more parochial and limited the domain of words seems."[76] God is, to be sure, a God of words, but also of deeds, of beauty, of vision—of words beyond words.[77]

Applying these observations directly to the impact history of Revelation, we might say that there is a complementary relationship between Revelation's imaginative, theopoetic interpretations and Revelation's transformative, theopoetic power. In other words, the body of centuries of visual and musical artistry is a major part of the evidence of what Revelation—and indeed all of Scripture—can do to us. The Christian church would benefit greatly, not only from greater attention to the arts,[78] but also from greater appreciation for the poetic, or theopoetic, character of Christian theology and practice.

The reception/impact history of Revelation manifests the dynamic tension between spiritual and political readings of Scripture, and of approaches to theology more generally, suggesting the need for a both/and rather than an either/or approach. Christian scriptural interpretation and existence are each inevitably and irreducibly both spiritual and political, coming together especially in worship as the fundamental theopolitical Christian practice.

One of the most striking features of Revelation's interpretation through the centuries is the concrete, this-worldly, political character of so many of those readings. To be sure, there are allegorical readings of Revelation as a story of the soul's journey to God, but much more often there have been blatantly political readings of the Apocalypse. This is certainly in large measure a function of the book's provocative images, especially its vividly portrayed characters, from the four horsemen to the two witnesses, and from the dragon and two beasts to the whore of Babylon. Such figures have called out for identification and thus for connection to the real world of ecclesial and secular politics, not primarily of the first century, but of the twenty-first, and before that of the eighteenth, the sixteenth, the twelfth, and so on. The political focus is likely due as well to the strong themes of resistance and hope that permeate the Apocalypse. Furthermore, as Udo Schnelle points out, "The Revelation of John only apparently portrays an event in distant worlds; the truth of the matter is the exact opposite, for it is entirely grounded in the present, this-worldly reality in which the churches to which it is addressed live. This immediacy explains its unique power and its enduring effects in the history of the church."[79]

For most interpreters, the political figures and struggles they have found in Revelation have also been part of a profoundly spiritual experience, normally understood (not surprisingly) as an apocalyptic battle between good and evil, God and the devil. In other words, most interpretations of Revelation have been simultaneously political and spiritual interpretations, and so much so that even describing these interpretations with those two different adjectives seems inaccurate.

Rather, I would suggest that reading Revelation has almost always been a unified politico-spiritual, or theopolitical, act, and that it should be. Moreover, the book of Revelation functions as a canonical reminder that *all* forms of Christian scriptural interpretation, theology, and existence are always simultaneously *coram Deo* and *coram mundo*; they are theopolitical practices. In recent years biblical scholars have discovered—though skeptics would say invented—the theopolitical dimensions of other biblical writings, such as the letters of Paul, the Gospels, the prophetic books, and other parts of the Christian Old Testament. Interest in, and conviction about, this hermeneutical tide will ebb and flow in the coming years, rightly or wrongly. But Revelation is the same yesterday, today, and forever. It is a theopolitical text.

This is true also because the heart of Revelation is worship, and worship is a theopolitical practice. Worship is the time within the flow of Christian existence when, *coram Deo*, personal and community narratives, identities, loves, and allegiances are expressed, reinforced, and shaped for action *coram mundo*, that is, for participation in the *missio Dei*. But here is the not so good news: to the degree that Scripture (especially Revelation) is misread, the church mis-worships and then mis-acts in the world. The other way around is also true: to the degree that the church mis-worships and mis-practices, it will also misread Scripture, especially the Apocalypse.

This does not mean that there should now be no eschatological dimension to our reading of Revelation; may it never be! Christian worship is meant to stimulate hope as well as faith and love. Judith Kovacs concludes her survey of Revelation's reception history in these words as an alternative to fixation on the book as "simply a blueprint for the future": "Could it not be that our Christian life would be enriched—in its worship of the Triune God, its sense of what his justice requires, and its expectation of a blessedness we cannot at present imagine—if we meditated carefully on the last book of the Christian canon?"[80] That is, Revelation enhances our liturgy, ethics, and eschatology, roughly equivalent to faith, love, and hope (on which see the following section).

The impact history of Revelation vividly illustrates the inherent hermeneutical dynamic of all of Scripture, namely the creative tension between the contingent and the coherent, or between the particular and the universal.

The previous reflection suggests that there is a profound unity-in-diversity within much of the tradition of Revelation's interpretation. The similar approaches to Revelation in various eras, especially the desire to correlate the book's symbolism with contemporary events and people (i.e., decoding, or employing a hermeneutic of correspondence), demonstrate something at the very core of Revelation: its simultaneous contingency and coherency, or particularity and universality. This is built into the very fabric of the document in several ways.[81]

First, Revelation is addressed to seven particular churches in Asia Minor, and yet the number seven almost certainly represents the church universal—historically speaking, in the first century, and theologically speaking, throughout all time. Second, each of the well-known particular messages to the various churches is addressed not only to that church, but also to the churches, as both the conclusion to each message states ("Let those with ears hear what the Spirit is saying to the churches") and the character of Revelation as a circular letter implies. Once again, these "churches" are not limited, at least theologically, to the first century. The universal claims of the text about the victory of the slaughtered Lamb and the coming new heaven and earth impinge on each church, but they do so in different ways from church to church. The lax church at Laodicea needs to hear a different word-on-target from the Lord than does the persecuted church at Smyrna, but they both need to hear the same overarching story.

Thus, at the very least, we should conclude that it is completely appropriate, natural, and *not* misguided to read Revelation in its particularity, that is, not merely as a document for the universal church but as a word from God to and for our *particular* situation centuries or even millennia later. In fact, to do so is to allow Revelation to fulfill its prophetic and canonical function, and not to do so would be to fail to acknowledge it as Scripture and thereby to treat it merely as a first-century apocalyptic text. The challenge, then, is to hear Revelation addressed to us without manipulating its content to our own ends.[82] That is, how do we allow Revelation to speak to us in its universal particularity without turning it into a ventriloquist's puppet that merely says what we want it to say, whether we want it to predict the day of Christ's return or the downfall of a particular political power? A disciplined imagination, a hermeneutic of analogy, and the practice of ruled reading will help prevent hermeneutical ventriloquism, though there are no absolute guarantees.

The impact history of Revelation demonstrates the validity and
even necessity of something like the fourfold sense of Scripture.

As one trained in the historical-critical method, I am among those who should be suspicious of other approaches to the text. The reception/impact history of Revelation might reinforce that suspicion in some. Commenting on what he thought to be the curious nature of certain motifs in current theological interpretation, one prominent New Testament scholar chimed in on his blog, "Give me that old-time historical-critical exegesis."

It might be wiser to look at the situation somewhat differently. "No book in the Bible raises the question of the nature of the exegetical task more acutely than the Apocalypse."[83] A plurality of interpretive approaches and interpretations is not only an indicative reality; it is also something of an ecclesial, and perhaps even a divine, imperative. Acknowledging that Revelation has spoken with multiple voices, in manifold ways, is a starting point for proposing some means to take full advantage of the variety, but also the *bounded* variety, of the word of God for the people of God. In addition to the four elements of a ruled reading noted above (context, canon, creed, and community), we who are producers of textual (rather than artistic) interpretations might benefit from utilizing the structure of the fourfold sense of Scripture as a way of reading Revelation theologically and responsibly. That structure supplements questions about the literal sense of the text with questions about faith (*the* allegorical, or doctrinal, sense), hope (*the* anagogical, or eschatological, sense), and love (*the* tropological, or moral, sense).

Such a proposal means, at the very least, that we continue our careful study of the historical, social, literary, and rhetorical dimensions of Revelation as a first-century text. It means as well that we look for analogies—though not precise correspondences—between the situations and claims of the first-century texts and our own day.[84] We then ask what the Spirit speaking in Revelation is calling us to believe, to hope for, and to do, and how all of those aspects are interconnected.

We might do well to consider N. T. Wright's interesting spin-off on the senses of Scripture when he writes about the fourfold love of God in reading Scripture, or what we might call the four senses of the hermeneutical task: interpreting Scripture as a practice of loving God with heart, soul, mind, and strength.[85] This will keep the interpretation of Revelation, and of Scripture as a whole, from becoming the speculative enterprise that it sometimes has become. There is no true interpretation without embodiment or actualization—becoming a living exegesis of the text. In the case of Revelation, that is no simple matter, and those who guide others in its interpretation and actualization need to understand the gravity of the task.

The reception/impact history of Revelation demonstrates the high degree of responsibility given to (or taken by) those who interpret the Apocalypse. Like all of Scripture, it should be read carefully as a prophetic word of both challenge and promise meant to increase our faith, hope, and love.

The so-called copyright at the end of Revelation—"I warn everyone who hears the words of the prophecy of this book: if anyone adds to them, God will add to that person the plagues described in this book" (22:18)—should also serve as a warning to interpreters. The warning is not to shun any interpretations except so-called literal readings (which are in fact always quite allegorical), but rather to take the interpretive task very seriously, and encourage others to do the same.

In the introduction to my book on Revelation, I recount a few horror stories related to the interpretation of the last book of the Bible, and I am sure there are many more that could be told.[86] My point was, and is, simply that there are enormous practical and pastoral implications in the interpretation of Revelation, perhaps more than there are for most biblical books. People's emotional, spiritual, physical, and even economic well-being can be negatively impacted in extraordinary ways by the interpretation of Revelation. Thus *lector caveat*, and even more so, *praeceptor caveat*—"Teacher beware!"

This need for interpretive care is ultimately grounded in a theological conviction: Revelation is a word from God. As such it must be handled carefully, appropriately (cf. 2 Tim 2:15). Craig Koester's review of Revelation's reception history includes a brief but fascinating interpretation of medieval readings of Revelation, especially Luther's, suggesting that there is a dialectic of warning and promise in those readings. The former views Revelation as a mirror for the church to confront itself, the latter as a storehouse of God's promises of sustenance in difficult times. Perhaps that is ultimately the dynamic of all Scripture, and of the Spirit's speech to all the church at all times.[87] This dynamic work of ongoing inspiration moves the church to a more complete participation in the life and mission of God, expressed concretely in lives of faithfulness, hope, and love.

Conclusion

As an open text, a hybrid document, Scripture writ large and projected in high definition, Revelation has been heard, and really beckons loudly to be heard, in the ways suggested by the preceding reflections. Much of the rest of Scripture, perhaps, only whispers the same message. Maybe the apocalyptic summons can alert us to the whispers of the rest of the canon as we seek to hear the prophetic Spirit continuing to speak words of challenge and promise to the church and the churches—and to the world. There is ultimately a unity in the diversity of their messages: the summons to follow the slaughtered Lamb into God's promised new creation.[88]

2

Models for Intertextual Interpretation
of Revelation

Steve Moyise

Introduction

The intertextual interpretation of biblical texts is not a new phenomenon but has always been practiced by the Christian church. Texts are not viewed as isolated units of meaning but are interpreted in the light of other texts (canon) and traditions ("rule of faith," creeds). This was not an innovation by the church but was widely used in the ancient world. In Jewish circles, it was later formulated in terms of certain exegetical rules (*middoth*) that governed the relationship between texts, while in the church, it found expression in the exegetical schools of Antioch and Alexandria and the fourfold meaning of Scripture practiced by medieval exegetes. As George Aichele puts it: "The canon opens a semiotic space within which creative interpretation of biblical texts is encouraged."[1]

However, the dominance of historical criticism in biblical studies over the last two centuries has changed all this. No longer can an interpretation be deemed correct because it is in agreement with traditional Christian doctrines. Rather, it must demonstrate that it was what the original author had in mind or (at the very least) could plausibly have had in mind. On this view, it is not only unnecessary to relate a text like Isaiah 7:14 ("Look, the young woman is with child and shall bear a son") to Matthew 1:23 ("Look, the virgin shall conceive and bear a son"), it is positively to be avoided. The meaning of Isaiah 7:14 is determined by its grammatical form and historical context and not by associating it with later texts or traditions. Texts can be *applied* to analogous situations, but changes in meaning are said to be a distortion of the original and are generally regarded as self-serving.

It is into this situation that the introduction of intertextual theory in biblical studies is best understood. The term (*intertextualité*) was first coined by Julia Kristeva in 1967 as a way of describing the dialogical relationship between "texts," broadly understood as a system of codes or signs. Moving away from traditional notions of agency and influence, she suggested that such relationships are more like an "*intersection of textual surfaces* rather than a *point.*"[2] No text is an island and, contrary to structuralist theory, a text cannot be understood in isolation but as part of a web or matrix of other texts. Each new text disturbs the fabric of existing texts as it jostles for a place in the canon of literature. Intertextuality suggests that the meaning of a text is not fixed but open to revision as new texts come along and reposition it.

Thus it was inevitable that the Christ-event and the texts that followed would reposition or reconfigure what went before. It was not simply an imposition on the texts, as historical critics have tended to argue; it is what texts do. This does not of course legitimate the *particular* reconfigurations found in the New Testament or in the councils and creeds that followed. But it challenges the view that such developments are automatically invalid because the meaning of earlier texts has been altered. Therefore, the use of intertextual theory in biblical studies has not only led to fresh insights,[3] it has also helped to rehabilitate what historical critics have often referred to as "pre-critical" interpretation.

However, as Anthony Thiselton points out, the application of such a broad understanding of intertextuality would result in an "infinite chain of semiotic effects"[4] and would therefore not be a viable mode of study. Thus in practice, the only way of applying intertextual theory to biblical texts is to reduce the number of intertexts to something more manageable. One way of doing this is to require the intertext to meet certain criteria, such as a level of common wording or a parallel sequence of ideas or themes. The interaction is then explored by considering the "semiotic effects" produced by the various "voices" in the text. Here, such things as the meaning of the intertext in its original setting, its relationship with other texts in the history of its tradition, and its role or function in the new work are understood as "voices" to be heard and in some way configured. In addition, modern interpreters will bring intertexts of their own, such as the history of the text's interpretation or specific events, such as the Holocaust or 9/11. Scholars differ in how much weight they give to these various "voices," resulting in different strategies or models of intertextuality.[5]

In what follows, I will discuss three models for the intertextual interpretation of the book of Revelation. The first model consists of a number of interpretations where priority is given to John's "voice," namely, his rhetorical purposes for writing. On this view, the various scriptural allusions have been chosen by John because they support his point of view; they are not offered as independent "voices" to be considered along with his own. As Meir Sternberg puts it, using someone else's words involves "tearing a piece of discourse from its original habitat and recontextualizing it within a new network of relations."[6] The violent language is deliberate and suggests a discontinuity: words are being forced to function in a context for which they were not designed.

A second model rests on the thought that a particular intertext has provided the "trigger" or "catalyst" for John's interpretations. Meaning is not therefore being imposed on the intertexts; they really do say what John wants them to say. For example, the book of Revelation opens with the words: "The revelation of Jesus Christ, which God gave him to show his servants what must soon take place" (Rev 1:1). This appears to imply that what follows will be something essentially new, but Greg Beale argues that this is a deliberate allusion to Daniel 2:28, 45, and so what follows should be read "within the thematic framework of Daniel 2 . . . or at least as closely linked to that framework."[7] In other words, John is not saying something essentially new but is seeking to clarify what is written in Daniel. On the other hand, other scholars think the allusion is more general, although it does serve to link John's book with what has gone before. Thus there are least two different approaches within this model. Some try to explicate John's meaning by focusing on the original context of the allusion, while others look to a wider intertextuality among related biblical writings. But in both cases, *something* in the biblical witness acted as a trigger for John's writing; it is not simply a matter of his own rhetorical purposes.

The third model of intertextual interpretation wishes to widen the field to include those texts or events that have influenced the modern interpreter. Faced with the task of configuring a number of "voices," modern interpreters are forced to make decisions about which are the most important or relevant,[8] which in turn raises questions about their own beliefs, commitments, and purposes. Historical critics strive to minimize the influence of these, but all historical reconstruction depends on certain prior commitments. This is why, for example, commentators are divided as to whether John is responding to a period of intense persecution from the Roman authorities (Rev 6:9-11) or laxity and collusion with them (18:4-5). On the other hand, a number of scholars, especially feminist interpreters, believe it is more honest to openly acknowledge one's own commitments and offer them—and one's interpretations—for public scrutiny. Thus this form of intertextuality can be best understood as a configuration of "voices" that also includes one's own.

Interpretations That Focus on John's Rhetorical Purposes

Perhaps the most obvious feature of the book of Revelation is the sheer quantity of violent language that it contains. As early as the seven messages (traditionally known as "letters"), John's adversary Jezebel will be thrown into great distress and her children (probably disciples) struck dead (Rev 2:22-23). In Revelation 6:4, the opening of the second seal will "take peace from the earth, so that people would slaughter one another." The blowing of the fifth trumpet brings forth a swarm of locusts to torture those who do not have the seal of God so that they will long for death but not find it (9:1-6). Revelation 14 speaks of a great harvest where those who worship the beast will be "tormented with fire and sulfur" and the "smoke of their torment goes up for ever and ever" (14:10-11). The chapter ends with a vision of the harvesting of the earth that results in a quantity of blood "as high as a horse's bridle, for a distance of about two hundred miles" (14:20). Revelation 19 describes a battle where a figure on a white horse destroys his enemies, and the birds of the air are invited to "eat the flesh of kings, the flesh of captains, the flesh of the mighty, the flesh of horses and their riders—flesh of all, both free and slave, both small and great" (19:18). Distressingly for many readers, the description "His eyes are like a flame of fire" (19:12) identifies the rider as the figure that appeared to John in the inaugural vision (1:14)—namely, the risen Christ—but here the figure's robe is bloody and from his mouth comes a sharp sword to strike down the nations and "tread the wine press of the fury of the wrath of God" (19:15).

George Caird

Much of this language draws on the various plagues, disasters, and judgments of the Old Testament, and various strategies have been employed by scholars to show that John intends to reinterpret them. One influential approach is that of George Caird, who drew attention to the fact that in the throne vision of Revelation 4–5, John *hears* that the "Lion of the tribe of Judah, the root of David, has conquered" (Rev 5:5), but *sees* a "Lamb standing as if it had been slaughtered" (5:6). Caird argues that this juxtaposition is deliberate, so that by "one stroke of brilliant artistry John has given us the key to all his use of the Old Testament."[9] What John *hears* is the Old Testament view of a conquering Messiah but what he is now enabled to *see* is the Christian view of victory through suffering. Caird says that it is as if John were saying to us, "Wherever the Old Testament speaks of the victory of the Messiah or the overthrow of the enemies of God, we are to remember that the gospel recognizes no other way of achieving these ends than the way of the Cross."[10]

Thus Caird's intertextuality is not so much the pitting of one text against another but the pitting of the Old Testament against Christian tradition. He has no interest in exploring what "lamb" traditions John might have had in mind; he simply asserts that for John, the lamb is a "symbol of self-sacrificing and redemptive love."[11] This is then used as the hermeneutical key for reinterpreting the other violent passages in the book. For example, although the "harvesting of the earth" passage draws on such texts as Joel 3:9-14 and Isaiah 63:1-6, Caird does not think that John is referring to the *judgment* of unbelievers but the *salvation* of believers: "Any Christian at the end of the first century would without a moment's hesitation recognize that the coming of the Son of Man with his angel reapers meant the gathering of God's people into the kingdom."[12] How then does he explain the huge quantity of blood that results? By identifying it not with the blood of Christ's enemies but the blood of the martyrs, thereby demonstrating that John sees the victory of the saints in the same terms as Christ's victory: "John has achieved yet another rebirth of images, and has found a way of telling his friends that Christ, who turned the Cross to victory and the four horsemen into angels of grace, can transform even the shambles of martyrdom into a glorious harvest-home."[13]

In his discussion of Revelation 19, Caird acknowledges that the battle draws on a number of Old Testament texts, including Isaiah 63, where it is clearly God who is treading the wine press and whose garments are soaked in the blood of his enemies. He remarks that it has "commonly been assumed that John must have kept close to his model, and that the blood here is the blood of the Rider's enemies also."[14] But John has the faculty for "kaleidoscopic changes of metaphor"[15] and so along with Revelation 14, Caird interprets the blood as that of the martyrs: "His blood has made their robes white, and theirs has made his red."[16] Interestingly, he can speak of the "gorging of the birds" as a fulfillment of the defeat of Gog and his armies from Ezekiel 39 but argues that its purpose here is to indicate the speed and swiftness of the result. Drawing on the Gospel saying where Jesus says, "Wherever the corpse is, there the vultures will gather" (Matt 24:28), Caird thinks that John's point is that "divine retribution is not less reliable than the birds."[17] Thus Caird's work is a good example of an intertextuality that assigns priority to John's point of view and rhetorical purposes. It corresponds to what Thomas Greene refers to as "heuristic" imitation, where texts "come to us advertising their derivation from the subtexts they carry with them, but having done that, they proceed to *distance themselves* from the subtexts and force us to recognize the poetic distance traversed."[18]

Jeffrey Vogelgesang

It has commonly been recognized that major sections of Revelation correspond closely to major sections of Ezekiel and in much the same order (throne vision, eating a scroll, sealing, scattering of coals, judgment of harlot Babylon, consequence for merchants and traders, defeat of Gog, gorging of birds, description and measurement of new temple/city, river of life, healing leaves).[19] Jeffrey Vogelgesang detects a pattern in John's usage that he calls "democratization," where what is bound and limited in Ezekiel is open and universal in Revelation. For example, God's promise to dwell with his people in Ezekiel 37:27 has become "peoples" in the plural in Revelation 21:3.[20] In his description of the tree of life, John follows Ezekiel's expansion of Genesis by assigning a healing role for the leaves, but adds "of the nations" (Rev 22:2). However, it is John's statement that the New Jerusalem does not have a temple, "for its temple is the Lord God the Almighty and the Lamb" (21:22), that is of most significance. John has been drawing extensively on Ezekiel 37–48 in Revelation 19–22 but then denies the very thing that these chapters are all about:

> John made detailed use of Ezekiel 40–48 in constructing the new Jerusalem vision. Yet a greater contrast with that vision, where seven of nine chapters describe the temple, its ordinances and its priests, and the glory of God dwelling therein, cannot be imagined.[21]

Alison Jack

Alison Jack thinks that John makes a dramatic change to Ezekiel's dry bones passage in Revelation 11. Ezekiel uses the imagery to refer to the restoration of Israel (Ezek 37:11) but John applies it to the resurrection of the two witnesses: "But after the three and a half days, the breath of life from God entered them, and they stood on their feet, and those who saw them were terrified" (Rev 11:11). It is an interesting allusion, since the wording appears to be dependent on the LXX of Ezekiel 37:5, 10, whereas a number of his other references to Ezekiel show dependence on the Hebrew.[22] Jack first draws on Neusner's definition of midrash as a form of interpretation that "holds together two competing truths, first, the authority of Scripture, and second, that equally ineluctable freedom of interpretation implicit in the conviction that Scripture speaks now."[23] But she then goes on to apply two themes from postmodern literary theory (marginalization and deconstruction) to John's application of the words to the two witnesses, concluding that "Ezekiel's message of comfort has been inverted, delayed and spiritualized into a heavenly reward for those who enter the world of suffering John creates."[24] This cannot be referred to as midrash, typology, or fulfillment since it is essentially a destabilizing reading. Neither can it reasonably be said to be drawing out the "semantic potential" of the text, since it forces it to function in a way that is contrary to Ezekiel 37. In Jack's view, John rhetorical purposes have overwhelmed the intertext.

Robert Royalty

Lastly, Robert Royalty uses the stricture of Revelation 22:18-19 ("I warn everyone who hears the words of the prophecy of this book: if anyone adds to them, God will add to that person the plagues described in this book . . .") to argue that John intends to silence every voice except his own. The text draws on Deuteronomy 4:2 ("You must neither add anything to what I command you nor take away anything from it") and 29:19, 20 ("All who hear the words of this oath . . . , thinking in their hearts, 'We are safe . . .'"; "All the curses written in this book will descend on them"). But according to Royalty, John is not evoking these warnings in order to allow Deuteronomy to "speak" to his readers. Rather, he is forcing the texts to conform to his own purposes, while simultaneously denying such interpretative freedom to his readers: "Revelation 22:18-19 is emblematic of the attack on John's opponents and the way the Apocalypse uses the Bible. John attempts to control interpretation of his text even as he deconstructs the Hebrew scriptures, the scroll that he has swallowed."[25] Thus whereas Caird and Vogelgesang applaud John's reinterpretations of Scripture (by making them more Christian), Royalty finds them ethically dubious. He concludes that unless the book of Revelation is itself deconstructed, its intertextuality represents the "death of scripture," for only John's authoritarian voice remains.[26]

Interpretations That Focus on John's Intertexts

Greg Beale

In contrast to such revisionary readings, many scholars believe that John alludes to Scripture because he thinks that the ancient "voices" continue to speak to the present situation. We have already noted Greg Beale's suggestion that Revelation 1:1 is a deliberate allusion to Daniel 2:28, 45, and that it is intended to inform readers that what follows is to be read in the light of that chapter. His approach is also to look for continuity and fulfillment in John's other Old Testament allusions. Thus his title for the discussion of the harvest of Revelation 14:14-20 is "Unbelievers Will Assuredly Suffer God's Thoroughgoing Judgment at the End of Time."[27] He thinks that the plain meaning of the words coincides so closely with the meaning of Joel 3:9-14 and Isaiah 63:1-6 that no reinterpretation is necessary or indicated by the text. Indeed, he thinks that John's two descriptions of the harvest (Rev 14:14-16 and 14:17-20) may well stem from the LXX's use of the plural "sickles" in Joel 4:13, whereas the Hebrew (3:13) has the singular ("Put in the sickle, for the harvest is ripe. Go in, tread, for the wine press is full. The vats overflow, for their wickedness is great"). Not surprisingly then, Beale takes the blood on the rider's garment in Revelation 19:13 to be that of his enemies, a view that he supports by citing a number of rabbinic references that understand Isaiah 63 to be God's judgment on his enemies. Beale says, "Christ's conviction of the impious will lead to his destruction of them, which will be as thoroughgoing as the crushing of grapes in a winepress."[28]

Beale does not think that Revelation 5 sets up a lion/lamb juxtaposition where military imagery is reinterpreted by the language of self-sacrifice. Both themes are present and correspond to what Christian tradition has referred to as Christ's first and second coming. Thus while Christ's initial victory was won in an "ironic manner" through his death as the Lamb of God, his future victory will be more straightforward. He will "judge decisively and openly both his earthly and cosmic enemies, including Satan himself."[29] In a similar way, Frederick Murphy asks "whether the warlike traits of a lion are replaced by the meekness of the Lamb or whether the messiah retains warlike qualities?"[30] His conclusion is that neither is replaced: "Christ won his victory over Satan and made possible the victory of Christians through his suffering and death. This is nonviolent. But he will also exercise force against the partisans of evil (chapter 19) and will punish them as they deserve."[31] Thus Scripture is not introduced in Revelation 5 in order to change its meaning; it is used because it significantly coincides with what John wants to say.

Richard Bauckham

In his aptly named book, *The Climax of Prophecy*, Richard Bauckham seeks to demonstrate that many of the passages in Revelation that have often been regarded as *impositions* on the Old Testament have been misunderstood. Thus the violent language of Revelation is appropriate when its genre is properly registered. Revelation is an example of a Christian war-scroll, where John makes "lavish use of militaristic *language* in a non-militaristic *sense*."[32] It is John's literary vehicle for communicating his message, and it is clear throughout Revelation that no actual violence takes place. Christians are not called to take up arms in their fight against evil, but the language of victory is nevertheless appropriate, for they are indeed engaged in a battle:

By reinterpreting the militant Messiah and his army John does not mean simply to set aside Israel's hopes for eschatological triumph: in the Lamb and his followers these hopes are both fulfilled and transformed. The Lamb really does conquer, though not by force of arms, and his followers really do share his victory, though not by violence.[33]

A rather different example is Bauckham's interpretation of the song of Moses and the Lamb in Revelation 15. It has perplexed commentators that what follows this description bears no relationship to Exodus 15 but appears to be a "pastiche of stereotypical hymnic phrases gathered primarily from the Psalms."[34] Bauckham, however, argues that it *is* based on Exodus 15 but that John was led by verbal association from Exodus 15:11 ("who is like you, O Lord, among the gods?") to three other texts, namely, Psalm 86:8-10, Psalm 98:1-2, and Jeremiah 10:7. From these three texts, by the "skilful use of recognized exegetical methods," John has discerned the content of the song to be sung in the new age. Bauckham defends the connection with Exodus 15 by citing five things that they have in common,[35] but his main point is that the language of the song is drawn from the three link passages. The significance of this is that these are among the most universalist passages in the Old Testament. Thus John's exposition of Exodus 15 via the three link passages has revealed the content of the new song and it is about universal salvation rather than judgment:

> Great and amazing are your deeds, Lord God the Almighty!
> Just and true are your ways, King of the nations!
> Lord, who will not fear and glorify your name?
> For you alone are holy.
> All nations will come and worship before you,
> for your judgments have been revealed. (Rev 15:3-4)

Paradise Restored

Perhaps the most explicit indication that Revelation should be seen in continuity with Old Testament texts can be found in John's references to the creation stories in Genesis. The first occurs in his message to the church in Ephesus, where those who overcome are given the promise that they will "eat from the tree of life that is in the paradise of God" (Rev 2:7). We are immediately reminded of Adam and Eve's expulsion from the Garden of Eden lest *ha-adam* ("the man" or "the human") "reach out his hand and take also from the tree of life, and eat, and live forever" (Gen 3:22).[36] The text does not say why this would be a bad thing. It is clearly related to the couple's act of disobedience, which has led to *ha-adam* knowing good and evil, but that does not appear to be bad in itself. According to the comment that follows ("See _ha-adam_ has become like one of us, knowing good and evil." Gen 3:22), the heavenly beings also possess such knowledge. Claus Westermann thinks that the original source of the Genesis tradition only knew of one tree (Gen 3:3, 5, 11) and the couple are banished for partaking of it.[37] The reference to the "tree of life" in Genesis 3:22 has caused the editor to add a second tree in Genesis 2:9 ("Out of the ground the Lord God made to grow every tree that is pleasant to the sight and good for food, _the tree of life also_ in the midst of the garden, and the tree of the knowledge of good and evil"). Gerhard Von Rad agrees but nevertheless tries to offer an explanation from the standpoint of the final form of the text. He says that the "severe denial of eternal life also has a merciful reverse side, namely, the withholding of a good which for man would have been unbearable in his present condition."[38]

The "tree of life" is largely absent from the rest of the Old Testament. Four verses in Proverbs (3:18; 11:30; 13:12; 15:4) state that various aspects of the wise or righteous are like _a_ tree of life, but the indefinite reference appears to mean "like a living tree," rather than a specific allusion to the Genesis story. The same can be said for Isaiah 65:22, where God's people are given the promise that they will be able to build houses and plant vineyards because their days will be "like a tree," a reference to longevity (the LXX has changed this to "the tree of life"). However, it is in the book of Ezekiel that the "tree of life" tradition is most prominent. There are references to the Garden of Eden in Ezekiel 28 and 31, but it is Ezekiel 47:12 that refers explicitly to the tree(s) of life:

> On the banks, on both sides of the river, there will grow all kinds of trees for food. Their leaves will not wither nor their fruit fail, but they will bear fresh fruit every month, because the water for them flows from the sanctuary. Their fruit will be for food, and their leaves for healing.

The relationship of this passage with the Genesis story is complex. Parallels include the wonderful fruit-bearing trees, a special river that waters them, and a particular reference to their fruit acting as food. On the other hand, there are many differences: Ezekiel does not refer to a particular "tree of life," the river flows from the sanctuary, the fruit appears every month, and a healing role is given to the leaves. Nothing in the promise to the church at Ephesus suggests that John has this plurality of therapeutic trees in mind, but when we turn to his vision of the New Jerusalem, we read:

> Then the angel showed me the river of the water of life, bright as crystal, flowing from the throne of God and of the Lamb through the middle of

the street of the city.[39] On either side of the river is the tree of life with its twelve kinds of fruit, producing its fruit each month; and the leaves of the tree are for the healing of the nations. (Rev 22:1-2)

The reference to a tree bearing fruit every month and the special healing property of its leaves confirms that John has Ezekiel 47 in mind. Indeed, many commentators suggest that John's singular reference to "the tree of life" must be intended as a collective, since its location is said to be on "either side of the river." As Beale says: "The one tree of life in the first garden has become many trees of life in the escalated paradisal state of the second garden. . . . But since these trees are all of the same kind as the original tree, they can be referred to from the perspective of their corporate unity as '*the* tree of life.'"[40] On the other hand, it is noteworthy that the singular is used here, as in the promise to the church at Ephesus, and also in its two further occurrences in Revelation 22:14, 19. It would seem that although John draws much of his imagery from Ezekiel 47, he does not want to lose the allusion to the singular "tree of life" from the Genesis account. It is possible that he is also drawing on traditions such as *1 Enoch* 24–25, where after the judgment, the elect will once again be granted access to the tree of life in the (new) paradise of God (see also *4 Ezra* 8; *T. Levi.* 18).

A second important allusion to the Paradise story occurs in Revelation 12. Drawing on a range of biblical and non-biblical sources, John sees a magnificent woman about to give birth to a son whose destiny is to "rule all the nations with a rod of iron" (Rev 12:5, drawing on Ps 2:9). Opposing this stands a "great red dragon, with seven heads and ten horns," poised to devour the child the moment it is born. When it is thwarted in this (the child is snatched away to God's throne), it turns its attentions first to the woman and then to her offspring (*sperma*). Although this might bring a faint recollection of Genesis 3:15 ("I will put enmity between you and the woman, and between your offspring and hers"), it is the specific identification in Revelation 12:9 that is significant: "The great dragon was thrown down, *that ancient serpent*, who is called the Devil and Satan, the deceiver of the whole world—he was thrown down to the earth, and his angels were thrown down with him" (emphasis added). Since the identification is repeated in Revelation 20:2, just before its final destruction in the lake of fire, it is clear that John is consciously forming an *inclusio* with the Garden of Eden story. In Genesis the serpent deceives Eve, and in Revelation it becomes the "deceiver of the whole world" (12:9), although it will finally be destroyed in the lake of fire. When John adds that Death will also be thrown into the fire

(Rev 20:14) and nothing "accursed will be found there anymore" (Rev 22:3), it would seem that the judgments of Genesis 3 have been lifted and the purposes of creation finally realized.[41]

Interpretations That Focus on the Reader's Intertexts

What the interpretations discussed above have in common is that they offer closure. They acknowledge that a number of factors need to be borne in mind when interpreting an allusive text such as Revelation but regard that work as essentially complete in itself. John's ideas about the Lion and the Lamb might once have jostled in his mind, but what we have in Revelation is his resolution of them. While there might be disagreement as to whether the purpose of the juxtaposition is best understood as replacement (not might but suffering), temporal sequence (suffering followed by might), or genre (might by means of suffering), the intertextuality is now closed. The reader (or community or church) is not required to add anything to this and if Royalty is correct, that is precisely what John intended.

However, the modern interpreter now finds the book of Revelation as part of a canon of Scripture. Physically, it is bound together with other books, sometimes with cross-references printed in the margins or footnotes. Theologically, it is to be read as part of a unified testimony of prophets and witnesses to the work of God in Israel, Christ, and the church. Thus while historical critics might confine their investigations to John's interpretation of Ezekiel (for example), the canon "opens a semiotic space within which creative interpretation of biblical texts is encouraged."[42] As a result, Paul Decock suggests that "Ezekiel is as much a commentary on Revelation as Revelation is a comment on Ezekiel."[43] And to the relief of many, the image of the conquering Christ in Revelation 19 does not stand alone buts sits alongside other images of Christ, whether from the Gospels, Acts, or the authors of the New Testament Epistles. But the interpretative freedom created by canon also has constraints, for "canonical intertextuality provides a carefully controlled context, and it produces a carefully limited range of ideologically satisfactory meanings."[44]

Nevertheless, what is ideologically acceptable to one community is heresy and distortion to another. For example, the various interpretations of the Lion/Lamb juxtaposition that we have discussed are clearly influenced by the interpreter's vision of God and/or Christianity. Some tend toward universalism (and perhaps pacifism) and are extremely uncomfortable with the language of conquest and rule. Thus the lake of fire is interpreted as annihilation rather than torment, and what looks like acts of vengeance are taken as warnings from a loving God. Threat and coercion are the strategies of the beast, but the gospel knows of no other victory than that of the cross. As David Barr asks, "if violence is not acceptable now how can it be acceptable at the Parousia?"[45] Such a community of interpreters would argue that a *Christian* reading of Scripture must remain true to the words of the Sermon on the Mount: "Love your enemies and pray for those who persecute you, so that you may be children of your Father in heaven; for he makes his sun rise on the evil and on the good . . ." (Matt 5:44-45). The violence of Revelation must be reinterpreted, just as the Fourth Gospel's emphasis on Jesus' divinity needs the balance of Mark's emphasis on Jesus' suffering.

Other church traditions regard this as sentimental and one-sided. There is good, and there is evil, and the message of the gospel is salvation for one and damnation for the other. Of course, the *spiritual* victory was won by Christ's self-sacrifice but in the final victory, all opposition will be crushed like clay pots (Rev 2:27; 12:5; 19:15). This is not to be explained as John's human desire for vengeance; it is the judicial act of a loving but just God. As Murphy puts it, God will "exercise *force* against the partisans of evil . . . and will *punish* them as they deserve."[46] The difference between Revelation and other New Testament writings is one of emphasis rather than content. The Jesus of the Gospels also speaks of cataclysmic disasters (Mark 13:7-8) and individual punishments (Matt 22:13), even if such sayings are generally in the minority.[47] John, for reasons at which we can only guess, has recorded a series of visions where judgment sayings are in the majority. Therefore, when Revelation states that Jesus is both Lion and Lamb, no sophisticated hermeneutic is needed to explain it. It corresponds to the justice and mercy of God, as taught by Jesus and the rest of the Bible.

Finally, as well as exploring interactions with texts and beliefs, the intertexts of the modern reader will also include other cultural phenomena. For example, the proliferation of nuclear weapons in the second half of the twentieth century has added a new voice to the interpretation of apocalyptic visions. Whatever we believe about the justice and mercy of God, we now know that humanity has the capability of causing its own apocalyptic disaster. We might be sophisticated enough to know that stars cannot literally fall to the earth (and so perhaps could John) but we *can* envisage a nuclear war where a "third of the earth was burned up, and a third of the trees were burned up, and all green grass was burned up" (Rev 8:7). Similarly, we might think it scientifically impossible for a third of the rivers to turn to blood but we can envisage an environmental catastrophe in which rivers are made bitter and a third of their creatures become extinct. We can agree with historical critics that this is unlikely to be what John had in mind but it is hard to see why we should ignore such factors

as we seek to interpret the book today. The error of much futurist interpretation is to collapse the intertextuality and assume that John had our
specific circumstances in mind. But there is no reason why those circumstances should not have a role in the intertextual matrix that constitutes
the context of our interpretation.

Lastly, such an intertextual interpretation does not necessarily have
to exclude historical reconstruction from consideration. The point is that
it is not treated as an ancient "fact" that somehow *controls* future interpretation. Historical reconstruction is done in the present and so offers
itself as a possible intertext for the reader. For example, scholars are currently divided as to whether the background for interpreting Revelation
is a period of severe Roman persecution or a period of laxity and cooperation. Since there is no consensus on this question, interpretation is
rather like an experiment or performance. Just as a particular specimen
looks different under ultra-violet light than under ordinary light (or so I
am led to believe by *CSI*), so Revelation will look different under different
historical hypotheses. The question is whether these multiple "viewings"
add to our understanding of the book or are mutually exclusive. Historical
critics assume that they are mutually exclusive; intertextual critics assume
that they are not.

Conclusion

The use of intertextual theory in biblical studies is permissive rather than
prescriptive. It offers analogies of how texts, broadly understood as a system of codes or signs, can interact with one another. Some think the
content of the book of Revelation demands a focus on John's rhetorical
purposes, while others think the "trigger" or "catalyst" for John's interpretations come from the intertexts themselves. A third group believes that
such decisions are mainly influenced by the interpreter's own commitments and beliefs. Such decisions are inevitably influenced by how one
understands the nature of Jesus' message, the relationship between the
Testaments, and the relationship of both to (particular) church beliefs. As
such, it is also a matter of ideology, since our (western) culture is extremely
sensitive to the question of who gains and who loses from particular
interpretations. As Aichele says, the problem is that ideology "creates an
illusion of reality; it makes the meaning of the texts seem obvious by providing a set of conventional codes that allows the reader to recognize the
text as a work, to identify it, and to make sense out of it."[48]

After the events of 9/11, it is not surprising that the portrayal of
Christ as a divine warrior in Revelation is problematic. Revenge is a powerful emotion and becomes even more dangerous when people believe

that God is on their side. Should our response to such atrocities be to "forgive them; for they do not know what they are doing" (Luke 23:34) or to ask "how long will it be before you judge and avenge our blood on the inhabitants of the earth?" (Rev 6:10)? The use of intertextual theory does not answer such questions, but it can make the process of interpretation more transparent by naming the intertexts and the weight that it is being accorded to them. This at least means that an interpretation is subject to public debate and not simply asserted as the "true" meaning of the text. Derrida offers a salutary challenge to those who think they have correctly configured all the "voices" of a text:

> There is always a surprise in store for . . . any criticism that might think it had mastered the game, surveyed all the threads at once, deluding itself, too, in wanting to look at the text without touching it, without laying a hand on the "object," without risking . . . the addition of some new thread.[49]

This is a call for humility rather than a call to abandon interpretation. If interpretation requires configuring multiple "voices," then there are always going to be other ways of doing it. But there is no reason why these interpretations cannot be in dialogue with one another. This was the purpose of the conference and as far as I am concerned, it was successful. My understanding has been enriched by the other participants, even if I did not always agree with the point being made. It was an illustration of the intertextuality that I have tried to articulate in this chapter.

3
The Reception of Daniel 7 in the Revelation of John

Thomas Hieke

Introduction
Purpose and Method

The kingdom of God will destroy all the oppressive powers of the present and lead the holy ones to victory. This is the message of the seventh chapter of the book of Daniel, and it is also the point that is made in the Revelation of John.[1] Indeed, John the Seer patterns the presentation of his visions after Daniel's prophecy, and Daniel 7 is the chapter that is most often quoted or alluded to in his book. Therefore, in what follows, by outlining the gist of Daniel 7 and showing how it clearly corresponds to the concerns of the Seer on Patmos, I shall explore the political and theological message of comfort for the community addressed.

This chapter will reflect a process of reading in a text-centered way and therefore will not focus on the production of the text of Revelation, nor will it ask whether an allusion is "intentional" or not.[2] Instead, it looks at intertextual references and describes what effects they have for a "critical" reading that meets the standards of intersubjective verifiability and that presupposes at least both texts: Daniel 7 and the Revelation of John.

The Message of Daniel 7

Chapter 7 is the core[3] of the proto-canonical book of Daniel and functions as a pivot between Daniel 2–6 and 8–12.[4] In Daniel 7 a narrative frame (7:1 and 7:28) binds together the vision (7:2-14) and its interpretation given by an *angelus interpres* (7:15-27).

DIAGRAM 1
OUTLINE OF DANIEL 7

---

1 Narrative frame: Daniel, visions
  2-6 Four beasts, first three beasts
    7 fourth beast
      8 ten horns, another horn
        9-10 judgment by the Ancient One
      11ᵃ the arrogant words of the horn
      11ᵇ destruction of the fourth beast
    12 End of the rest of the beasts
        13 the Ancient One and the one like
        a human being
          14 DOMINION AND KINGSHIP FOR THE ONE
          LIKE A HUMAN BEING
  15 Narrative frame: Daniel's troubles
    16-17   Interpretation of the four beasts
        18 THE KINGDOM FOR THE HOLY ONES
        OF THE MOST HIGH
      19 Daniel's inquiry about the fourth beast
      20 the ten horns and the other horn
      21 Daniel's observation of the horn's war with
      the holy ones
        22ᵃ until the Ancient One came
        22ᵇ⁻ᵈ JUDGMENT AND KINGDOM FOR
        THE HOLY ONES
      23 interpretation of the fourth beast
      24-25 the ten horns and the other horn
      26 judgment and destruction of the horn
        27 KINGSHIP AND DOMINION FOR THE
        HOLY ONES
  28 Narrative frame: Daniel's reaction

Content

Daniel 7 communicates the following message: after times of terror under the regimes of inhuman powers, a divine intervention will destroy all the violent enemies and hand over dominion and kingship to the holy ones of the Most High. Their kingdom will be an everlasting one that establishes a reign with a human face.

The "reality" behind the text refers to the faithful ones in the people of Israel who come into close contact with the celestial sphere and are hence called "holy ones," a term used in other passages for celestial beings.[5] Here, the "holy ones of the Most High" are the righteous ones[6] that are assessed as "the good ones" according to the books that were opened in Daniel 7:10. They approach the Ancient One, represented by the "one like a human being":

> Thus the "one in human likeness" did not *descend* or *come from* God as if he had been an angel in the divine presence, but rather he *ascended* or *came to* God and *was brought* into his presence. In effect, the author is saying that "the holy ones of the Most High," faithful Israel responsive to the demands of the reign of God even in the face of their present humiliation and suffering, will come into the divine presence in order to receive everlasting dominion in holiness, nobility, and grandeur, and so will replace the depraved, brutal, and vile kingdoms of the pagan world which were opposed to the reign of God and to his holy People.[7]

> The man-like figure (כְּבַר אֱנָשׁ) is a symbol for Israel, who is described in the interpretative section as "the Holy Ones of the Most High," "the Holy Ones," and "the people of the Holy Ones of the Most High."[8]

The pragmatics of this highly encoded text are clearly directed *ad intra*: this is not a tractate trying to convince someone from outside or to claim publicly the dominion of one's own community over the world. The text's intention, rather, is to provide consolation for a community under pressure, a community that knows to decipher the roles and metaphors of the characters it finds therein.[9] This message of consolation includes the admonition to remain holy, that is, to keep the commandments of the Torah. "Holy ones" is probably an intertextual reference to the central verse of Leviticus 19:2 that calls the Torah as a whole to the fore: "You shall be holy, for I the LORD your God am holy."

Reception in Early Jewish Literature

The issue of the reception of Daniel 7 and the figure of the "one like a human being" can be addressed here only briefly.[10] The expression "Son of Man" occurs in the book of Parables/Similitudes (*1 En.* 37–71) in three different formulations—the Elect One, the Righteous One, the Anointed One or Messiah—all signaling an eschatological figure.[11] *1 Enoch* 46 appears as an interpretative continuation of Daniel 7, and the "Son of Man" functions as a mediator between the realm of God and the human world and so differs from angels as well as from human beings. The figure is an individual celestial being especially associated with righteousness and justice: "This is the Son of Man, to whom belongs righteousness, and with whom righteousness dwells" (*1 En.* 46:3). However, the Son of Man takes over functions and roles that go by far beyond those seen in Daniel 7. In cooperation with God, the Son of Man works as the eschatological judge,[12] providing salvation for the righteous ones and punishment for the kings and mighty ones who persecute the faithful ones and who do not obey God.

In a similar way, *4 Ezra*, a writing contemporary with the Revelation of John, reinterprets Daniel 7: the visionary sees something like a figure of a man coming up out of the heart of the sea and flying with the clouds of heaven (*4 Ezra* 13:3). This figure brings eschatological judgment and appears as a celestial being with divine qualities; he is the one the Most High has been keeping for many ages and who will deliver his creation. God calls this figure "my son" (see *4 Ezra* 13).[13] In fact, both texts, *1 Enoch* 37–71 and *4 Ezra* 13, give witness to common assumptions about the interpretation of Daniel 7 in first-century Judaism,[14] with the concept of the "one like a human being" enlarged and developed to a "Son of Man concept." Thus the symbol of the collective becomes an individual figure and is identified with the Messiah, a celestial, preexistent, and transcendent being taking over divine attributes and functions (a development that also occurs in the fragmentary *Aramaic Apocalypse* from the Qumran literature [4Q246]).[15] This line of reception demonstrates that the imagery of Daniel 7 is open enough to be associated with new hopes for salvation, hopes that concentrate on an individual redeemer coming from God. This line also leads to the reception of Daniel 7 as background material of the visions of the Seer on Patmos.[16]

The Reception of Daniel 7 in the Revelation of John

Understanding the relationship between the Old Testament background provided by Daniel 7 and its use by John the Seer is vital if we are to apprehend the full meaning of the book of Revelation.[17] Therefore, Diagram 2 maps out the relationship between the two books and prepares the ground for a comparison of the major themes of kingship and dominion, thrones and books, the Son of Man, and the animal imagery in Revelation 11–13.

DIAGRAM 2
OVERVIEW FOLLOWING THE SEQUENCE IN REVELATION

Dan 7:13	Rev 1:7	Coming with the clouds
Dan 7:13	Rev 1:13	One like a son of man
Dan 7:9	Rev 1:14	Hair white as wool; flames of fire (see Dan 10:6)
Dan 7:10	Rev 5:11	A thousand thousands . . ., and ten thousand times ten thousand
Dan 7:2	Rev 7:1	The four winds
Dan 7:21	Rev 11:7	The beast conquers the holy ones/the two witnesses
Dan 7:14	Rev 11:15	The kingdom of our Lord (see Dan 2:44; 7:22, 27)
Dan 7:7, 24	Rev 12:3	Ten horns
Dan 7:25	Rev 12:14	A time, times, and half a time (see Dan 12:7)
Dan 7:3, 7 Dan 7:24	Rev 13:1	A beast (Rev)/Four beasts (Dan) from the sea; ten horns
Dan 7:4-6	Rev 13:2	Four beasts in Daniel, but one mixed beast in Revelation
Dan 7:8, 11, 20	Rev 13:5	A mouth uttering haughty and blasphemous words
Dan 7:25	Rev 13:6	A mouth uttering blasphemies (see Dan 11:36)
Dan 7:21, 25	Rev 13:7	The beast/horn making war on the saints and conquering them
Dan 7:13	Rev 14:14	The one like a human being on the cloud(s)
Dan 7:20,.24	Rev 17:3, 7, 12, 16	Ten horns
Dan 7:11	Rev 19:20	The destruction of the beast in fire
Dan 7:9, 22 Dan 7:27	Rev 20:4	The holy ones receive judgment and the kingdom A thousand years (Rev)/eternal kingdom (Dan)
Dan 7:9	Rev 20:11	Throne(s)
Dan 7:10	Rev 20:12	Books were opened; the book of life (see Dan 12:1)
Dan 7:18, 27	Rev 22:5	The saints will reign forever and ever

The Animal Imagery in Revelation 11–13

| Daniel 7:21 | Revelation 11:7 | *The beast conquers the holy ones/the two witnesses* |

In Revelation 11:7 the "beast" (τὸ θηρίον; here: coming from the "bottomless pit," ἐκ τῆς ἀβύσσου) as a code for hostile powers (or the antichrist[18]) appears for the first time. It originates from the animal imagery of Daniel 7, but several elements from Daniel appear in Revelation 11–13 in a new context. The "beast from the bottomless pit" in Revelation 11:7 was never mentioned before, but, given that its appearance is not explained, it may be assumed that the text presupposes readers would be able to reconstruct its scriptural provenance.[19] By combining the information about the "bottomless pit" from Revelation 9:1-12 with the beasts from Revelation 13 and Daniel 7 and with the horn from Daniel 7:21 that made war with the holy ones and prevailed over them, this intertextual web will be found to form the new image of "the" beast that conquers and kills the two witnesses. Activating Daniel 7 as one of the background texts of Revelation 11:3-14 generates a good deal of consolation for those who know the outcome of Daniel 7: "The" beast(s) will not have the last word, it (they) will be destroyed, and the holy ones will gain the kingdom. Revelation 11 keeps this hope alive in 11:15 when loud voices in heaven proclaim that the kingdom of the world has become the kingdom of our Lord and of his Messiah.

| Daniel 7:7, 24 | Revelation 12:3 | *Ten horns* |

In Revelation 12, the visionary "creates" another monster: the great red dragon.[20] Regarding the biblical intertext, the Greek word δράκων points in two directions: (1) The word recalls the passages from the Greek Old Testament that speak about God's victory over the primeval monsters (see Pss 74:13; 148:7: the dragons of the water; 74:14; 104:26; Isa 27:1: the Leviathan; Job 26:13; 38:39 LXX; 40:25). (2) In the addition "Bel et draco" to the book of Daniel (Bel 1:23-27 = Dan 14:23-27), the protagonist kills a "dragon" that the Babylonians revered like a god. He does so by a ridiculous process: the silly dragon devours the poisonous cakes Daniel had prepared from pitch, fat, and hair. Therefore, if one keeps these two aspects of "dragon" in mind, the dragon in Revelation 12 loses some of his impressiveness, even though his description makes him sound dreadful. The "ten horns" of the dragon are borrowed from the fourth beast of Daniel 7:7, 24, and the seven heads may stem from the sum of seven heads of the four beasts also found in Daniel 7.[21] However, activating the Old

Testament references provides consolation: although the dragon seems to prevail, he will be defeated in the end, like the dragon Daniel killed in Babylonia, and like the beasts from Daniel 7.

Daniel 7:20, 24   Revelation 17:3, 7, 12, 16   Ten horns

In Revelation 17 the "ten horns" reappear in the scarlet beast with seven heads, on which the great whore sits. This beast is essentially identical with the beast from the sea in Revelation 13-16 and 19 (see below on Rev 19:20), but the imagery as a whole represents a code for the Roman Empire and its oppression on the Christian communities. As in Daniel 7:24, the ten horns represent ten kings to come, but as in the Danielic *Vorlage*, the figure is a vague number, and the ten kings cannot be keyed to historical persons or events.[22] Rather, the text seems to introduce a realistic element—"there will still be some kings to come"—although the writer then immediately reduces the reign of these ten kings to the unrealistic length of one hour (!). This wishful thinking wants to comfort the audience that the end of the oppression will soon come. The same holds true for the following verses, which sketch an upheaval of the ten horns and the beast against the whore: they will destroy her. Here the text of Revelation provides rather elusive and hazy ideas about the desired end of the Roman Empire.

Daniel 7:3, 7	*Revelation 13.1*	*A beast (Rev)/ Four beasts (Dan) from the sea*
Daniel 7:24		*Ten horns*
Daniel 7:4-6	*Revelation 13:2*	*Four beasts in Daniel, but one mixed beast in Revelation*

The animal imagery comes to its culmination in Revelation 13, where the Seer creates *one* beast rising out of the *sea* (not from the "bottomless pit" as in Revelation 11:7) and describes it with the help of the four beasts from Daniel 7. The salient characteristics of their appearance are merged into one monster; the ten horns reappear (see Dan 7:20, 24); and the seven heads correspond to the total number of heads in Daniel 7 (the first, second, and fourth beasts have one head each, while the third beast has four).[23] The change from four beasts to one mirrors the political situation in that the four kingdoms that once existed have been superseded by the mighty Roman Empire and the current pressure it exerts.[24] It incorporates all the evil and violent elements of the previous empires and conquers the whole earth, which admires the beast. Without the background of Daniel 7, a reader of Revelation 13 could not grasp or cope with the overwhelming imagery of the composite monster and would reject it as a delirium. By activating the intertextual link, the report of the visionary on Patmos looks like the natural continuation of what Daniel saw in former times. The reader can say, "See, it happens again!" but can look forward, with Daniel 7 in mind, knowing that *in the end* God will be the victorious party in the battle.

Daniel 7:8, 11, 20	*Revelation 13:5*	*A mouth uttering haughty and blasphemous words*
Daniel 7:25	*Revelation 13:6*	*A mouth uttering blasphemies (see Dan 11:36)*

In the meantime, however, the beast is given a mouth uttering haughty and blasphemous words, just as the "little horn" in Daniel 7:8, 11, 20, 25 speaks great things and words against the Most High.[25] Moreover, in Revelation 13:6 the beast even attacks God's name and dwelling and the heavenly beings. This was also what the dragon (being an image of the devil) did in Revelation 12, and both passages seem to draw upon Daniel 8:9-10: "Out of one of them [the four horns representing the Hellenistic successors of Alexander the Great] came another horn [the Seleucid king Antiochus IV Epiphanes], a little one, which grew exceedingly great toward the south, toward the east, and toward the beautiful land. It grew as high as the host of heaven. It threw down to the earth some of the host and some of the stars, and trampled on them." Thus Revelation 13 proclaims exactly what Daniel 7-8 insinuates: the community's daily experience of persecution and oppression is a reflection of a cosmic battle involving even the stars.[26] This idea would no doubt sound exaggerated if it were not prefigured in Scripture, but as readers remember Daniel 7-8, the truth of the conclusion must be faced as both prophecies seem almost the same.

Daniel 7:21, 25	*Revelation 13:7*	*The beast/horn making war on the saints and conquering them*

The identification of the composite beast of Revelation 13 and the "little horn" of Daniel 7 continues insofar as both are allowed to make war upon the saints and to conquer them (Daniel 7:21; see also above on Revelation 11:7). In a highly symbolic language both texts mirror the experience of their present, that is, being oppressed in their freedom by the ruler of a foreign empire. For Daniel 7, the "little horn" is Antiochus IV Epiphanes, and for the visionary on Patmos, events under Antiochus are paralleled by the prosecution of the Christians under Nero and other Roman emperors.[27] And again, the reader of Revelation who activates the intertextual

links can take a good portion of consolation from the Danielic background: *in the end*, the oppressors will be destroyed, and the kingdom will
be given to the saints of the Most High.

Daniel 7:11   Revelation 19:20   The destruction of the beast in fire

The composite beast from Revelation 13 reappears in chapters 14–16 and
19. In 13:14-15 it is represented by εἰκών (an image) and recalls the production of a golden statue by Nebuchadnezzar in Daniel 3, and his command that all should worship his image or be killed.[28] In ensuing chapters
(see Rev 14:9, 11; 15:2; 16:2, 10, 13), this image can be identified by the
fact that it is worshiped by most of the people.

    In Revelation 17, a scarlet beast appears as the riding "horse" of the
great whore. It has seven heads and ten horns that represent kings (see
above on Rev 12:3) and hence reflects the imagery in Daniel 7. As it comes
from the "bottomless pit," like the beast in Revelation 11:7, it is essentially
identical with "the" beast mentioned elsewhere in Revelation. For the historical author and the addressees of the text at the end of the first century
C.E., the common equivalent in "reality" is probably the Roman emperor.

    The beast from Revelation 13–16 and its image reappear in Revela-
tion 19:19-20 in order to be burned in the lake of fire that burns with
sulfur. A reader acquainted with Daniel 7:11 would expect this end of
the beast in fire, for in this verse the fourth beast is slain and its body
is given over to burning. However, Revelation 19:20 boosts the imagery
insofar as the beast and the false prophet who deceived those who worshiped the beast's image are both thrown *alive* into the lake of fire. So,
with the vision of Daniel 7 in mind, the reader certainly gets the impression that the destruction of the beast in fire is the just and appropriate
end of the beast's career. The people who did not worship the beast and
its image and as a consequence were killed finally come to life again
and reign with Christ a thousand years (Rev 20:4). The devil, however,
will also end in the lake of fire and sulfur, and together with the beast
and the false prophet, he will be tormented day and night forever and
ever (Rev 20:10).

The Son of Man in Revelation

The long and ongoing discussion about the meaning of the phrase "Son
of Man" and its development cannot be summarized here.[29] However, it is
possible to consider the implications of the wording that a model reader
can derive from the texts. The phrase in Daniel 7:13 reads כְּבַר אֱנָשׁ, and
its appropriate translation is "one like a human being."[30] The meaning of

the phrase is "a human figure seen in a vision." The Greek translations both read ὡς υἱὸς ἀνθρώπου, "a son of man," that is, a human being.

In Daniel, the phrase occurs again only once in the Hebrew part. In Daniel 8:17, בֶּן־אָדָם or υἱὲ ἀνθρώπου is the Ezekiel-like address of the visionary after his prostration.[31] Hence, the "son of man"-theme does not occur too often in Daniel, but does in Revelation, although only two occurrences (Rev 1:13 and 14:14) need to be discussed here. Both passages refer back to Daniel 7:13, but in each the phrase is not a title ("Son of Man") as in most other occurrences in the New Testament.[32] However, it is important to grasp the content of the symbolism that connects Daniel 7:13 with the passages in Revelation.

Daniel 7:13   Revelation 1:7   Coming with the clouds

Revelation 1:7 describes the expected coming of the risen Christ (the *Parousia*) and borrows the motif of the clouds from Daniel 7:13 to signify this event.[33] This clear reference shows that the text intends to identify Jesus Christ with the "one like a human being" from Daniel 7:13, although it does not say so explicitly and does not use the title "Son of Man" here[34] (but see Revelation 14:14 below); nevertheless, there are some other passages from the Hebrew Bible that mention that the LORD rides on a cloud[35] (Isa 19:1; see also Ps 97:2) or that the clouds are the dust of his feet (Nah 1:3). That it is Jesus Christ (not God) who will come with the clouds is clarified by another echo from prophetic literature: "those who pierced him" originates from Zechariah 12:10 and recalls the crucifixion in a Christian context. Maybe one can read Revelation 1:7 also as an abbreviation of all those New Testament passages that speak about the coming of the Son of Man on/with the clouds of heaven (see Mark 13:26 par. Matt 24:30/ Luke 21:27; Mark 14:62 par. Matt 26:64; Acts 1:9). However, the clouds are not a divine prerogative, but a means of transportation to and from heaven; according to 1 Thessalonians 4:17, at the moment of the *Parousia* those who are still alive "will be caught up in the clouds . . . to meet the Lord in the air."

Daniel 7:13   Revelation 1:13   One like a son of man

Daniel 7:9   Revelation 1:14   Hair white as wool; flames of fire (see Dan 10:5-12)

Just as the coming with the clouds in Revelation 1:7 alerts the reader to keep Daniel 7 in mind (or reread it), a few verses later, when John the Seer describes his first vision, the "one like a human being" (ὡς υἱὸς ἀνθρώπου) from Daniel 7:13 is called forth. As this figure is a riddle in Daniel 7, the wording ὅμοιον υἱὸν ἀνθρώπου functions as a mystery in Revelation 1:13 too,[36] and, according to Adela Yarbro Collins, "[t]he phrase is not used in a titular or even quasi-titular manner."[37] The visionary does not immediately identify the one who is speaking to him, and in order to dramatize the appearance, a variety of images from the Old Testament is collected for its portrayal.

The "hair white as wool" (Rev 1:14) comes from Daniel 7:9, where it is an attribute of the Ancient One,[38] and the "flame of fire" (φλὸξ πυρός) belongs to his throne.[39] By the subtle mixing of the attributes of the Ancient One and the one like a human being, both figures are identified in Revelation 1[40]—or, in other words, the Seer sees something new that is not completely new but has its roots in the prophetic literature of "Holy Scripture." This provides authenticity for the vision because for the ancient reader the text does not invent something but conveys something the prophets of old have already seen, although here the visionary claims to see more clearly who the persons are and to whom the images refer—namely to the risen Jesus Christ. Revelation 1:13-17 borrows much from the book of Ezekiel here, but the sequence of the scenery comes from Daniel 10:5-12[41]: the appearance of a heavenly figure, the overwhelming sight that strikes the Seer down to the ground as if dead, the consolation of the heavenly figure, and the encouraging words "Do not be afraid" (Rev 1:17). The following words, "I am the first and the last," stem from Isaiah (41:4; 44:6; 48:12) and are attributed to the LORD God. Nevertheless, considering all the links to Old Testament literature so far examined, the figure that Revelation 1:13-17 describes still remains a mystery. While it carries traces from the "one like a human being" (different from the Ancient One in Dan 7), it looks in parts like the Ancient One himself, or like the heavenly being from Daniel 10, and it utters words that the LORD God spoke in Deutero–Isaiah. Who is this person? In Revelation 1:18 the person finally reveals its identity: "I was dead, and see, I am alive forever and ever." It is the risen Jesus Christ in whom all the images about heavenly and human-like beings coincide. It also becomes clear that Jesus Christ forms an inseparable unity with the Ancient One, the LORD God, the Father.[42] This is "new" and a "revelation"; however, the attributes and the imagery are familiar to all those who are acquainted with the Scriptures. Thus the text develops its message about the coming of Jesus Christ from a scriptural basis and gains reliability and the reader's confidence.

Daniel 7:13   Revelation 14:14   The one like a human being on the cloud(s)

The wording ὅμοιον υἱὸν ἀνθρώπου appears only once more in Revelation (14:14). The vision begins with a concomitant, a white cloud (νεφέλη

λευκή). Clouds are an accompanying motif in theophanies in the Old Testament (see, e.g., Exod 16:10; Lev 16:2; Num 11:25) and at the Transfigu-
ration of Christ (Mark 9:7 par. Matt 17:5 par. Luke 9:34-35)[43]—hence the
appearance of the cloud introduces the revelation of a divine being. The
"cloud" and the color "white" evoke the text of Daniel 7 (the "one like a
human being coming with the clouds" in Dan 7:13; the white clothing of
the Ancient One in Dan 7:9). The singular "cloud" may be due to the idea
that the "one like a human being" is *sitting* on it.[44] It is obvious that Daniel
7 and its reception in the traditions of early Judaism form the primary
background for the understanding of the imagery, despite the difference
between "coming" (Dan 7:13) and "sitting" (Rev 14:14). The "sitting" on
the cloud introduces the juridical function of the "one like a human being"
(see the background text of Joel 4:12-13: God sits to judge all the neighbor-
ing nations; the sickle being a metaphor for the eschatological judgment).
Again, the text of Revelation attributes functions and qualities to the "one
like a human being" that the Old Testament ascribes to God himself. The
result is a very close relationship, approaching an identification between
the "one like a human being" and God, and—once the identification of the
"one like a human being" with Christ is established—a high Christology.

In Revelation 14, the "one like a human being" occurs together with
six angels as one of seven heavenly beings. There are three angels before
and after the center of the chapter, which contains a heavenly voice (Rev
14:13) and the "one like a human being" (Rev 14:14).[45] The heavenly voice
in 14:13 remains a riddle for the moment; however, as the following verse
recalls the "one like a human being" from Daniel 7, one could identify
the speaker of the voice with the "Ancient One," that is, God. Another
speaker is the "Spirit" (τὸ πνεῦμα), but both messages go in the same direction and supplement each other: The beatitude praises the faithful ones
who lose their life for the sake of Christ ("in the Lord")—they will rest from
their labors, and their faithfulness will be rewarded. This scene probably
corresponds to the court of the Ancient One in Daniel 7:10, where the
books were opened—among these must be the book of life—and everyone
who is found written in the book will be delivered (as Dan 12:1 states).

After the speaking voice (to be identified with the Ancient One or
God) and the speaking spirit (to be identified with the "Holy Spirit"), the
next verse in the center of the chapter (Rev 14:14) mentions "one like a
human being" seated on a white cloud. The wordings "one like a *human
being*" and "another angel" (occurring several times in the chapter) make
it clear that the figure sitting on the cloud is *not* an angel.[46] In order to
identify this figure, the reader has to recall both Revelation 1 and Daniel
7. In Daniel 7:13-14, the "one like a human being" was given dominion

and glory and kingship, and in Revelation 1:7-18 the "one like a human being" was identified with the risen Jesus Christ (see above, p. 57). Hence, Revelation 14:14 presupposes the combinations of biblical passages and the identifications the reader has made so far. The person sitting on the white cloud is Jesus Christ; the "golden crown"[47] represents the kingship he was given by God—and from this position, Christ will execute the final judgment over the earth and the human beings together with the other three angels mentioned in the rest of the chapter (Rev 14:15-20).

The agricultural images used for this judgment—the sickle (δρέπανον) and the wine press (ληνός)—clearly derive from Joel 4:13 ("Put in the sickle, for the harvest is ripe. Go in, tread, for the wine press is full").[48] This verse stands in a highly eschatological context describing the "day of the Lord" as a cosmic judgment of all the people on earth. The wine press as a metaphor for the eschatological judgment also plays an important role in Isaiah—"Why are your robes red, and your garments like theirs who tread the wine press?" (63:2)—and the red color comes from the blood of the nations whom the Lord smashed in wrath and anger on the day of vengeance. The wine press is an attribute of Jesus Christ judging the nations as "king of kings and Lord of lords" and reappears in Revelation 19:11-16.[49] Hence, the visionary works his way along the whole panoply of eschatological imagery, mastering the material in a creative way. The reader who is acquainted with the underlying biblical hypotexts can believe that the book of Revelation conveys truth because it accords in so many ways with what has already been seen and mentioned by the prophets of old and written down in Holy Scripture.

Kingship and Dominion

Using a variety of expressions, Daniel 7 announces that the "kingship" (מַלְכוּ, βασιλεία) will be given to the "one like a human being" (Dan 7:14), the "holy ones of the Most High" (7:18), the "holy ones" (7:22), and "the people of the holy ones of the Most High" (7:27). All these descriptions in some way pick out an identical object and are meant so to be understood by the faithful ones within Israel. The text oscillates between a singular unity with traces of an individual ("the one like a human being") and a collective unity ("the holy ones") and revolves around the "kingdom of God." This constellation provides an ideal basis for Christian scriptural exegesis: The Seer on Patmos can easily identify the mysterious scene of Daniel 7 to Jesus and his message of the kingdom of God. Certainly, the reception of Daniel 7 in Early Jewish literature (see above, especially *1 En.* 37–71 and *4 Ezra* 13) paves the way for an understanding of the "one like a human being" as an individual, as the "Son of Man," so from here it is only a short step toward the identification with Jesus Christ. Once it is clear for the Christian reader of Revelation that the prophecies of old, as well as the writings of the Seer on Patmos, both speak about Christ, the other motifs of the prophetic imagery are easily applied to the Christian community—they are the "holy ones" who will prevail in the end.

Daniel 7:14	Revelation 11:15	The kingdom of our Lord (see Daniel 2:44; 7:22; 7:27); (see also Psalm 2:2; Zechariah 14:9)

The proclamation during the trumpet blown by the seventh angel in Revelation 11:15 reads: "The kingdom of the world has become the kingdom of our Lord and of his Messiah, and he will reign forever and ever." This verse is a conflation of various prophecies: for example, Daniel 2:44 and 7:14 (eternal kingdom); Psalm 2:2 (the Lord and his Anointed); and Zechariah 14:9 (the Lord will become king over all the earth). From Daniel 7, a reader would expect that the eternal kingdom of the Lord will also bring salvation for the holy ones (they also get the kingship according to Dan 7:22 and 7:27), and indeed, Revelation 11:18 speaks not only about the destroying of those who destroy the earth, but also about the reward for God's faithful servants (τοῖς προφήταις καὶ τοῖς ἁγίοις καὶ τοῖς φοβουμένοις τὸ ὄνομά σου, τοὺς μικροὺς καὶ τοὺς μεγάλους: the prophets and holy ones and all who fear your name, both small and great). Thus, the text of Revelation 11:15, 18 takes over the promises of Daniel 7 and the other prophecies, declares them still valid, and prolongs them to the future: the eternal kingdom of God, about which Daniel had in the past received revelation, will finally become reality through God and his Anointed, Jesus Christ. Moreover, a reader acquainted with the Daniel text will conclude that the faithful ones, the holy ones who fear the Lord's name, will get their salvation and reward, although in Daniel 7 the idea that the holy ones (or the saints) receiving the kingdom and ruling in eternity is still absent. Revelation comes back to this concept some chapters later.

Daniel 7:9, 22	Revelation 20:4	Thrones; the holy ones get judgment and the kingdom
Daniel 7:27		A thousand years (Rev)—eternal kingdom (Dan)

The comforting concept that the faithful and steadfast ones will finally get the kingship and hence rule forever and ever is also developed in Revelation, specifically in two steps. Revelation 20:4 returns to the thrones that were set in order to establish a court: "Then I saw thrones, and those seated on them were given authority to judge." This text reminds the readers of Dan 7:9, and furthermore of Daniel 7:22, where the judgment is given to the holy ones of the Most High. Revelation 20:4 mentions the conditions under which one will be counted among the number of salvation: "I also saw the souls of those who[50] had been beheaded for their testimony to Jesus and for the word of God and those who had not worshiped the beast or its image and had not received its mark on their foreheads or their hands. They came to life and reigned with Christ a thousand years." Hence, the first step of the kingship for the holy ones (the saints that meet the conditions mentioned[51]) is a rule of thousand years.[52] Although this is already an amount of time that cannot be overseen by human beings (something like eternity), it is nevertheless a limited period. There are still acts of judgment to be made after the thousand years, and these will result in the final destruction of all powers that oppose God and the holy ones. The reader that has Daniel 7 in mind is still waiting for the everlasting dominion and kingdom of the righteous ones.

| Daniel 7:18, 27 | Revelation 22:5 | *The saints will reign forever and ever* |

The very last sentence of the great vision at the end of the book of Revelation, just before the interesting epilogue (Rev 22:6-21[53]) closes the Bible (!), mentions the everlasting kingship of the saints (the holy ones): "And there will be no more night; they need no light of lamp or sun, for the Lord God will be their light, and they will reign forever and ever" (Rev 22:5). This state of affairs—the reception of the kingdom and an eternal reign—is repeatedly mentioned in Daniel 7 (see 7:18, 7:27), so the reader of Revelation, aware of the intertextual links to Daniel 7, will conclude that the promises of Daniel 7 are indeed still valid and that their fulfillment lies closely ahead. The faithful ones, also called the "holy ones," will get their light from the Lord God himself, and they will take over what Daniel already prophesied: they will get the eternal kingdom of God.

Thrones and Books

Daniel 7:9, 22	Revelation 20:4	*Thrones; the holy ones get judgment and the kingdom*
Daniel 7:27		*A thousand years (Rev)—eternal kingdom (Dan)*
Daniel 7:9	Revelation 20:11	*Throne(s)*
Daniel 7:10	Revelation 20:12	*Books were opened; the book of life (see Dan 12:1)*

Within the eschatological imagery of Revelation 20, verse 4 briefly mentions a court scene that one can only fully understand with the background of Daniel 7 in mind.[54] The terms κρίμα, "judgment," and θρόνους, "thrones," facilitate the link to Daniel 7:9 and 7:22. From these verses and the entire chapter, the reader can glean the necessary information about the ones who will sit on the thrones: the holy ones of the Most High, the ones who will get the everlasting kingdom. The Seer identifies this group with those "who had been beheaded for their testimony to Jesus and for the word of God," that is, the early Christian martyrs, and all believers who "had not worshiped the beast or its image and had not received its mark on their foreheads or their hands." Again, with the help of Daniel 7, a message of comfort emerges for all who remain faithful to Christ and the word of God: even if they die, they will be resurrected and reign together with Christ.

The construction of a messianic interregnum of a thousand years follows in Revelation 20, a "Millennium" that attracted a lot of attention.[55] While the discussion cannot be pursued here, it can be said that the text itself does not seem to make much of the thousand years. They are not an autonomous stage between the two eras, since Christ reigns in the Millennium *and* afterwards in the era of the New Jerusalem, and the true Christians are not killed by the "second death," but reign together with Christ in the thousand years *and* in the following period.[56] The thousand years separate the *first* resurrection of the martyrs and the faithful ones (who then will sit on thrones and reign with Christ) from the *final* judgment over Satan and Death. Revelation 20:7-15 describes this second stage of judgment. The great *white throne* in Revelation 20:11 may be a conflation of the throne of the Ancient One and his white clothing in Daniel 7:9, but in the light of Daniel 7, the whole situation of the Ancient One with his fiery throne, the court, and so on, enriches the reading process.

Here, as in Daniel 7:10, *books* are opened—for a true judgment it is necessary to build the sentence on reliable data, and the data about the works of the dead, according to which they are judged, are recorded in these books. This idea may come from Isaiah 65:6: "See, it is written before me: I will not keep silent, but I will repay; I will indeed repay into their laps"[57] or from Malachi 3:16: "Then those who revered the LORD spoke with one another. The LORD took note and listened, and a book of remembrance was written before him of those who revered the LORD and thought on his name." The "book of remembrance" is an anthropomorphic metaphor; however, it is a necessary image that helps people to imagine how God can remember all the faithful deeds and works of those who died under persecution without having their reward on earth.

While the "books" (plural) in Revelation 20:12 record the works of the individual, the "other book" (referred to as the "book of life") probably lists the names of all those who are saved from the "second death." This "book of life" belongs to the Lamb (see Rev 13:8; 17:8; 21:27), and

it records all those, from the foundation of the world, who do not worship the beast (see Rev 13); that is, the holy ones who remain faithful and
will be saved. Those who worshipped the beast—the beast itself, the false
prophet, and, finally, Death and Hades—will be thrown into the lake of
fire. The "book of life" recording the names of those who will be saved is
nothing unknown to the reader of the book of Daniel: chapter 12 begins
with an eschatological judgment carried out by Michael, the great prince
(the archangel), resulting in a hard time of anguish, but Daniel is comforted with the announcement that his people—everyone who is found
written in the book (Dan 12:1)—will be delivered. This idea is taken over
by the seer John and applied to his *very final* judgment scene where even
Death and Hades are destroyed. The purpose is consolation for those who
remain faithful to the Lord Jesus Christ, and who do not take part in the
imperial cult; even if they may die or are killed before the *Parousia*, they are
assured that their names are recorded in the Lamb's book of life.

Other Elements

| Daniel 7:10 | Revelation 5:11 | A thousand thousands . . . and ten thousand times ten thousand |

In Revelation 5:1-14, John sees a "Lamb standing as if it had been slaughtered." The Lamb[58] is identified with the Lion of the tribe of Judah, the
Root of David, and all these images are codes that stand for Jesus Christ.
He, the (guiltless and pure) Lamb, is worthy to open the seven seals of
the book and thus to start the eschatological process of judgment. The
Lamb is praised by "the voice of many angels surrounding the throne and
the living creatures and the elders; they numbered myriads of myriads
and thousands of thousands" (Rev 5:11). The structure of this pericope
resembles that of Daniel 7:13-14: the main figure (the Lamb/the one like
a human being) appears in the center of the heavenly world, approaches
God (the Ancient One/the Most High) and gets dominion, might, and
kingship (symbolized by the scroll in Rev 5:8). The scene closes with praise
by all heavenly beings that stand by (see Dan 7:14 and Rev 5:9-14). The
hymn in Revelation 5 is more elaborate, and the scene is the beginning
of the apocalyptic drama, while Daniel 7:13-14 forms its closing climax.[59]
The connection between Revelation 5 and Daniel 7 is underscored by the
number of the bystanders (heavenly beings next to the fiery throne in Dan
7:10; angels and living creatures in Rev 5:11): χίλιαι χιλιάδες ("myriads of
myriads" or "ten thousand times ten thousand") and μύριαι μυριάδες (a
"thousand thousands").[60] Especially the repetition (or multiplication) of
the greatest number in Greek expressed in one word (μυρίος) demonstrates

that the expression really wants to say "countless, innumerable." Again, the text of Revelation uses features that its readers know from Scripture, here Daniel 7, and this construction mediates the reliability and trustworthiness of the Patmos visions.

| Daniel 7:2 | Revelation 7:1 | *The four winds* |

The four winds of the earth are a common motif,[61] but if one takes the intertextual link from Revelation 7:1 to Daniel 7:2 seriously—both passages speak about the τέσσαρες ἄνεμοι—the passage in Revelation 7 gets an additional note of consolation, as in Daniel 7 the stirring up of the sea by the four winds leads to the appearance of the beasts that stand for terror and destruction. Hence, the four winds are heralds of a time of distress. In Revelation 7:1, however, four angels hold the four winds back, and this creates the opportunity for the calm before the storm and enough time for the sealing of those who will be saved. Terror and distress will come, and the war of the beasts will rage—as the four winds in Daniel 7 indicate—but God will make sure that his servants (Rev 7:3) will not be hurt.

| Daniel 7:25 | Revelation 12:14 | *A time, times, and half a time (see Dan 12:7)* |

In Revelation 12:14, one finds the strange date "for a time, and times, and half a time," which occurs in Daniel 7:25 and Daniel 12:7. In Daniel, this wording covers the time that the "holy people" (Dan 12:7) or the "holy ones" (Dan 7:25) must suffer and stand the attacks of the enemy (enemies). It is a symbolic analogy to the scheme of the four empires,[62] and since from this scheme it is clear that the addressees live under the fourth empire, they also live in the fourth section of the time of distress, that is, in the part "half a time." This means that the time of terror will be soon over and that "the end" is close by. Hence, the phrase does not provide a date or an amount of time, but indicates that the end is coming soon. The Revelation of John implies this meaning by using the same wording in 12:14: here, "a time, and times, and half a time" covers the time that the persecuted woman (i.e., the church of Jesus Christ) will be hidden and nourished in a safe place until the end (and also the end of persecution) will come soon.

Conclusion

In a visionary court scene, together with several explanatory speeches, Daniel 7 communicates a message of consolation directed to the author's own community, which is under pressure and feels itself to be in a time of terror. It is clearly stated that for a short amount of time foreign powers (encoded as the monstrous beasts) will prevail over the faithful, but in the end, God (encoded as the Ancient One and the Most High) will intervene, a heavenly court will judge and destroy the enemies, and all those of the people who remain faithful to the LORD (encoded as the holy ones) will gain possession of the kingdom. This everlasting kingdom differs fundamentally from the earthly empires under which the community suffers. The faithful ones that keep the commandments of the Torah and hence remain holy are encoded as the "holy ones of the Most High." They are represented in the heavenly court scene by the "one like a human being," and this imagery demonstrates that the new rulers who were given their dominion from God will reign in a truly human way; their everlasting kingdom will have a "human face."[63]

From a methodological or hermeneutical viewpoint, it is necessary to keep in mind that it will not be possible to pin down one or more exact historical situation(s) as a possible background for the imagery. The language and the chosen codes are highly symbolic and carry a (probably) intended vagueness that enables multi-faceted applications.

This observation clearly paves the way for the different ways Daniel 7 was received in Early Jewish literature. In the Book of Parables (*1 En.* 37–71) and *4 Ezra* 13, the scenery is taken over, but the concept changes: The "one like a human being" develops to a "Son-of-Man concept," that is, the symbol of the collective becomes an individual figure and is identified with the Messiah, a celestial, preexistent and transcendent being taking over divine attributes and functions. Obviously the imagery of Daniel 7 is open enough to be associated with new hopes for salvation, hopes that concentrate on an individual redeemer coming from God.

An intensive knowledge of the text of Daniel 7 directly leads to a better understanding of the Revelation of John, and the imagery found in the New Testament Apocalypse appears as a natural continuation of the visions of Daniel. The occurrences of Daniel 7 in Revelation are neither a mere copy nor are they quotations from Daniel 7, but they are organic enhancements that fit several purposes and have various effects.

* * *

First, as the text of Revelation seemingly tells something new, but which in fact has its roots in prophetic literature of Holy Scripture, the reader senses that the Seer on Patmos saw something that Daniel already had seen centuries before. The text evokes this impression and does so in order to suggest the truth of John's visions. An ancient mind is suspicious about everything new that has never been seen or heard of before, but here a reader acquainted with Scripture (and Daniel 7) must conclude that the "revelation" he or she is hearing is in accordance with Scripture.

Second, the "revelation of Jesus Christ" introduces the "new" person Jesus Christ in a very subtle way. The "one like a human being" is presented in Revelation 1:13 as a "riddle" and thus imitates the riddle in Daniel 7. The reader of Daniel 7:13 first wonders about the "one like a human being" before the Ancient One, until it becomes clear from the context that the "one like a human being" represents the "holy ones of the Most High" who will finally receive the everlasting kingdom. This knowledge is now introduced to the first vision in Revelation 1, and in the end the "Son of Man" comes out as the "living one" who was dead and is now alive forever and ever. By this subtle transformation, the risen Jesus Christ is identified with the "one like a human being" of the court scene of Daniel 7. Already in the prophetic chapter one notes a tendency to put the Ancient One who is the Most High in very close and inseparable unity with the "one like a human being," and Revelation fosters this move by attributing functions and qualities of God to the "one like a human being" who is the "Son of Man." The result is a "high Christology."

Third, a step parallel to the identification of the "one like a human being" with Jesus Christ comes with the identification of the "holy ones (of the Most High)" with the author's Christian community. They are the holy ones who did not worship the beast and had not received its mark on their foreheads or their hands; they are the faithful ones who cling to Jesus and his words. They will rule together with Christ in the Millennium and afterwards, and thus they are the ones who receive the everlasting kingdom of Daniel 7.

Fourth, as a consequence of these identifications a message of consolation emerges (just as the message of Daniel 7 communicates comfort). Although a time of terror and distress may come, although the faithful ones must even die as martyrs for the sake of Christ, finally God will victoriously intervene and destroy the enemies, and the "holy ones" will get their reward and will rule in eternity.

Fifth, hence, Revelation takes over the promises of Daniel 7 (and of other prophecies such as those of Isaiah and Ezekiel), declares them to be still valid, and prolongs them to the future. The eternal kingdom of God, which was in part revealed to Daniel in the past, will finally become reality through God and his Anointed Jesus Christ.

*   *   *

The prophetic and apocalyptic vision of Daniel 7 is reactivated in Revelation for the Christian community. The community gets the "truth of Scripture," the believers get a message about Christ and themselves from Scripture, and they are comforted by the message that they are on the way of Scripture that is the way of God. God will finally punish all earthly powers of terror and will hand over his kingdom to the ones who qualify as true *human* beings.

4

Faithful Witness, Alpha and Omega

The Identity of Jesus in the Apocalypse of John

Richard B. Hays

Introduction

A Profusion of Images

Who is Jesus in the Apocalypse of John? This visionary book deploys a kaleidoscopic profusion of imagery to depict its chief protagonist. Jesus is portrayed as exalted revealer of prophetic mysteries, faithful witness and martyr, firstborn from the dead, Son of God, the Coming One, the Son of Man, the future judge of the world and giver of life, the Lion of the tribe of Judah, the root of David, the Lamb who was slaughtered, the shepherd who guides his people to springs of the water of life, the child given birth by the woman clothed with the sun, the conquering Rider on a white horse, the bright morning star, the Lord of lords and King of kings, the one who is Alpha and Omega, and much more.[1]

Faced with such a diverse array of images—which could, on an unsympathetic reading, be regarded as chaotic and self-contradictory—studies of the Christology of the book of Revelation have tended to pursue one of two interpretative strategies: (1) seek to identify different *sources, traditions, or social settings* from which the book's depictions of Jesus are derived;[2] or (2) focus on specific titles or images as the *key* to the book's Christology.[3] The present essay will take a different approach. I do not deny that John the Seer draws upon sources and traditions. I do not deny that some images in the book (e.g., the Lamb) are weightier than others. Nor do I deny that some of the images stand in a certain tension with others. I would suggest, however, that it is most *theologically* fruitful to read the Apocalypse's christological imagery as manifesting a complex unity. Its christological unity is best grasped through a reading that treats the book as a literary whole, acknowledges diversity and intertextual interplay, and lets the tensions stand—just as wise readers do when encountering any complex work of literature.[4] Jesus in the book of Revelation is a multi-faceted character whose identity unfolds gradually within the work as a whole; to understand his identity, we are required to absorb the full range of representations that we encounter throughout the book; to interpret those representations, insofar as we are able, within the imaginative frame of reference ("encyclopedia of reception")[5] of the Christian communities of Asia Minor at the end of the first century C.E.; and to ask how the complex person we encounter in this complex text might engage or challenge the symbolic world in which we live and move.

It is this last part of the interpretative task from which biblical interpreters often shrink. But the Apocalypse does not want to permit its readers a position of wise neutrality: it pronounces blessing on those who keep the words of the prophecy (Rev 22:7) and dire warnings to those who fail to hear what the Spirit is saying. The Apocalypse summons readers to enter sympathetically into the intertextually rich symbolic world of the story it tells, in all its grandeur and confusing complexity. Only by doing so will we come to understand its depiction of the identity of Jesus.

Within a single short essay we cannot explore all the facets of Jesus' identity that such a reading might discover. I want to propose, therefore, that we attend to two major strands of the book's narrative representation of Jesus: *Jesus as sharer in the identity of God*, and *Jesus as faithful witness*. After examining these two strands, we will offer some concluding reflections about how these very different motifs play in counterpoint to illumine the identity of Jesus.

Jesus as Sharer in the Divine Identity

We begin in an unusual and slightly daunting place. In the prophetic word to the church in Thyatira, Jesus (the glorious "one like a Son of Man," 1:13) chastises the community for tolerating the false prophetess Jezebel and issues this dire warning:

> Beware, I am throwing her on a bed, and those who commit adultery with her I am throwing into great distress, unless they repent of her doings; and I will strike her children dead. And all the churches will know that I am the one who searches minds and hearts, and I will give to each of you as your works deserve. (Rev 2:22-23)

Here we encounter the threatening, judgmental Jesus that many contemporary readers of Revelation find so problematic. Before grappling with this aspect of Jesus' identity, however, I want to draw attention to an easily overlooked feature of Jesus' self-description in this prophetic word. Jesus' stern judgment against the "children" of Jezebel is meant to teach the churches to recognize two aspects of Jesus' identity and action: "I am the one who searches minds and hearts" (ἐγώ εἰμι ὁ ἐραυνῶν νεφροὺς καὶ καρδίας) and "I will give to each of you according to your works" (δώσω ὑμῖν ἑκάστῳ κατὰ τὰ ἔργα ὑμῶν). Each of these actions is elsewhere in Jewish tradition and in early Christianity ascribed exclusively to God. The parallels to two passages in Paul's Letter to the Romans are particularly striking. In Romans 8:27, Paul declares that the "the One [i.e., God] who searches hearts (ὁ δὲ ἐραυνῶν τὰς καρδίας) knows what is the mind of the Spirit, because the Spirit intercedes for the saints according to the will of God." And earlier in the same letter, Paul declares that God's wrath is being stored up against those who refuse to repent (cf. Rev 2:22, ἐὰν μὴ μετανοήσωσιν), because God is the one "who will repay to each one according to his works" (ὃς ἀποδώσει ἑκάστῳ κατὰ τὰ ἔργα αὐτοῦ, Rom 2:6).

I am by no means suggesting that Revelation is literarily dependent on Romans. Instead, Revelation's close parallels to Paul's statements about God simply demonstrate that these affirmations of God's supernatural perspicacity and just repayment according to works were commonplace maxims in the ancient Jewish and Christian cultural encyclopedia. Indeed, the maxim about God's repayment of human works is a near citation of Proverbs 24:12, where the wider context, particularly in the LXX rendering, bears especially close relation to Revelation's affirmation about Jesus:

> the Lord knows the hearts of all (κύριος καρδίας πάντων γινώσκει),
> and he who formed breath in everyone,
> he himself knows all things,
> who renders to each one according to his works (ὃς ἀποδίδωσιν ἑκάστῳ
>   κατὰ τὰ ἔργα αὐτοῦ).

My point here is a simple one: the prophetic warning in Revelation 2:23 ascribes to *Jesus* a power (knowing hearts and rewarding or punishing deeds) that Israel's Scripture ascribed to *God alone*.[6] Similar transferred ascriptions appear pervasively in Revelation, and they hint that Jesus is the possessor of divine power and prerogative. Precisely because this example appears unobtrusively in Rev 2:22-23, without fanfare or authorial comment, it all the more powerfully discloses the symbolic world from which John's prophecy issues. In that world, Jesus knows and does what only God can know and do.[7]

Other similar transferrals of divine attributes to the person of Jesus, both in descriptions of actions and in visual imagery, are more explicit.

One of the major christological motifs in the Apocalypse is the identification of Jesus as the "one like a Son of Man," the figure who appears in the eschatological prophecy of Daniel 7:13-14, "coming with the clouds of heaven" to receive universal dominion.[8] From the opening lines of the book, Revelation identifies Jesus as the embodiment of this figure, beginning with a solemn declaration that echoes and fuses Daniel 7:13 and Zechariah 12:10:

> Look! He is coming with the clouds;
> every eye will see him,
> even those who pierced him;
> and on his account all the tribes of the earth will wail. (Rev 1:7)

In Daniel 7, the Son of Man figure is a representative of an eschatologically triumphant Israel; the "one like a Son of Man" is the visionary symbolization of Israel's final vindication and triumph over enemies and oppressive empires.[9] But when Jesus first appears in John's vision as the glorious Son of Man (1:9-20), the iconography of his appearance includes an important additional detail that suggests divine identity:

> Then I turned to see whose voice it was that spoke to me, and on turning I saw seven golden lampstands, and in the midst of the lampstands I saw *one like the Son of Man*, clothed with a long robe and with a golden sash across his chest. *His head and his hair were white as white wool, white as snow*; his eyes were like a flame of fire, his feet were like burnished bronze, refined as in a furnace, and his voice was like the sound of many waters. In his right hand he held seven stars, and from his mouth came a sharp, two-edged sword, and his face was like the sun shining with full force. (Rev 1:12-16)

The imagery of the head and hair white as wool is drawn *not* from Daniel's description of the "one like a Son of Man" but rather from his portrayal of "the Ancient of Days" seated on the throne in the heavenly throne room (Dan 7:9), and John's depiction of the Son of Man as a fiery presence (eyes "like a flame of fire" and a face "like the sun") is also reminiscent of the God of Israel in Daniel's vision: "His throne was fiery flames, and its wheels were burning fire. A stream of fire issued and flowed out from his presence" (Dan 7:9-10). Thus, from Jesus' first appearance on the stage of the drama of Revelation, he is *intertextually* marked as bearing the visible signs of divine identity. Or, to put the point another way, the figures of the Ancient of Days and the Son of Man—two distinct figures in Daniel 7—are iconographically blended in Revelation's portrayal of Jesus.[10]

John's depiction of Jesus' fiery countenance is repeated in the prophetic address to the church in Thyatira: "And to the angel of the church in Thyatira write: These are the words of the Son of God, who has eyes like a flame of fire, and whose feet are like burnished bronze" (Rev 2:18). This is the only place in the entire book where the title "Son of God" appears, and, as we have seen, it is precisely to this church that Jesus asserts his divine power to search hearts and mete out judgment according to each person's works (2:22-23).

The role of the Son of Man as judge of the world is signaled again in the vision of Revelation 14:14-20, where "one like a Son of Man" seated on a cloud wields a sickle to reap the harvest of the earth—another well-known symbol for final judgment. This passage is sometimes taken as evidence of an angelomorphic Son of Man Christology—that is, a conceptuality in which the Son of Man is an angelic figure of intermediate status between God and humanity—because here the Son of Man figure acts in response to the bidding of "another angel" who comes out of the heavenly temple (14:15) and because the Son of Man's reaping action is paralleled by an apparently different angel who swings a sickle to "gather the clusters of the vine of the earth" and to throw them "into the great wine press of the wrath of God" (14:17-20).[11] As Loren Stuckenbruck comments, it is "logically problematic to modern readers why the author has not attempted to introduce terms which would keep his christological and angelological categories more separate."[12] This vision may be compared to the Matthean interpretation of the parable of the wheat and the weeds, where the Son of Man sends angelic reapers to perform the eschatological harvest and to throw the weeds "into the furnace of fire" (Matt 13:36-43). In Matthew, the distinction between the Son of Man and the angels is clearer than in the vision of Revelation 14:14-20. Nonetheless, readers of Revelation who have followed the prophecy from its beginning in chapter 1 will clearly identify the Son of Man figure on a cloud (Rev 14:14) as Jesus, and for such readers there can be little doubt of his dominion over the angels, as well as the whole earth.

The problem that Stuckenbruck identifies arises chiefly when Revelation 14:14-20 is treated as a separate form-critical unit of material rather than as part of a total composition. It is certainly possible that the passage may derive from an earlier source in which the Son of Man is an angelic figure, but within the literary context of the book of Revelation, he can be none other than Jesus, who has already been disclosed as bearing the divine identity. Within this reading, the function of Revelation 14:14-20 is to assert once more the role of Jesus as the exalted Son of Man who will execute just judgment on the earth.

This divine role has been repeatedly assigned to Jesus throughout the text. It appears especially in the letters to the seven churches (e.g., Rev 2:5, 16, 22-28; 3:2-5, 16, 21) as well as at other points in the visionary sequences (e.g., 6:16-17; 11:15-18), and it culminates in the christological vision of the rider on a white horse who "judges in righteousness" (19:11). For that reason, even though there is no explicit mention of Jesus in the brief description of final judgment of the dead in 20:11-15, the reader of the whole book will surely surmise that the book of life (20:12, 15) is none other than *the Lamb's* book of life (13:8), and that when Death and Hades are thrown into the lake of fire (20:14), the agent of their overthrow must be none other than Jesus, the Living One who now holds "the keys of Death and Hades" (1:18).[13]

It should be emphasized that final judgment in the book of Revelation means not only punishment of the wicked but also the granting of life, consolation, and rewards to the faithful. This is emphasized throughout the letters to the seven churches (Rev 2:7, 11, 17, 26-28; 3:4-5, 10-12, 21), and it is given particularly powerful emphasis in 7:9-17, where the *Lamb* (Jesus) is portrayed—in a paradoxical formulation—as the *shepherd* who will protect and guide his people to "springs of the water of life" (echoing Psalm 23), where God will "wipe away every tear from their eyes" (echoing Isa 25:8). This vision anticipates the book's climactic image of the New Jerusalem, where God himself will dwell with mortals, wipe away all tears, and abolish death and pain forever (Rev 21:1-4). Readers who have fully grasped the christological depth of the Apocalypse will almost certainly understand that if "the dwelling (σκηνή) of God is among human beings," then God's embodied presence in their midst cannot be understood apart from the embodiment of the divine presence in Jesus.

The mysterious coinherence of the identity of God and the identity of Jesus (*Verbindungsidentität*, to use the term proposed by C. Kavin Rowe),[14] is nowhere expressed more remarkably than in Revelation's deployment of the divine title "the Alpha and the Omega." This terminology appears only in the opening and closing sections of the book. Its first occurrence is the sonorous declaration of Revelation 1:8, where the speaker is none other than the one God of Israel, the cosmic Creator and ruler: "'I am the Alpha and the Omega (τὸ ἄλφα καὶ τὸ ὦ),' says the Lord God, who is and who was and who is to come, the Almighty (ὁ παντοκράτωρ)." Similarly, when the title reappears in 21:6, the speaker again is a voice from the divine throne who self-identifies as "God" (21:7). In this second instance, the "Alpha and Omega" title is supplemented and interpreted by the appositional expression, "the Beginning and the End" (ἡ ἀρχὴ καὶ τὸ τέλος). But in the third and final appearance of this divine title (22:13), we encounter a highly significant variation. Here the speaker is one who is "coming soon . . . to repay according to everyone's work" (22:12)–precisely the office already claimed for Jesus in 2:23. And in this final reiteration, the title "the Alpha and the Omega" has now acquired a third synonymous epithet, "the First and the Last" (ὁ πρῶτος καὶ ἔσχατος). So the final cadence sounds like this: "I am the Alpha and the Omega, the First and the Last, the Beginning and the End" (22:13). But ὁ πρῶτος καὶ ὁ ἔσχατος has already appeared as a title specifically for Jesus, "the one who was dead and came to life," in 1:17 and 2:8. Thus, however remarkable it may seem, the reader should not be surprised when the same revelatory voice that speaks as Alpha and Omega finally announces, "*It is I, Jesus*, who sent my angel to you with this testimony for the churches" (22:16). In the end of the book of Revelation, it is *Jesus* who can say, "I am the Alpha and the Omega, the First and the Last, the Beginning and the End."

Readers who have already heard Jesus assert himself to be "the First and the Last" (1:17, 2:8)–if their ears are attuned to echoes of Isaiah's prophecies–will already have heard a theme preparatory to the climactic christological cadence of Revelation 22:13. The title "the First and the Last" (ὁ πρῶτος καὶ ἔσχατος) is strongly reminiscent of the divine declaration in Isaiah 44:6:

Thus says the LORD, the King of Israel,
and his Redeemer [!], the Lord of Hosts:
"I am the first and I am the last (MT: אֲנִי רִאשׁוֹן וַאֲנִי אַחֲרוֹן)
besides me there is no God."

Or again, readers might recall Isaiah 48:12:

Listen to me, O Jacob, and Israel, whom I called:
I am He; I am the first, and I am the last (MT: אֲנִי־הוּא אֲנִי רִאשׁוֹן אַף אֲנִי אַחֲרוֹן)

Thus, even in the early part of the Apocalypse, in the letters to the churches, Jesus has already spoken the self-description that belongs only to the One who can say "besides me there is no other God."[15] By fusing "First and Last" with "Alpha and Omega," Revelation 22:13 clearly brings Jesus into a shared identity with the God of Israel, who has said, "My glory I will not give to another" (Isa 48:11). The only possible implication, within the symbolic world of Revelation, is that Jesus and God are one; their identity is a *Verbindungsidentität*. Otherwise, the claims made here by and for Jesus are simply blasphemous profanations of the name of God.[16]

A similar phenomenon appears in John the Seer's depiction of worship around the heavenly throne in Revelation 4 and 5.[17] In chapter 4, the four living creatures around the throne and the twenty-four elders offer praise to "our Lord and God" who is "worthy . . . to receive glory and honor and power": ἄξιος εἶ, ὁ κύριος καὶ ὁ θεὸς ἡμῶν, λαβεῖν τὴν <u>δόξαν</u> καὶ τὴν <u>τιμὴν</u> καὶ τὴν <u>δύναμιν</u>" (4:11). But when the new figure of the slaughtered Lamb appears in the throne room in chapter 5, the elders are joined by a great chorus of angels singing, "Worthy (ἄξιον) is the Lamb that was slaughtered to receive power (τὴν <u>δύναμιν</u>) and wealth and wisdom and strength and honor and glory (<u>τιμὴν</u> καὶ <u>δόξαν</u>) and blessing" (5:11). The Lamb that was slaughtered—clearly a symbol of Jesus Christ—is now deemed worthy of receiving precisely the same praise addressed to God in the first part of the throne room vision. And this point is finally driven home explicitly by the sung acclamation of "every creature in heaven and on earth and under the earth and in the sea." They all sing together:

> To the One seated on the throne *and to the Lamb*
> be blessing and honor (<u>τιμὴ</u>) and glory (<u>δόξα</u>) and might forever and
>   ever. (Rev 5:13)

And lest this acclamation be thought an aberration, it receives the "Amen" endorsement of the four living creatures and the elders in the final verse of the chapter (5:14). So the Lamb is included within the praise addressed to God.

The startling character of this inclusion is highlighted all the more forcefully by Revelation's incorporation, later in the book, of what Stuckenbruck has called "the refusal tradition," in which an angelic figure rejects the attempt of the human visionary to offer veneration or worship and redirects worship to God alone (Rev 19:10, 22:8-9; cf. Tobit 12:16-22; *Apoc. Zeph.* 6:11-15; *Ascen. Isa.* 7:18-23, 8:1-10, 15; *2 En.* 1:4-8; *3 En.* 1:7, 16:1-5).[18] The stark contrast between all creation's worship of the Lamb and the angel's emphatic refusal of worship ("You must not do that! . . . Worship God!" [Rev 19:10, 22:9]) shows that the worship of Jesus, the Lamb, cannot be thought to violate the prohibition of idolatrous worship.[19]

The Lamb's sharing in the divine identity is reinforced at the end of the book in John's vision of the new Jerusalem, where "the river of the water of life" flows "from the throne of God and of the Lamb" (22:1). Most strikingly, "the throne of God and of the Lamb will be in it [the city], and his servants will worship *him* (αὐτῷ)" (22:3). Here, in view of the compound antecedent (God and the Lamb) we would expect the plural pronoun αὐτοῖς. But the seemingly ungrammatical singular αὐτῷ makes a deeper point of theological/christological grammar: God and the Lamb are one.[20] That is why this Lamb can be named "Lord of lords and King of kings" (17:14; cf. 1:5).

But what is the significance of the fact that this Lamb who mysteriously shares the exalted identity of God is at the same time "the Lamb that was slaughtered"? The answer to that question is closely bound together with Jesus' identity as the one who faithfully testified to God's truth through his death.

Jesus as Faithful Witness

The opening salutation formula of the book offers "grace and peace . . . from Jesus Christ, the faithful witness, the firstborn from the dead, and the ruler of the kings of the earth" (1:4-5). The programmatic prominence of the epithet "the faithful witness" (ὁ μάρτυς ὁ πιστός) leads us to expect that the Christology of the Apocalypse will place heavy emphasis on Jesus' role as one who testifies to the truth. The actual expression "faithful witness" appears as a christological title, however, in only one other place in the book: the letter to the church in Laodicea is introduced as "the words of the Amen, the faithful and true witness (ὁ μάρτυς ὁ πιστὸς καὶ ἀληθινός)" (3:14). And the same qualities are ascribed—probably in titular form—to the rider on a white horse who comes to execute the final triumph of God: "Then I saw heaven opened, and there was a white horse. Its rider is called Faithful and True (πιστὸς καὶ ἀληθινός)" (19:11). We should not make the mistake of supposing, however, that Jesus' role as faithful witness is confined to those few passages in which he is given this specific designation.

The concept of witness-bearing (μαρτυρία) is central to the message of Revelation, and to its hortatory purposes. John the Seer describes himself as one "who testified to the word of God and to the testimony of Jesus Christ, everything that he saw (ὃς ἐμαρτύρησεν τὸν λόγον τοῦ θεοῦ καὶ τὴν μαρτυρίαν Ἰησοῦ Χριστοῦ ὅσα εἶδεν)" (Rev 1:2). So John himself is a witness, and that to which he bears witness is said to be "the μαρτυρία of Jesus Christ." Commentators debate whether the genitive construction here is objective ("the testimony about Jesus Christ") or subjective ("the testimony given by Jesus Christ"). Both meanings are possible, and I would suggest that a careful reading of the book as a whole will require us to hear both senses simultaneously.[21]

On the one hand, John tells us that his exile on the island of Patmos is "because of the word of God and the testimony of Jesus" (1:9), that is, presumably because of his own prophetic activity of proclaiming Jesus, not Caesar, as the true Lord and King. Similarly, we are told later that the dragon is making war on "those who keep the commandments of God and hold the testimony of Jesus" (12:17). Perhaps the clearest example of this objective-genitive sense is found in Revelation 20:4, where the Seer witnesses "the souls of those who had been beheaded for the testimony of Jesus (διὰ τὴν μαρτυρίαν Ἰησοῦ) and for the word of God." In this class of references, we should include also John's depiction of the souls under the altar in the heavenly throne room, those "who had been slaughtered for the word of God and for the testimony which they held" (6:9). In all of these instances, "the testimony of Jesus" constitutes an act of countercultural resistance through public prophetic proclamation of Jesus as Lord, an act of resistance that leads to persecution and (ultimately) martyrdom.[22]

On the other hand, there are also several suggestions in the text that Jesus himself is one who bears testimony, as the opening declaration of his role as "Faithful Witness" certainly indicates. In part, this refers to his role as the revealer of the visions given to the Seer: "I, Jesus, have sent my angel to testify (μαρτυρῆσαι) to you concerning these things for the churches" (22:16). This sense of Jesus as the revealer of testimony is confirmed in his final words in the book: "The one who testifies to these things (ὁ μαρτυρῶν ταῦτα) says, 'Surely I am coming soon.' Amen. Come, Lord Jesus!" (22:20). Here it appears that the entire book of Revelation constitutes Jesus' own testimony. Thus, there is a strong case to be made that "the testimony of Jesus" encompasses both the proclamation about him and the revelation that he supplies.

Beyond these grammatical observations about the multivalence of the construction διὰ τὴν μαρτυρίαν Ἰησοῦ, however, I would propose that "the testimony of Jesus" must include the memory or message of Jesus' own faithful suffering and death. This is suggested first of all by the interesting fact that the martyr Antipas in Pergamum is described as ὁ μάρτυς μου ὁ πιστός μου (2:13)—precisely echoing Revelation's programmatic description of Jesus himself as ὁ μάρτυς ὁ πιστός (1:5). It is likewise noteworthy that the martyred souls in Revelation 6:9 are said to have been *slaughtered* (ἐσφαγμένων) on account of their testimony—precisely the same verb used to describe the identity of the slaughtered Lamb in 5:6, 9, 11. Again, we should observe carefully how John describes the triumph of God's faithful over the adversarial dragon in chapter 12: "they have conquered him *by the blood of the Lamb* and *by the word of their testimony* (διὰ τὸν λόγον τῆς μαρτυρίας αὐτῶν), *for they did not cling to life even in the face of death*" (12:11). Here is an unmistakable statement that the "testimony" that conquers evil is not merely a verbal message; instead, it is an embodied testimony, enacted through a confession that refuses the way of violence and undergoes death, just as Jesus did, at the hands of earthly powers.[23] That is why witnesses of this kind can be said to have the Lamb's name written on their foreheads (14:1); they are the ones who "follow the Lamb wherever he goes" (14:4)–which surely means following his example of testimony through the way of the cross.

Consequently, when John declares that he has "testified to the word of God and to the testimony of Jesus Christ, *everything that he saw*" (1:2), we must surmise that the ματυρία he *saw* includes the vision of Jesus as the slaughtered but triumphant Lamb–that is to say, Jesus as the crucified Lord. And precisely in his identity as slaughtered Lamb, Jesus provides the pattern, the example, and prototype for those who follow him wherever he goes. Their identity as suffering witnesses is patterned on Jesus' identity as Faithful Witness, which finds its definitive embodiment in his own death on a cross.

Only in that sense can we rightly understand his prophetic promise to the church at Laodicea: "To the one who conquers I will give a place with me on my throne, just as I myself conquered and sat down with my Father on his throne" (3:21). To "conquer," as in 12:11, is to follow Jesus' own example of conquering through a faithful submission to death.[24] This paradoxical symbolic inversion lies at the heart of the entire book of Revelation. To put the point aphoristically, I would suggest that the conquering power of the Lamb in Revelation can be best understood when it is interpreted through the intertextual lens of the Gospel of John, in which Jesus conquers the world (John 16:33) by being lifted up on the cross in such a way that his death will draw all humanity to himself (John 12:32-33). Thus, the Passion Narrative is the christological subtext that undergirds all of the Apocalypse's references to Jesus as Faithful Witness/Martyr.

The Lamb on the Throne
God Crucified and Triumphant

These preliminary explorations in the Christology of the Apocalypse have demonstrated something of the depth and complexity of this visionary work. I would like to draw out some of the implications of my reading by making four points–two methodological observations and two substantive claims.

(1) *The necessity of intertextual interpretation.* The Christology I have described is not entirely to be found in the explicit surface statements and affirmations of the text. It arises from reflective intertextual interpretation of the Apocalypse as a document embedded in a particular encyclopedia of production, a discursive space shaped by dialogue with precursor texts. For example, the full import of describing Jesus as "the First and the Last" can be discerned only in relation to the precursor texts in Isaiah that emphatically declare the God of Israel to be "the First and the Last." Readers unfamiliar with Israel's Scripture are likely to underinterpret the radical

and shattering christological implications of Revelation's imagery. Consequently, interpretation of the message of Revelation requires the recovery and amplification of numerous intertextual echoes that will be inaudible to many readers today. One effect of recovering these echoes will be to highlight the astonishing claim that Jesus is a sharer in the divine identity.

(2) *The implications of canonical reading.* A related but distinguishable point is that the Christology of Revelation is brought rightly into focus by a reading that places it firmly within the canon of the New Testament—or at least within the narrative world of the four canonical Gospels. The image of the triumphant "Lamb that was slaughtered" is unintelligible apart from the Gospel narratives of Jesus' crucifixion and resurrection. And it should be noted that the interpretation of Jesus' crucifixion as the "slaughter" of a "lamb" almost certainly presupposes a canonical/intertextual reading of the passion story in light of Isaiah 53:7:

> He was oppressed, and he was afflicted,
> yet he did not open his mouth;
> like a lamb that is led to the slaughter (LXX: ὡς πρόβατον ἐπὶ σφαγὴν
>   ἤχθη),
> and like a sheep that before its shearers is silent,
> so he did not open his mouth.

Most Christian readers effortlessly and unreflectively perform this sort of intertextual reading, so that the otherwise puzzling figure of the slaughtered Lamb on the throne occasions no particular difficulty. But it should be noted that apart from the narrative context provided by the Gospels, as well as by Isaiah 53, this aspect of the christological imagery of the Apocalypse would be at best opaque.

Further, I would suggest that a similar point can be made about the image of Jesus as "Faithful Witness." Such an interpretation of Jesus presupposes not only the explicit description of Jesus as a revealer in the Apocalypse but also the influence of at least two other streams of New Testament Christology. First, the image of Jesus as "Witness" appears prominently in the Gospel of John, climactically in the trial scene before Pontius Pilate: "For this I was born, and for this I came into the world, *to testify to the truth* (ἵνα μαρτυρήσω τῇ ἀληθείᾳ)" (John 18:37; cf. also John 3:31-33, 8:18). And second, Paul's references to the faithfulness of Jesus Christ (πίστος Ἰησοῦ Χριστοῦ) in his obedient self-giving death may undergird Revelation's portrayal of Jesus as the faithful one.[25] Further, as I have already noted (note 14), the image of Jesus as faithful oppositional witness in the face of Roman power is brought fully to expression in the Pauline tradition in 1 Timothy 6:13.

One of the major hermeneutical implications of reading Revelation within the canonical framework of the New Testament is to serve as a check and corrective on interpretations that seek to read the violent militaristic imagery of the Apocalypse literalistically. If Jesus wins his victory over the world through his faithful death on a cross (as all the rest of the New Testament documents insist), and if Revelation's figurative depictions are to be read in intertextual concert with these other texts, then the triumphant rider who is "clothed in a robe dipped in blood" (Rev 19:13) must be wearing a garment drenched with his *own* blood, and the "sharp sword" that comes "from his mouth . . . to strike down the nations" (19:15) must be the proclaimed word of the gospel (as in Eph 6:17), not a literal sword of iron that kills enemies.[26]

The larger point, however, is not only that placing Revelation within the New Testament canon leads to a nonviolent reading of the text, but that the book's vivid depictions of God, Christ, and the church must all be construed as part of a larger narrative whole. Such a reading will cause hermeneutical implications to run both ways. On the one hand, the wider New Testament narrative creates hermeneutical constraints on the interpretation of Revelation's symbolism; on the other hand, Revelation's apocalyptic worldview broadens and deepens the radical implications of the New Testament's other stories and letters—it discloses vividly that our lives are placed in a cosmic frame of reference.

(3) *The narrative embodiment of proto-Chalcedonian Christology.* I turn now to two substantive findings of this brief study of the Christology of the Apocalypse. One of the most striking features of the analysis we have pursued here is that it seems to show that the presentation of Jesus in this book is what we might call "proto-Chalcedonian." Jesus in Revelation is a figure who shares fully in the divine identity, yet at the same time, he is a human figure who suffered a martyr's death at the hands of an earthly Empire. Only so can he rightly say of himself, "I was dead, and see, I am alive forever and ever; and I have the keys of Death and Hades" (1:18). Thus he is simultaneously the example par excellence of human faithfulness (the prototypical martyr) *and* the Alpha and the Omega, the one who is worthy to receive worship and honor that belongs to God alone. This is not merely a retrospective projection of a later doctrinal standard onto a primitive Christian text; rather, this paradoxical duality of the identity of Jesus is embedded deeply in the symbolic logic of the text itself.[27] The book of Revelation does not attempt to explain its paradoxical Christology through any sort of ontological analysis or second-order conceptual reasoning; rather, its presentation of Jesus' identity operates in the realm of narrative and poetic figuration. It is not hard to see how the book's

symbolic representations—along with similar material in the other New Testament documents—subsequently stimulated (indeed, we might say, *demanded*) second-order reflection. But the Apocalypse itself offers vision and proclamation, not "theology" as a mode of discourse. At best, we could say that theology and Christology are implicit in the text's *poiēsis*.

(4) *The politics of eschatological justice.* Finally, Revelation's portrayal of the identity of Jesus impacts our understanding of *politics.* The theme of the conference that gave rise to the essays in this book was "The Book of Revelation: Theology, Politics, and Intertextuality." I have sketched here the manifold ways in which careful *intertextual* reading can inform our grasp of the *theology* implicit in the book. In these concluding remarks, I also want to highlight the way in which the Christology of the Apocalypse points toward certain *political* implications.[28] In the interpretation of the Apocalypse, it becomes evident that literary, theological, and political readings are inextricably interwoven.

The two components of the christological paradox we have examined converge to encourage the formation of a confessing community of followers of the Lamb, a community that poses a fundamental challenge to the powers of the present world. On the one hand, Jesus as Faithful Witness/ Martyr stands in opposition to the false and blasphemous claims of the dragon, the Empire that exercises "authority over every tribe and people and language and nation" so that "all the inhabitants of the earth will worship it, everyone whose name has not been written from the foundation of the world in the book of life of the Lamb that was slaughtered" (13:7-8). Jesus the Lamb dies as a victim of this false power, but precisely by so doing exposes its evil and its illegitimacy. On the other hand, because this same Jesus is in fact "the ruler of the kings of the earth" (1:5), the "Lord of lords and King of kings," his victory over the oppressing earthly powers is both assured and final (17:14). Thus, both in his humanity (Faithful Witness) and his divinity (Alpha and Omega), Jesus stands triumphant: "the kingdom of this world has become the kingdom of our Lord and of his Messiah, and he will reign forever and ever" (11:15).[29] The derisive lament over the fall of Babylon the great—with its military power, its mercantile wealth, its immorality, and its violence (18:1-24)—is the apocalyptic disclosure of God's final judgment on the present political order. This politics of wealth and violence, the politics of "Babylon, the mighty city" (18:10), is judged and supplanted by God's new *polis*, the New Jerusalem, in which God dwells with his people and wipes away all tears (21:1-4). This eschatological vision of justice looms over present political reality and subjects it to judgment.[30]

The consequent effect of Revelation's political vision is summed up eloquently by Oliver O'Donovan: "It conveys to us a hope that in the life which we are summoned to live with Christ we may experience, as a social reality, that authority of truth and righteousness which our experience of political society on earth has consistently denied us." Consequently, those who proclaim the message of the Apocalypse to challenge the injustice of the prevailing political powers are "confronting a false political order with the foundation of a true one."[31] Those who "follow the Lamb wherever he goes" (14:4) will find that the Christology of this mysterious visionary Apocalypse leads us ultimately to justice and life. The slaughtered Lamb, the Faithful Witness, is also the One who stands, as Alpha and Omega, at the beginning and end of history. For that reason—and only for that reason—we can join John the Seer in patient endurance while we live, act, and bear witness in light of his apocalyptic vision of the healing of the nations.

5
God, Israel, and Ecclesia in the Apocalypse

Joseph L. Mangina

Introduction

The Apocalypse puzzles me. This strange work is "a cataract, a primeval forest, a demonic power, something directly down from Himalaya, absolutely Chinese, strange, mythological; I lack completely the means, the suction cups, even to assimilate this phenomenon, not to speak of presenting it adequately. What I receive is only a thin little stream and what I can then give out again is only a yet thinner extract of this little stream."[1] Those words are not mine, but the young Karl Barth's, and he was writing not about the Apocalypse but about Calvin. Yet his bafflement about the Reformer matches mine about Revelation—remarkably, the only book of the Bible on which Calvin never lectured.

There is something else that puzzles me, however, and that is the church. The flaws of the church are all too clearly manifest. There is no need for me to rehearse them for you. And yet despite the church's flaws, we confess our faith in her every time we recite the creed. The church (more precisely, Christ's nuptial relation to the church) is what Paul in Ephesians calls a *mega mysterion*, a great mystery. The church is not simply an addendum to or consequence of the gospel. The church is itself a part of the gospel, and participates in the gospel's character as a *mysterion*. That this should be true in Ephesians, or even, say, 1 Corinthians, with its high doctrine of the church as Christ's body, does not surprise us. But is it the case for Revelation?

In this paper, I will argue that it is indeed the case. The mystery that is the apocalypsing of Jesus Christ includes the mystery of the church. In the victory of Jesus, the Lamb, God is engaged in the apocalyptic remaking of the world, and the *ekklēsia* is present at this new creation. She has her own distinctive role to play in the drama. And yet, curiously, it is not by inhabiting the role of "church" that she participates in it. Rather, the church—in Revelation, the churches—are drawn into their destiny by inhabiting the scriptural role of Israel. Apocalyptic reality is Jewish-messianic reality. As a consequence, those caught up in this reality cannot help but be Messiah's people.

Therefore, I will try to set out some of the ways in which this is so, partly by exploring the theme of Israel in particular passages of Revelation, partly by offering a broader set of reflections on the relations among apocalypse, church, and history. Multiple questions present themselves. How can the apocalyptic church of John the Seer's time, expecting the imminent "end of the world," be the same community as that which has lived and borne witness over two millennia? What relevance have John's visions for a church that has a story, a past? More epigrammatically: what has *apokalypsis* to do with *ekklēsia*? While such questions cannot be resolved in a single essay, I hope that thinking of the church as Israel may help us in framing them properly.

My point of departure in developing this theme is a programmatic article written by George Lindbeck in the late 1980s, simply "The Church."[2] This densely-argued piece pursues multiple agendas. It is a proposal about scriptural hermeneutics; it is a contribution to an ongoing research program on the role of narrative in theology; it seeks to advance the cause of Jewish-Christian dialogue. Most of all, however, it functions as a proposal in ecumenical theology, Lindbeck's particular vocation dating from his years as an official (Lutheran) observer at the Second Vatican Council. At the heart of this essay is a lapidary and precisely worded definition of the church: "the messianic pilgrim people of God typologically shaped by Israel's story."[3]

It will be worthwhile spending some time unpacking this definition.

The phrase "pilgrim people" is a conscious echo of *Lumen Gentium*, the Dogmatic Constitution on the Church of the Second Vatican Council.[4] In recent Roman Catholic theology, it is frequently said that the idea of communion lies at the heart of the council's understanding of the church.[5] It was, however, the image of church as God's pilgrim people that most impressed itself upon observers at the time. Lindbeck's essay is an attempt to give greater precision to this image—to turn it into a proper concept. He does so by arguing that the church is continuous with, indeed identical to, the historical people Israel. The early Christians were a Jewish sect. Their sacred writings were the Hebrew Scriptures. As a consequence, Lindbeck writes, it was natural that they should understand their communities as *ekklēsia*, as *qahal*, the assembly of Israel in the new age. . . . Thus the story of Israel was their story. They were that part of the people of God who lived in the time between the times after the messianic era had begun but before the final coming of the kingdom. Whatever is true of Israel is true of the Church except where the differences are explicit.[6]

A prominent feature of this account is the use of the concept "story," which does a great deal of work for Lindbeck. In this ecclesiology, "story" has a logically primitive status. The church's story is what the church is. While there are many true things that can and need to be said about the church—that she is the body of Christ, that she is one, holy, catholic, and apostolic, etc.—these predicates do not float in mid-air. They require a subject; they need a people to be their bearer. As a corollary of this rule, Lindbeck insists that the primary referent of the word "church" in the New Testament is concrete communities. "Church" does not mean an ecclesial event or a mode of being or a promissory utterance. While any or all of these may be involved when it comes to the actual stuff of Christian living, it is not these predicates or relational terms that define the *ekklēsia*. A church is visible; a church is sociologically "dense." All this follows from the scriptural point of departure. "An invisible Church is as biblically odd as an invisible Israel," Lindbeck insists.[7] The subject of ecclesiology is nothing less than "empirical churches in all their crass concreteness."[8]

We should pause to note the antisupersessionist and antitriumphalist motivations behind this proposal. It is anti-triumphalist, because while the church continues Israel's story she is not the fulfillment of that story. Only Jesus Christ is that. This means that one cannot (on New Testament grounds) contrast the shame of Israel with the splendor of the church, for the church shares in Israel's imperfections. When Paul writes to the Christians in Corinth, he invokes not only the water that graciously flowed from the rock, but the possibility of being struck down for disobedience like the sons of Korah. Both of these are "examples [*typoi*] for our instruction" (1 Cor 10:11).

Assigning typological primacy to Christ also serves Lindbeck's goal of being anti-supersessionist. If the church as such does not fulfill Israel's story, this means she herself is still waiting, and that the last word has not been spoken about the fate of unbelieving Judaism. While Lindbeck offers no detailed exegesis of Romans 9–11, he obviously would assign hermeneutical priority to Paul's affirmation that "all Israel will be saved," over the sharp and seemingly final judgment on the synagogue expressed in Matthew's Gospel (27:25!).

If we stand back from the details of this proposal, what do we see? As I mentioned earlier, the concept story plays a prominent role here, as does its quasi-sociological counterpart, peoplehood. Peoples have narratives, and while things change in narratives (they would hardly be narratives otherwise) peoplehood remains more or less a constant. As Lindbeck writes:

> Israel and the Church were one people for the early Christians. There was no breach in continuity. A new age had begun, but the story continued and therefore also the people which it identified. The French remain French after the revolution, the Quakers [who started out as a church of the poor] remain Quakers after becoming wealthy, and Israel remains Israel even when transformed by the arrival of the eschaton in Christ. The Church is simply Israel in the time between the times. The continuity of the story and the identity of the people are unbroken.[9]

It is at this point that worries begin to arise. These are of two sorts. First, the *ekklēsia* in the New Testament is always the *ekklēsia tou theou*. The church is "of God," in a way that is not the case with either the Quakers or the French. To be sure, Lindbeck himself admits that a full dogmatic ecclesiology would have to begin with "the people of God as worshiping community created by the Father through the Son in the power of the Holy Spirit, constituted by the proclamation of the gospel in word and sacrament, and bearing joyous fruit in works of suffering love."[10] This is a winsome description, and yet one wonders if God's triune activity has been neutralized in advance by the empirical "facts on the ground." Divine action cannot come in as an afterthought, but must be integrated into one's reading from the very outset.

The other worry is that, just as God plays a very muted role in this essay, so the difference made by Messiah's coming seems curiously thin. Perhaps the French do remain French after the revolution—though even here, the horrors of the Revolutionary Tribunal and the guillotine would seem to represent an awesome "breach in continuity." How much more so "the arrival of the eschaton in Christ"! The New Testament seems consistent in saying that the ministry and death of Jesus, the Jew, represented a wrenching dislocation in the life of the people. This is not to say we may not speak of continuities; but the continuities will be discerned in light of

> the revelation of the mystery (*apokalypsin mysteriou*) that was kept secret for long ages but is now disclosed, and through the prophetic writings is made known to all Gentiles, according to the command of the eternal God . . . (Rom 16:25-26)

Talk about either Israel or the church must be situated between God's election on the one hand, his eschatological purpose on the other.

As we turn to the Apocalypse, we will find that John the Seer fully shares the conviction of other New Testament writers that the *ekklēsia* is Israel. Lindbeck is correct about this. But she is Israel in so far as she suffers divine things and undergoes what the Seer calls "tribulation" (*thlipsis*). It is time to have an ear for what the Spirit is saying, not only to but about the churches.

Stars and Lampstands
The Visible Church as the Heavenly Church

The place to begin, of course, is with the letters to the seven churches, the ecclesiological *locus classicus* in Revelation. There we have no difficulty seeing many aspects of Lindbeck's vision confirmed. The churches of Asia are seven real assemblies, located in seven actual cities of Asia Minor. They are concrete, visible, and vulnerable—threatened from without, conflicted within. The church in Pergamum dwells "where Satan's throne is," and has already given up one martyr (Rev 2:13). Both there and in Thyatira the question of food sacrificed to idols is a major issue, as it was for Paul (2:14, 20), and in Philadelphia, the church struggled over the relationship between Jewish and Christian identity. Members of the community in Smyrna are facing the prospect of imprisonment (2:10). The Christians in Ephesus have grown cold, those in Sardis are dead despite their glittering reputation, and the Laodicean church is famously lukewarm, good for nothing but to be spat out with disgust (2:4; 3:2, 16).

Reading the messages to the seven churches occasions much the same shock of recognition we have when reading Paul's letters. We know these people. We can relate to situations like these. It is not that the historical distance is dissolved. On the contrary, the very real differences in culture and social setting serve to highlight basic, shared features of the human struggle. The churches of Asia had to deal with questions of food, drink, authority, doctrine, discipline, and confronting the local gods (food sacrificed to idols, "Satan's throne"). So do ours. This comes in part of inhabiting a common, material, historical world. It is because first-century Christians are so different from us that they are so much the same. *Plus ça change, plus c'est la même chose.*

That the *ekklēsiai* are visible social bodies does not mean, however, that we can account for them in purely sociological terms. As communities (*Gemeinschaften*) they appear to be mere voluntary associations in the patchwork of urban Roman society. But they are more than this. They are the recipients of a letter, a prophecy, addressed from "the one who is and who was and who is to come," from Jesus Christ, and from the seven spirits of God (1:4-5). Sean McDonough has shown that the formula "the one who is" is a rabbinic cipher for YHWH, ultimately traceable to the "I AM" saying in Exodus 3:14.[11] And in so far as the churches are addressed as the beloved (1:5b; 3:19) of Israel's God, who can they themselves be except Israel?

This point is confirmed when we examine the letters to the seven churches. The very language used in these letters is coded to Israel's Scriptures. The Ephesians are promised "the tree of life, which is in the paradise of God" (2:7). The Christians in Pergamum are offered some of the "hidden manna," while those in Philadelphia will be made "a pillar in the temple of my God" (2:17; 3:12). Nor is it only these positive images that point to Israel's story. Even the threats are Scripture-shaped. Instead of calling his rival prophet in Thyatira by her (presumably Greek) name, John calls her "Jezebel," casting himself, perhaps, in the role of Elijah. Likewise, some people in Pergamum are followers of "Balaam," a shady character who "put a stumbling block before the people of Israel" (2:15). If nothing else, the summoning of the churches[12] to repentance is a sure sign that they inhabit the role of Israel: "For the time has come for judgment to begin within the household of God" (1 Pet 4:17).

In a broad sense, then, we may say that the churches of Asia are the inheritors of Israel's story. Does that story ever appear as such—is there any reference in the Apocalypse to the chronological sequence of Israel's life before God? This is much less clear. David L. Barr has made the intriguing suggestion that, in the letters to the seven churches, one can detect a rough progression through biblical history: thus Ephesus = creation (the tree of life); Smyrna = exodus (imprisonment); Pergamum = wilderness-conquest (Balaam, the sword); Thyatira = kingship (Jezebel/Ahab); Philadelphia = the temple (pillars); and Laodicea = exile (being poor, blind, and naked). This is ingenious; I find it attractive. But it is also tenuous.[13] Nor does Barr insist on the point. Less important than any progression is the sheer presence and density of the images themselves. The churches display elements of Israel's story because they participate in that story, because they are involved in a struggle that resembles Israel's in important ways. Just what this looks like will depend on one's particular location. In Smyrna, the drama of imprisonment and release may well play out the scenario of the exodus. In lukewarm Laodicea, the threat of some final exile hangs over the church. The "mapping" of the church onto Israel's story is contextual, typological, and synchronic, rather than a matter of strict chronology.

The most important thing of all, however, is that the churches do not *map themselves* onto Israel's story; they are mapped onto it by the One who is speaking to them. Deriving any "ecclesiology" from the letters to the churches would be a hopeless enterprise indeed if we did not take into account the christological and pneumatological actuality in which the churches find themselves.

This becomes apparent already in the opening vision (1:9-20). A Danielic figure appears to John on Patmos. He is robed in splendor. His face shines like the sun in full strength. He walks among seven golden lampstands, and holds seven stars in his right hand. The symbols in Revelation are not always explained, but these are—and it is the Speaker himself who explains them:

> As for the mystery of the seven stars that you saw in my right hand, and the seven golden lampstands, the seven stars are the angels of the seven churches, and the seven lampstands are the seven churches. (1:20)

The word mystery, *mysterion*, can be taken here in what might be called an epistemological sense. A mystery is a puzzle, a riddle, a dark saying. Much later in the book we are told that the Whore bears "a name of mystery," to wit "Babylon the great, mother of whores and of earth's abominations" (17:5). Mystery here places us in the realm of trope or metaphor: *this is that*. But the term mystery may also be taken in an ontological sense. When the angel with the little scroll appears, he declares that when the seventh trumpet sounds "the mystery of God will be fulfilled, as he announced to his servants the prophets" (10:7). Here "mystery" seems to approach its meaning in a work like Ephesians, where *mysterion* refers to God's purpose to unite Jew and Gentile in a single body, a thing long hidden but now revealed (cf. Eph 3:1-13).

That the seven churches should be called "lampstands" seems clear enough. Seven churches are seven lamps—this could be nothing else but the seven-branched candelabrum that illumined the desert tabernacle, and that later adorned the temple in Jerusalem. Far more than the Star of David, the menorah was the universally-recognized symbol for Judaism in the ancient world. (On the Arch of Titus in Rome, commemorating the sack of Jerusalem by the Roman army in 70 C.E., one can clearly see the candelabrum being carted off as part of the plunder.) The symbolism is obvious. The seven churches are the menorah, and the menorah (by metonymy) is Israel. It would be hard to imagine a more direct identification between Israel and the *ekklēsia*.

This interpretation would be incomplete, however, if we did not include a reference to Zechariah 4, a passage with strong intertextual echoes in Revelation. John's "two witnesses" (Rev 11) are clearly an echo of Zechariah's two olive trees, identified as "the two anointed ones who

stand by the Lord of the whole earth" (Zech 4:14). But there is also a link
through the figure of the menorah. Zechariah sees a golden lampstand
bearing seven lamps. When he asks his accompanying angel what this
means, he is told: "These seven are the eyes of the LORD, which range
through the whole earth" (Zech 4:10b). Earlier in the same vision, the
prophet is given a message for the leader of the returning exiles: "This is
the word of the LORD to Zerubbabel: Not by might, nor by power, but by
my Spirit, says the LORD of hosts" (Zech 4:6).

The fourth chapter of Zechariah, then, offers a cluster of messianic
and pneumatic images that bear fruit in the Apocalypse. In the latter book
not only do the seven eyes of YHWH become the Lamb's seven eyes, but
these eyes themselves are understood as *pneumata*, as spirits/Spirit: "the
seven spirits of God sent out into all the earth" (Rev 5:6). The overall
effect here is quite curious. At one level the sevenfold lampstand clearly
stands for the churches themselves, as we are told explicitly at Revelation
1:20. But at another level, the intertextual resonances with Zechariah 4
tend to draw the churches into the divine reality itself. The seven churches
"are" at once the eyes of YHWH, the eyes of the Lamb, and the seven
spirits of God sent into all the earth—a trinitarian ecclesiology, indeed!
The seven little assemblies in Asia Minor exist, as it were, *internally* to the
drama of God's will being powerfully realized on earth that the Apocalypse narrates. They are the recipients and beneficiaries of that action, but
at the same time they are participants in it.

We attain the same result when we examine the mystery of the seven
stars, identified by Christ as "the angels of the seven churches." I doubt
we should linger very long over their ontological status.[14] Like the Letter to
the Hebrews, a work with which it shows some remarkable affinities, Revelation locates angels firmly within the creaturely realm. They are not to
be worshiped (19:10; 22:9). And yet what would the Apocalypse be without its angels?—the seven angels of the trumpets and of God's wrath, the
armies of Michael, the "myriads of myriads and thousands of thousands"
who worship God and the Lamb. The role of angels in the book may
be considered an intensification of their more general role in Scripture.
Angels, it can plausibly be argued, serve as sites of apocalyptic irruption.
Their presence is thickest at those times and places where ordinary earthly
causality breaks open, allowing humans to discern the unsuspected nearness of heaven. It is no accident that angels appear at the empty tomb
in the resurrection narratives in the Gospels. In Revelation, they suggest
both the nearness of heaven and the imminence of "the time."

It is significant, then, that each of the seven churches comes equipped
with its personal angel, and that these angels have been variously

interpreted as guardians, as presiding rulers,[15] or even as representations of the common spirit of the assembly. I do not think it matters a great deal which of these readings we choose. The important thing is that the angelic element in the church indicates its determination by the things of heaven rather than the things of earth.[16] The *ekklēsia* is itself a site of apocalyptic rupture, a site where the heavens are opened. In this regard, it is significant that while the *content* of the letters is clearly directed to the churches themselves, the letters are actually *addressed* to the churches' angels ("to the angel of the church at Ephesus write . . ." etc.). A mere religious community, a *Gemeinschaft*, is in the end governed by the powers of the present age; it is subject to "fate." But—to borrow a concept from Stanley Hauerwas—a community ruled by an angel is determined not by fate but by destiny.[17] It is thereby granted the freedom to live in genuinely human ways, in contrast to the various enslavements characterizing life under the beast and Babylon. We should note that such freedom derives not from the absence of lordship, a prevalent myth of the modern era, but from *who* is Lord: Jesus, ruler of Israel and the church, he who "holds the seven stars in his right hand."

Twice in the letters to the churches, Christ has alluded to a "door" that enables communion between himself and his followers (3:8, 19). Now John himself crosses this threshold—"and there in heaven a door stood open!" (4:1)—and his readers/hearers cross with him. No single vision in Revelation is more determinative of the churches' identity than the scene of heavenly worship that unfolds in chapters 4–5. Here God's sovereign rule over all things is not only stated, it is shown, in a dazzling display of metaphor. To ask whether this is a "religious" scene or a "political" scene is to miss the point. It is both.[18] John is showing his hearers both who is to be worshiped and who is in charge, and the answer in both cases is God, with the negative always implied: not the beast, not Caesar.

It would be inappropriate, even blasphemous, to try to make the church in any sense the direct *content* of the visions in chapters 4–5. The visions are radically and rapturously theocentric. Their point is the worship of God and the Lamb.[19] And yet the presence of the *ekklēsia* is signaled in multiple ways. This is most obviously the case in the image of the twenty-four elders, the "courtiers" of heaven, whose number likely represents the twelve tribes plus the twelve apostles (cf. 21:12-14). They do not speak, but twice we hear them sing. The first time they sing the praises of God as the one who "created all things, and by [whose] will they existed and were created," while the second time they hymn the victory of the Lamb:

You are worthy to take the scroll and to open its seals,
for you were slaughtered and by your blood you ransomed for God
saints from every tribe and language and people and nation;
you have made them to be a kingdom and priests serving our God . . .

                                                    (5:9-10a)

The allusion here, of course, is to God's declaration that Israel will
be to him "a kingdom of priests and a holy nation" (Exod 19:6). But the
song also echoes the doxology that irrupts spontaneously in the opening
lines of John's letter:

To him who loves us and freed us from our sins by his blood, and made
us to be a kingdom, priests serving his God and father . . . (1:5b)

Prophetic speech is ecstatic speech, in which the ordinary boundaries
between past and present or between heaven and earth are transgressed.
The Seer does not have a "theory" about how the churches in Ephesus or
Smyrna can be the people whom God led out of Egypt for priestly service.
He does not even assert that this is the case; it just *is* the case. Likewise, he
is not so eschatologically fastidious as to restrict the heavenly worship to a
place "up there" or to a time "at the End." To the extent that the congregations in Asia Minor worship the one Creator God and sing the praises of
the Lamb, they themselves are participants in that worship. Whether on
heaven or on earth, the determinative truth is that the Lion of Judah/the
Lamb "has conquered" (*enikēsen*, 5:5), a verb with no object, and whose
range is therefore unrestricted. The Lamb has conquered all enemies and
prevailed in every possible way. Therefore the *ekklēsia*, too, can enjoy a
foretaste of its identity as "the conquerors."

The Great Ordeal
The Church and the Struggles of History

So far, I have been tracing the powerfully vertical, eschatological thrust of
Revelation's understanding of *ekklēsia*. The church is Israel, but precisely
the messianic Israel, her identity shaped by God's and the Lamb's victory.
And yet the messianic era is a time of woes. This common New Testament
teaching is shared by the Apocalypse—and, by the book's logic of extremes,
also intensified by it. Nothing that has been said so far should be interpreted as saying that the church is spared the agonies of life in history.
The church's heavenly destiny must be lived out *on earth*. If this were not
the case, then the book would be an escapist fantasy with strongly gnostic
overtones, like the latter-day apocalypse *Left Behind*.

The Apocalypse does not, after all, conclude with chapter 5, which
would be the case if its eschatology were "realized." The Lamb's victory is

what entitles him to open the seals and preside over the slaughterhouse of history. This is harsh language, but then the central visions of Revelation are harsh. They depict God's unfinished business with the earth, otherwise known as the divine wrath (6:16-17; 14:10, 19; 15:1, 7; 16:1-21). However else we may read these passages, they are a guarantee that the Lamb's victory over the powers of evil is not just notional but real. There *will* be a new heaven and a new earth. Oppressors will not "get away with it" (20:11-15); victims will be comforted (7:17; 21:4); and the powers of death and hell will themselves be destroyed forever (20:14).

Where is the church in all of this? In one sense, it could be argued that the church is not present at all. One of Revelation's more curious semantic features is that the word *ekklēsia* is never used in the central body of the visions (3:22–22:16). Dispensationalist interpreters have an explanation for this: the church, the true Christians, have been raptured! A more plausible reason, however, is that John (or the Spirit) reserves *ekklēsia* for the audience of the work—whether the churches of Asia or any subsequent Christian communities and readers. *Ekklēsia*, the congregation of Israel, is who they are. The point of the visions is to show them what they must *become*. If the divine judgment of the world is the primary theme of these central chapters, the chief secondary theme is the destiny of God's people. To state it in narrative terms: Revelation opens with (*a*) the church as we know it, in the form of the seven churches of Asia, and concludes with (*a'*) the glorious New Jerusalem, the bride of the Lamb. The book describes a transformation. But in what does this transformation consist? How does (*a*) become (*a'*)?

It is totally characteristic of the Apocalypse that it does not flatly relate the answer to this question. Instead of saying, it shows. And this showing takes place in the form of a series of strategically located tableaux, or set-pieces, depicting the destiny of God's people. The first of these occurs in the interval between the sixth and seventh seals, and depicts the sealing of the 144,000, immediately followed by John's vision of the white-robed army of martyrs (7:1-17). The second occurs in the interval between the sixth and seventh trumpets, and narrates the mysterious story of the "two witnesses" (11:1-13). The third tableau opens with the assembling of this same 144,000 with the Lamb on Mount Zion (14:1-4), not long before the pouring of "the seven plagues, which are the last, for with them the wrath of God is ended" (15:1). In this one case, the tableau has a "sequel" in the jubillant victory celebration of God's people by the sea of glass (15:2-4).

In each of these pictures, the people of God occupy a position of penultimacy—before the seventh seal, before the seventh trumpet, before the seven bowls representing God's definitive judgment. If, as an ancient tradition of interpretation holds, these sequences are to be read as complementary descriptions of the same basic event, they have the effect of locating the church "near" the end but not "at" it. The place of the church is not in the last things but in the things-before-the-last. We might also note that each of these episodes situates the people of God in relation to one or more strands of Old Testament imagery. The episodes involving the 144,000 trade on images of *the exodus* and of the *messianic army;*[20] the tale of the witnesses reflects Revelation's concern for *prophecy;* both the latter story and that of the Lamb's army involve *conflict with pagan powers in the form of beasts,* one of the many echoes of Daniel in the Apocalypse.

Each of these episodes, then, displays the destiny of Israel in the messianic era. But again, who is this "Israel"? One of the few places the *name* "Israel" appears in Revelation is in John's vision of the 144,000. The vision comes at a critical moment, when it seems the seventh seal must soon be opened, unleashing the full fury of God's wrath (with bad results for the earthdwellers—cf. 6:12-17). Instead, four angels appear, restraining the "four winds of the earth" so that the "servants of God" can be marked with a seal upon their foreheads. John then hears the number of the sealed: "144,000, sealed from every tribe of the sons of Israel," followed by an impressive enumeration of the twelve tribes.

One hundred forty-four thousand—some modern readers have found this figure to be disappointingly small. But the number is not meant to be a literal accounting of the "saved." It derives from twelve (the number of Israel), squared (to denote perfection), and multiplied by a thousand (Revelation's number of magnitude or of power). Any "Israel" called to fight in Messiah's army against the powers of evil must be worthy of the calling. In the present passage, the army's perfection is represented numerically. Later in the book it will be symbolized in cultic and moral terms. The 144,000 are said to be "virgins" (a hyperbole, perhaps, for the sexual purity expected of soldiers on the eve of battle) and perfect truth-tellers, witnesses: "in their mouth no lie was found; they are blameless" (14:4-5).

So perfect is this community, indeed, that we might wonder whether John's vision has wandered into sheer fantasy. Perhaps there is no denotative referent for this community. Yet the language is clear. These "servants of God" can be none other than the present hearers of the prophecy, identified as God's "servants" as early as 1:1. It is *they* who have been sealed against the fury of the four winds and all other forms of tribulation. It is *they* who bear the Lamb's and his Father's name upon their foreheads, in sharp contrast to those who bear the mark of the beast (14:1; cf. 13:16). It is *they* who "follow the Lamb wherever he goes" (14:4).

The connection of the 144,000 to the Lamb is consistent throughout the Apocalypse. Indeed, it may already be hinted at in the description "servants of God," which echoes the "servant of YHWH" in the later chapters of Isaiah. It becomes even more apparent in the second half of the vision in chapter 7. When John looks a second time, he sees not the 144,000—a large number, but still a finite one—but rather "a great multitude that no one could count, from every nation, from all tribes and peoples and languages, standing before the throne and before the Lamb, robed in white . . ." (7:9-10). The finite has become the virtually infinite. And when John asks who this multitude is, he is told that they are "they who have come out of the great ordeal; they have washed their robes and made them white in the blood of the Lamb" (7:14).

Like the vision of the Lion of Judah/Lamb in chapter 5, this twofold vision tempts us to divide where the Apocalypse would unite. In both cases, the second half of the vision flows seamlessly out of the first. The Lion of Judah is a figure of royal rule—"he will rule the nations with a rod of iron" (2:25; 12:5; 19:15). While commentators are inclined to dwell upon the opposition between the Lion as a symbol of power, and the Lamb as a figure of weakness, surely the Lamb exercises power as well. He is, after all, credited with a "victory." Not unlike Paul, the Seer is capable of predicating the power of Christ, even if that power is exercised in the form of self-sacrifice (cf. 1 Cor 1:24, cf. 12:9). The unexpected fusion of military and cultic or royal and priestly imagery is the key to much of the power of the Apocalypse. So it is for the *ekklēsia*. The 144,000 ranged according to their several tribes are the army of God. The great multitude are also an army—a hint picked up by the *Te Deum*, which speaks of the "white-robed army of martyrs"—but an army that wins the battle by dying, being killed by the beast (11:7; 13:7). It is therefore misleading to ask if the "blood" in which the martyrs wash their robes is their own, or Christ's. Surely it is their blood *as a participation in* the blood of Christ, a sharing in his death, and therefore in his victory.

A similar result is obtained if we examine, more briefly, the tale of the witnesses in chapter 11. This passage may be usefully expounded using the medieval fourfold reading of Scripture. At the literal level, the two witnesses are two prophets who meet their death in the streets of Jerusalem, the "great city." Here is John's prophetic theme in a powerfully concentrated form. At the allegorical or spiritual level,[21] the story of the witnesses is clearly a display of the story of Jesus, whose ministry follows the same pattern of authoritative proclamation, death at the hands of this world's powers, climaxing in a great reversal—resurrection and ascension. At the moral level, the story functions as exhortation:

do what these prophets did! Bear courageous witness in the streets of your own "great city," whether Ephesus, or Smyrna, or Pergamum or even Rome itself! At the anagogical (i.e., eschatological) level, finally, the story functions for its hearers as a rehearsal of what they can expect will become of them. Tribulation and distress are, if you will, the "normal" condition of the Lamb's followers in history. But their future is one of consolation, even glory.

The church has its own story, its own history. The witnesses always meet their death at the hands of some specific historical polity: whether Rome in the first century, Uganda in the nineteenth, or El Salvador (supported by the United States) in the twentieth. If the church were not visible and concrete, she could not suffer, and so complete "what is lacking in Christ's afflictions."[22] Just so; for while the church has its own contingent history, this history is in turn a participation in the sufferings of the Lamb.

Realism of a Higher Order
The Church's Mission to the Nations

The *ekklēsia* as Israel and the *ekklēsia* as body of Messiah are not mutually exclusive, therefore, but mutually re-enforcing. Lindbeck again states the matter well. Regarding the New Testament, he writes:

> Jesus Christ alone is the antitype or fulfillment. He is depicted as the embodiment of Israel (e.g., "Out of Egypt have I called my son," Matt. 2.15), and the Church is the body of Christ. Thus Israel's story, transposed into a new key through Christ, becomes prototypical for the history of the Church which is its continuation rather than its fulfillment.[23]

This is insightful; we might only wonder about Lindbeck's use of the word "continuation." As a matter of historical fact, it can be argued that both the church and the rabbinic synagogue stand in an ambiguous relation to the Judaism of the temple. As Robert Jenson puts it, "we must remember that neither community was a direct historical continuation of the Israel that came to an end with the last destruction of the temple." Both, in a way, "superseded" the older Israel.[24] The *substantive* connection that each community claims must be worked out amid considerable historical discontinuity. Lindbeck's account would seem to underplay the element of both crisis and creativity displayed by church and synagogue alike, as they negotiated the transition to "life after the temple."[25]

These are important theological questions; yet they move in a different imaginative orbit from that of the Seer. John is not interested in continuations, but precisely in endings. "The time is near" (1:3). "There will be no more delay" (10:6). The Apocalypse is canonical Scripture for catholic Christianity, yet it has little interest in the church's history as such. Hans Urs von Balthasar captures something of the book's unique outlook when he writes:

> The book of Revelation concludes the biblical revelation-event; but it does not do so by continuing the Acts of the Apostles, by prolonging the latter, as it were, into the whole history of the Church and the world. Instead, the seer is lifted up, above the entire sphere of historical revelation in both Old and New Testaments, into a God-given vision that is separate from empirical history (though it integrates it), a vision of all that is taking place between heaven and earth. . . . It follows that the sequence of images seen in this vision is not built upon historical events of the seer's time, nor is it a symbolic representation of particular epochs of the Church's history.[26]

Here we recall once again that the word *ekklēsia* is absent from the main body of the visions. The audience (who are surely *ekklēsia*) are invited to contemplate not themselves as they are, but themselves as they will one day be. The eschatological future belongs to those who "have washed their robes and made them white in the blood of the Lamb." The church, if you will, is made forgetful of itself as it is drawn into the Apocalypse of God.

To say that the Apocalypse is uninterested in "continuations" does not mean that it is ahistorical. It means that its purpose is to create history, rather than to describe it. Take the book's pervasive emphasis on worship. The worship described in chapters 4 and 5 is radically theocentric. God is not only sovereign and awesome, but magnetic, calling forth the praise of every being imaginable—and no doubt many that we cannot imagine:

> Then I heard every creature in heaven and on earth and under the earth and in the sea, and all that is in them, singing, "To the one seated on the throne and to the Lamb be blessing and honor and glory and might forever and ever!" And the four living creatures said, "Amen!" And the elders fell down and worshipped. (5:13-14)

All this is depicted as happening in heaven. But John rehearses the vision precisely so that the *ekklēsia* on earth will join in the heavenly worship. Will join, moreover, at great cost to itself. The community that worships the Lamb in chapter 5, will be forced to discover (as the story unfolds) that worshiping the Lamb means following him. The community that "follows the Lamb wherever he goes" is led inexorably to a life of confrontation with the powers. The outcome of this encounter is not pretty:

the beast is "allowed (*edothē*) to make war on the saints and to conquer
them" (13:7). So much for fantasies of the church's being "effective" or
"successful" in the political realm, at least on the beast's or Caesar's terms!
The "perlocutionary force" of the Apocalypse may be seen as a purging
of fantasy—the very opposite of idealism. The book instead summons its
hearers to what might be called a "realism of a higher order."

Integral to such realism is the history of the nations (*ta ethnē*), a word
that appears with some frequency in the Apocalypse.[27] In the story John
tells, the nations are not, as we might anticipate, simply cast in the role of
enemies. To be sure, sometimes they appear in a negative light. When the
witnesses are murdered, it is said that people from all tribes and languages
and nations will gaze on the bodies and refuse them burial—yet even here,
it is the beast and not the nations that does the killing. When Babylon
falls, the cities of the nations fall too (16:19). Yet this is because the nations
are to some extent Babylon's victims (cf. 18:3, 23; 20:3). Other passages
are even more positive toward the pagan peoples. It is said of the heavenly
city that the "nations will walk by its light, and the kings of the earth will
bring their glory into it" (21:24-26). This could, to be sure, be seen as
a mere exacting of tribute. Such a reading would fit a larger interpretation of the book as a text of vengeance, imagining the church's triumph
and her enemies' humiliation. Yet it is hard to rhyme this interpretation
with the verse that follows, which speak of the leaves of the tree of life as
intending "the healing of the nations" (*eis therapeian tōn ethnōn*) (22:2).
This goes beyond Ezekiel, who speaks of leaves being used for healing, but
not of the nations (Ezekiel 47:12).

If the Apocalypse does not sentimentalize the nations—it does not
sentimentalize *anything*—neither does it demonize them. It simply acknowledges their presence, and the fact that they are subject to the lordship of
the Creator. If there is no such thing as an invisible Israel, there is also no
such thing as an Israel that exists apart from the Gentiles. This is as true
in Revelation as it is in the rest of the New Testament.

We may expand upon this point by comparing Luke's theology of
the Gentiles with that of the Seer. Luke, the originator of "salvation history," sees the church moving outward from historical Jerusalem to Judea,
Samaria, Greece, Asia Minor, and ultimately Rome. This world-ward mission is grounded in the identity of Jesus himself. The aged Simeon greets
the boy Jesus as "a light for revelation [*apokalypsin!*] to the Gentiles, and
for glory to your people Israel" (Luke 2:32). In his sermon at Pentecost,
Peter likewise cites the great messianic prophecy in which God declares "I
[will] make your enemies your footstool" (Acts 2:34-35, citing Psalm 110).
When Acts ends with Paul imprisoned in Rome, of all places, preaching

with all boldness, we see a parable of this prophecy being fulfilled. The nations are not yet subdued; yet they now have Jesus and his Spirit-led community to reckon with.

Like Luke, the Seer views the nations in light of prophecy, even if it typically cites another messianic psalm, the second, as a warrant. Twice the book says of Christ that he will "rule all the nations with a rod of iron" (12:5, 19:15, citing Psalm 2:9). It also says that he bestows this authority on his followers (2:26-27). There is no doubt but that Revelation sees the church as a locus of power—power is simply a characteristic of apocalyptic realities—and that the people of God are called to rule. The question is, rule in what form? In the Apocalypse, it is the martyrs who will one day rule (20:4ff.). Their share in the reign of Christ is the answer to their cry for justice, uttered early on in the course of John's visions (6:9-11). Apocalyptic literature is always a theodicy literature, not in the sense of providing a theoretical explanation for evil, but in the sense of offering a vision that sees beyond the horrors of "the present evil age."

As for the church that must live *in* this present age, it, too, exercises power—the power of the Word of God. When John eats the scroll in chapter 10, a sign of his having internalized the Word, he hears a voice saying: "You must prophesy again about many peoples and nations and languages and kings" (10:11). In this passage, John himself may be seen as embodying the church. In the episode that immediately follows, the two witnesses display the church's life and death in narrative form. Their witness is verbal—the fire that pours forth from their mouths and consumes their foes is surely the gospel (cf. 14:6)—but at the same time it is physical, consisting in their death. And all this before the astonished gaze of the nations.

Where the book of Acts narrates the church's outward movement from historical Jerusalem to the ends of the earth, Revelation's account proceeds downward: from the heavenly Jerusalem as the church's destiny, to the streets of the great city where her witness must be lived amid the muck and mire of history. As Balthasar points out, these perspectives are quite distinct. It would be unwise to seek to harmonize them. Nevertheless, they share in common the conviction that the destiny of Israel and the church is bound up with that of the nations. Neither, we may say, is "sectarian." Moreover, despite the air of apocalyptic necessity that hangs over Revelation—it purports to tell us the things that "must" (*dei*) soon take place (1:1)—it assumes the contingency that marks all historical life. John would hardly have written this urgent letter if he did not expect a response on the part of his readers. The church's existence, including her encounter with the nations, simply cannot be plotted in advance. It is a story, and it is in the very nature of stories that surprising things happen.[28]

Has Revelation an "Ecclesiology"?

We began with Lindbeck's working definition of the church as the "messianic pilgrim people of God, typologically shaped by Israel's story." I hope that I have been successful in showing just how apt that construal is, especially with respect to Revelation. The account I have given is hardly exhaustive. I have not, for instance, discussed the two powerful feminine images of the church: the woman clothed with the sun, and the bride of the Lamb, both with strong roots in the Old Testament. Any treatment of the church as Israel must take these into account. It is such images that, along with Paul's language in Ephesians 5 and elsewhere, make it necessary to refer to the church not just as an "it" but as a "she." The woman in Revelation 12 is Israel, Messiah's mother, but she also has other "offspring"—presumably the Christian assemblies to whom John writes (12:17). It is characteristic of the Apocalypse that even this maternal image appears in a quasi-military context. The woman's children find themselves in a continual state of warfare, as they are assaulted by the dragon.

This points up a possible limitation, to be sure, in Revelation's ecclesial vision. The book's gaze is directed upward (to God), outward (to the powers of the present age), and forward (to the consummation of all things). The ethics it proposes is one of "patient endurance" in the face of suffering. But has it anything to say to the situation inward: to the ethos or character of life within the church? Does Revelation's ecclesiology encompass relations *within* the community of the "servants of God"?

To a limited extent, yes. Early on, the prophet identifies himself as "I, John, your brother who share with you [literally 'your brother and *synkoinōnos*,' partner or comrade] in the tribulation and the kingdom and the patient endurance that are in Jesus . . ." (1:9). This description serves not only to validate John's credentials as a prophet; but also to foster a sense of solidarity between him and the churches, and among the churches. Indeed, Revelation's character as a circular letter serves this end. While each community receives its own, quite particular, message from Christ, it is also privy to the word he speaks to the other six. No community of the Lamb's followers exists in isolation. Whatever the differences in their situations, they are involved in a common struggle. The resultant outlook could rightly be called an "ethic of communal solidarity."

The question is, is this enough? While involvement in a common cause tends to draw people together, it can also become the occasion for rivalry and backbiting. One will find nothing in Revelation to parallel Paul's painstaking efforts to foster unity and reconciliation within his churches. Paul, to be sure, was the father—or mother[29]—of the churches he founded. John is more of an outsider. Yet even allowing for this difference, we note the absence of counsels to love, patience, and forbearance within the *ekklēsia*. This is simply not John's concern. Perhaps it would be just to say that the Apocalypse offers us an ethic of the first table of the Decalogue, the obligations toward God, and that it tends to slight the second table, detailing obligations toward the neighbor.

Yet not every voice within the canon of Scripture can say everything. The witness of Revelation is unique. It shows us the victory of God's people Israel in the victory of the slaughtered Lamb. It shows how small, beleaguered communities of Jesus-followers in the cities of Asia Minor (and communities today) participate in the destiny of Israel, the church, the nations, and creation itself. It is an extended exercise in "remembering the End."[30] While one would surely not wish Revelation to be the only book within the canon, the canon would be immeasurably impoverished without it. "Let anyone who has an ear listen to what the Spirit is saying to the churches" (1:7).

6

Revelation and Christian Hope

Political Implications of the Revelation to John

N. T. Wright

Introduction

My primary title, "Revelation and Christian Hope," would have appeared to many in earlier generations quite straightforward. Revelation is, after all, about heaven. Though it does indeed say some complicated and unexpected things about heaven, we gain an initial glimpse of heaven in chapters 4 and 5, and we then work our way through to the Celestial City itself, the New Jerusalem, in the final two chapters. So, in this deceptively straightforward view, the hope is "heaven," and Revelation offers something of a tourist guide to that destination and perhaps the route toward it.

So ingrained is this perspective that more than one commentator recycles an old joke about someone who has written a commentary on the book of Revelation finally breathing his last and being carried by angels to the Pearly Gates. There he is met by several other learned scholars who themselves, in their day, had written commentaries on the book. "So," they say, "you did one too. You will find things very different up here."

As for political implications within that view: well, that can go two ways. Either we say that, because we're bound for heaven, the rantings and ragings of bestial powers on earth are interesting but largely irrelevant to us. Or we treat those bits as code, rather than symbol, and decode them so that they refer to particular movements within our own day, leading up to Armageddon and the end of the world (which will of course happen next week).

When I say that this way of reading the book misses the point in more ways than one, I mean that it subverts the book theologically, politically and, not least, intertextually—the three main focal points of the conference for which this chapter was written. I suspect, in fact, that one of the reasons for the comparative neglect of Revelation in many Christian circles has been a direct result of the embracing of that pseudo-theology about "going to heaven" that has been the staple diet of much western Christianity, both Catholic and Protestant.[1] Since I have sometimes been misunderstood on this point, let me say that I have no problem speaking of Christians dying and "going to heaven," only with the notion that that is the final destination. As I have often said, heaven is important but it is not the end of the world. A glance at the last two chapters of Revelation itself makes the point graphically. Unlike many hymns and prayers, much iconography, and enormous unquestioned popular assumption, the final scene of the Christian Bible is not about humans leaving this earth and going up to a place called "heaven." It is about the heavenly city coming down to earth. And part of the reason for Revelation's sharp political content is that—again in contrast to the dualist escapism of much modern western Christianity—the coming of God's kingdom on earth as in heaven is not, for John the Seer, something for which we have to wait to the very end. It has already been inaugurated through the victory of the sacrificed Lamb who is also the Lion. The reason there is any question of political theology in this book is that Jesus is already Lord of lords and King of kings, and those who hail him as such need to learn what it means to bear witness to him in the face of the claims and threats of other lords and other kings. That is the burden of my song.

I shall approach this conclusion in four steps. First, I shall set the scene with some reflections on the notion of "apocalyptic." Second, I shall look in more detail at the hope that Revelation offers, and how it relates to the present vocation of the church as seen in the central chapters of the book. Third, I shall look at the unholy trinity of villains that emerge at the center of the book, and enquire what sort of political profile they present and what sort of political theology they might engender—in other words, what it means for the church, then and now, to recognize their deceitfulness and escape their clutches. Fourth, I shall offer some reflections on the place of Revelation within the Christian canon of Scripture. That will probably be enough for one chapter.

I should add a disclaimer. In writing about Revelation I am venturing to march right in and pluck one or two rather obvious flowers from a garden where others have planted, watered, and tended for generations. I hope that more experienced gardeners will forgive my blunderings, and help me gently toward further and deeper insight.

Apocalyptic and the Book of Revelation

The word "apocalyptic" has been pressed into service in relation to at least three quite different sorts of thing: an experience, a literary genre, and a worldview. These sometimes overlap, but should not be confused. (Nor should they be confused with the currently popular meaning of the word, which indicates terrible, cataclysmic upheavals. When journalists have sought to describe the events of 9/11, or subsequent occurrences such as earthquakes and tsunamis, they have often called them "apocalyptic events." But this phrase, in this context, neither denotes nor connotes the experience, the genre, or the worldview of which we are now speaking.)

First, and I believe foremost, the word can denote a phenomenon in which someone experiences a revelation of things not normally perceptible—sometimes seeing, sometimes hearing, sometimes both. We know about this because they write down what happened, but this first meaning has to do not with the writing down but with the event itself, a "revelation" or "unveiling," and to the spirituality or tradition which cultivates or hopes for such events. Some might call this a "religious" phenomenon, though our word "religion" is at least as misleading as "apocalyptic" itself. At its heart—this is very important for what follows—this kind of experience, and the cultivation of such events, presupposes that reality is more complex and multi-dimensional than it normally appears, and that, in particular, the sphere of normal human experience (call it "earth" for the sake of argument) is not separated from the sphere of the angels and their Creator by a great gulf, but rather that "heaven" and "earth" in fact overlap and interlock in a variety of ways.

The belief that heaven and earth could and sometimes did overlap and interlock is built into the very structure of ancient Israelite life, thought, and particularly worship. Israel's central symbol was the temple, at the heart of the land. The temple was the place where the two spheres of heaven and earth intersected, where God had chosen to dwell on earth. And the temple is central for John the Seer, right up to the point where it disappears because its function is swallowed up in the new, complete, heaven/earth reality.

The prophetic tradition thrived on this overlap. Elisha calms his worried assistant through a vision of horses and chariots of fire. Micaiah ben Imlach stands humbly in the heavenly council so that he can then stand boldly before King Ahab. Isaiah happens to be in the temple when what is always true suddenly becomes visibly true. Jeremiah finds the overlap crushingly painful but unavoidable. Ezekiel reports strange visions in which symbol and reality flow in and out of one another. And Daniel, the canonical climax of ancient Jewish apocalyptic, combines the wisdom by which he himself can perceive hidden secrets with a sequence of dreams for which he himself needs an angelic interpreter. The book thus moves from accounts of ancient wisdom confronting the principalities and powers to visions which enable the later reader to do the same. In each case, we might note, the meaning and result of these visions is not about the religious experience for its own sake but about (what we would call) the political and social implications.

Nothing in this whole matrix of ancient Israelite and Jewish apocalyptic implies what we properly call "dualism."[2] Heaven and earth are distinct, but that duality implies no ontological incompatibility. Earth's inhabitants have gone their own way, and their rulers have abused their power, but heaven's answer to that is not to pull up the drawbridge and provide a back-stair access for those who can escape, but to re-assert the claims of the God of heaven and earth on his whole two-sided creation. This always involves conflict with the powers that have usurped his rule on earth, whether pagan or Jewish. The prophets who experience these visions, and speak of them, may be ostracized, threatened, and/or punished, but they do not see themselves as part of a tiny little group waiting for the world to go to hell so that they can then be rescued or vindicated. In particular, the prophets are not saying that the world of space, time, and matter is coming, or has come, to an end, so that something radically new may happen, generating "antinomies," and forcing readers to choose between them. Part of the problem of "the day of Lord," in Jeremiah and elsewhere, is that it is precisely not, in that crude sense, "the end of the world." The morning after the fall of Jerusalem, the created world moves on into a new era of sorrow and shame.

I therefore do not recognize the common antithesis between "apocalyptic" and "prophecy," so beloved of an earlier generation. When we come to John's book, he declares up front that his work belongs in both categories, as well as that of "epistle" (Rev 1:1-3). The second meaning of "apocalyptic" is that of the *literary genre* that has come to bear that name. Scholars frequently use it to denote the genre of books that, broadly, stand in the tradition that developed beyond Daniel. Here there is a problem: were these also the result of Category One events? It is notoriously difficult to tell whether, in books like *1 Enoch*, *4 Ezra*, or *2 Baruch*, the writer has actually experienced the visions he records as (what we would call) a "religious" or spiritual phenomenon. Our suspicions are aroused by the heavy-handed reinterpretation of earlier books; by the exceedingly far-fetched visions that we find in, for instance, *4 Ezra*'s explicit re-reading of Daniel; and also by the obvious pseudonymity. Thus, though the literary genre to which these books belong appears to overlap with some parts at least of Daniel, it is I believe a significantly new development. It uses as an expository method what earlier writers had found themselves driven to say through vivid first-hand experience. Please note, I do not say it was any the worse for that. Bunyan's *Pilgrim's Progress* is a literary artifact, using the fiction of an extended dream. We are neither deceived nor disappointed when we realize this.

But in some of these works of "apocalyptic" genre, made accessible over the last fifty years in a plethora of new editions, we detect signs of what has sometimes been thought of as "apocalyptic" in the third sense, which is that of a particular *worldview*. Students have routinely been taught that an "apocalyptic mindset" is dualistic, sectarian, determinist, pessimistic, world-denying, looking to an immediate future not for transformation or healing but for rescue. This may be true of some of the works that use the apocalyptic form as a literary genre. But not only is it not true of those in my first category, it also denies precisely the heaven/earth overlap, that strange open commerce between the twin halves of God's good creation, upon which the visionaries rely and which contextualizes and makes sense of their work. I am not hereby committing, I trust, the romantic fallacy of making original experience good and subsequent formalization bad. I am merely noting that what has been thought of as "the apocalyptic mindset" does not fit many of the principal writers who stand at the head of the stream of apocalyptic writings.

And—here comes the point—I am convinced of two things. First, John the Divine seems to belong in the first category rather than the second. His is not an "apocalypse" like, say, *4 Ezra*. He writes in his own name, claiming no ancient alter ego. His fresh use of the ancient prophets is quite unlike *4 Ezra*, *2 Baruch*, and so on. He does occasionally report conversations between himself and an angelic interpreter, but never do we have that step-by-step interpretation of visions that, beginning with Daniel 7, became the stock-in-trade of later writers. He veers to and fro, as Daniel does, between fairly literal description (as in chapter 18) and reported visions that, uninterpreted, remain dense and impenetrable. He challenges his readers to work things out for themselves, providing clues (albeit sometimes rather obvious ones) rather than explicit one-on-one interpretations. His work has an immediacy that, though not of itself a guarantee of divine inspiration (a skeptic could always blame John's strange diet, or indeed lack thereof), seems to place him with Jeremiah and Ezekiel, two of his greatest inspirations, rather than with the works of his pseudonymously writing Jewish contemporaries. If, therefore, we come to John's book with the assumption that it exhibits "the apocalyptic mindset," we are bound to misunderstand and misinterpret it. John is no dualist, no pessimist. In our modern sense, he is no sectarian.

Second, the rather narrow band of thought that has taken up the word "apocalyptic" in some quarters of New Testament studies—I think of Ernst Käsemann, and his American followers J. Christiaan Beker and J. Louis Martyn—has not made the case for its own fresh meaning of "apocalyptic." Since these authors have written about Paul rather than Revelation I shall not stop on this point, except to say that we are overdue for a reaction based on actual analysis of apocalyptic texts rather than on the assumption of a particular worldview, which looks suspiciously like one variety of mid-twentieth-century systematic theology. A healthy dose of John Collins or Chris Rowland, to look no further, would be a good start. I have no doubt that Saint Paul was what we could call an "apocalyptic" thinker and writer. But I do not mean by that what Käsemann and his followers meant. (I note in passing that whereas for Käsemann "apocalyptic" always referred to the expectation of the imminent end of the world, in his American followers this has been transformed into an understanding of Jesus' death: a sign, I believe, of residual confusion within the putative category.) In exploring John the Seer as an "apocalyptic" writer, such constructs will not be helpful, primarily because they are generated by contemporary interests that have borrowed the word "apocalyptic" to give the appearance of historical-critical rootedness, but without exploring what those roots are or what sort of plants they sustain.

The question of the theological interpretation of "apocalyptic," and of this "apocalypse" in particular, must therefore remain in abeyance until we have gone further. The tale is told of Karl Barth being asked by a lady whether the serpent in Genesis actually spoke. "Madam," he replied, "it doesn't matter whether or not the serpent spoke. What matters is *what the serpent said.*" In similar fashion, the fact that something is "apocalyptic" may not be of such theological significance as we have supposed. What matters is *what the Apocalypse says.* The exception to this rule is in the presupposition I have spoken of already. The prophetic kind of apocalypse to which John's work belongs presupposes the overlap of, and interplay between, heaven and earth. On that hinges a great deal of theology, and of relevance.

The Hope and the Vision

So what, then, is the Christian hope that John holds out, and how does that hope sustain the calling and identity of the followers of Jesus in the present? The hope is expressed, again and again, in claims such as that of Revelation 11:15: "The kingdom of this world has become the kingdom

of our Lord and of his Messiah, and he will reign forever and ever." It
is important to note that this is stated at various points throughout the
book, even in the midst of trouble and suffering. It is true already. That
which is fully realized in chapters 21 and 22 is already anticipated in the
sequence that runs from chapter 5, where all creation praises the Lamb
that was slain because he has won the right to open the scroll of God's
eternal purposes, through the various outbursts of praise, to the final conclusion that, in the New Jerusalem that has come down from heaven to
earth, "the dwelling of God is with humans." In the present time God has
a temple in heaven, which is sometimes glimpsed by the Seer, but when
heaven and earth are joined there will be no temple, because the whole
city will be suffused with the presence of God. As Greg Beale has shown
powerfully,[3] drawing out its larger significance within biblical theology,
the city will be an enormous *cube*—quite unrealistic as an earthly city, even
supposing we allow it to be a gravity-free zone with gigantic skyscrapers,
but utterly appropriate, symbolically, both in terms of its ultimate perfection and, more particularly, of its being a huge replica of the Holy of
Holies. Heaven and earth are one at last.

The dramatic tension that drives most of Revelation is the sharp and
horrible realization that this state of affairs has not yet come to pass. But
from the very beginning we know that something has happened in and
through which it has *begun* to be true. Jesus the Messiah, the Lion of
Judah, has already conquered, is already enthroned. He is worthy to open
the seals that otherwise would hold back the divine purpose for the world.
Here, as in much of the New Testament, we encounter a christologically
based inaugurated eschatology. It is because Jesus has been raised from the
dead that his death is seen as salvific, redemptive, and above all victorious.
And here we discover, too, how mistaken is that reading of the New Testament which supposes that for the early Christians everything depended
on a future event still to come. Clearly there was a strong and vital future
hope. The eschatology was not realized. But *something had already happened*
as a result of which Jesus had already been installed as King of kings and
Lord of lords. That is what most twentieth-century scholarship failed to
realize. The implicit and often explicit denial of the bodily resurrection
of Jesus, as I have argued elsewhere, caused generations of liberal scholars
to place all the eschatological weight on the immediate future, whereas
for the earliest Christians the main pillar of hope was something that had
happened in the immediate past.

The way the hope is articulated, then, and the way it holds in place
the vocation and character of the church in the present, is through the
tension between the opening vision of heavenly worship in chapters 4 and

5 and the closing vision of the New Jerusalem in chapters 21 and 22. A word about each.

Chapters 4 and 5, we should stress, are not a vision of the ultimate future—despite, for instance, Charles Wesley's magnificent "till we cast our crowns before thee" (in the closing stanza of "Love Divine, All Loves Excelling"). They are a vision of the worship that all creation offers to its Creator right now, but invisibly within the heavenly throne room. They are the reality of which the throne rooms of this world, with their sycophantic worship, are the parody—a theme (reality and parody) that occupies John quite a lot. And the vision of the scroll indicates, remarkably enough, that the world's Creator is true to his original plan in Genesis, which was to rule the world, and govern its course, *through obedient humanity*. All others have failed, but the slaughtered Lamb steps forward, to do what in Scripture the Lion of Judah was to do: the messianic task, Israel's task, the human task. The result is that through his redemptive death humans from every nation have become "a kingdom and priests" (Rev 5:10) who will reign on the earth—a significant framing theme of the book (Rev 1:6; 20:6). This vocation derives from the vocation of the redeemed Israel in Exodus 19:6, looking back in turn to the vocation of the human race in Genesis 1 and 2. This is not, then, some specialized, off-beat task peculiar to John's vision. It is the articulation of what it means to be genuinely human, standing between the Creator and the creation, summing up creation's praises before God and bringing God's rule to bear upon creation. That is the hope that enables this people to praise God in the present despite their immediate circumstances, and to learn that their witness, even unto death if need be, is the means by which the world will be brought under the rule of the Lamb. This is the vision, and vocation, which frames in particular the revelation of the mystery of evil at large in the world and the task of God's people to discern it and refuse its seductions. The vision of chapters 4 and 5, in other words, is designed to set the context within which the little communities will take heart and, sharing in the worship already on earth, have courage to hold on, to resist those who speak from other throne rooms, and so to become victorious and to share at last in the New Jerusalem.

The New Jerusalem, for its part, offers the ultimate hope: the city (the place of human habitation, mutual interchange, and flourishing) that is also a garden, indeed *the* garden. This is not about going back to Eden, but about going on and discovering that the final city is the goal toward which, had they but realized it, Eden's original inhabitants were called to work. In a fresh blending of Genesis 2 and Ezekiel, the river flows through the city, and the tree of life grows on its banks. From Cain's building of the first city (Gen 4:17) to the original Babel of Genesis 11, we see humans grasping at the ideal from which the primal sin had debarred them, constructing instead murderous and arrogant parodies of that goal. This lies at the heart of the great contrast at the end of Revelation between Babylon and Jerusalem. Babylon represents the ultimate in that Cain-and-Babel story; the New Jerusalem represents the ultimate in the story that begins with the nomad Abraham, but which is anticipated in the city of David. The dualist reaction of romanticism is to demonize the city and celebrate withdrawn rural life as the only alternative. I recall Stevie Smith's line about those that went to build the New Jerusalem and ended up with New York. But that is not the biblical answer—any more than Richard Neuhaus's opposite position, that when we arrive in the New Jerusalem we will see a sign saying, "From the people who brought you New York City"! No. Now that the Lion of Judah has conquered, and according to Psalm 2 will conquer all the kingdoms of the earth, the true city can at last appear. And within that city the redeemed human beings—who appear to be a growing number, not a little withdrawn minority—will share in the rule of the Lamb (22:5).

When we understand this relationship between the vision of heavenly worship in chapters 4 and 5, on the one hand, and the final scenes on the other, the long and often puzzling middle section of the book—by which I mean all the way from chapter 6 to chapter 20—begins to fall into place. The seals are removed from the scroll, one by one, unleashing a sequence of divine judgments, which are necessary in order to overthrow and abolish the ingrained and powerful evil that has taken root in the world through human sin and its sinister empowerment. Among the many highly complex and artistic patterns that have been discerned throughout these chapters we may highlight the rather obvious one: that the judgments, like the plagues in Egypt, are the prelude to the rescue of God's people. The judgments come in three sequences of seven—the seals, the trumpets, and the bowls—which are almost certainly to be seen as different symbolic angles on the same events, rather than twenty-one different events. Thus each sequence draws to its climax in terms of terrifying events—thunder, lightning, earthquake, and so on (8:5; 11:19; 16:18, echoing 4:5). The judgments themselves are highly stylized, replete with biblical allusions and echoes, evoking the awesome judgments on Sodom, Egypt, Tyre, and above all Babylon. But in each case the sequence is interrupted by a vision of the redeemed, celebrating in worship, joining with the heavenly liturgy that had already been witnessed in chapters 4 and 5 and which continues to form the theological as well as liturgical ground plan for the book: God is the good and wise Creator; Jesus is the Lamb whose death has ransomed a royal priesthood.

The vision of hope is therefore the vision of a people, a community, a *polis*, which will finally be revealed as the New Jerusalem itself, the bride of the Lamb. The fundamental characteristic of this *polis* is worship of the true God for who he is and for what, through the Lamb and his death, he has now done. The remarkable sequence of songs of worship, spread liberally throughout the book, indicates the quality and content of that worship (and, incidentally, shows up the lack of quality and the poverty of content in much that today passes for "worship"). And since this worship already takes place in the present, the eschatology is indeed inaugurated. The question thus presses as to what this *polis* looks like in the present time, and how it conducts itself against the other cities, the other communities, that surround it. That is at the heart of the political question, to which we shall shortly turn. But, as quickly becomes clear, all this can only happen because a victory has been won that now opens the way for other victories to be won. What is this victory, over whom is it won, and what are the consequences? Up until chapter 12, it might have seemed as though the church simply faced all kinds of miscellaneous challenges, temptations, dangers, and threats. But from chapter 12 onwards it becomes clear that these are neither random nor isolated. They are part of a concerted campaign conducted by an ultimate enemy who will stop at nothing to prevent the purpose of the world's Creator from being carried out. Here John's symbolism, culled as usual from many other sources, is on full lurid display as he introduces us to the dragon, the beast from the sea, and the beast from the land.

The Challenge of the Beast

With chapters 12, 13, and 14 we are forced to recognize, if we had doubted it, that this book is written from, and to, a very precise context. Detailed studies have shown that, of all the interpretations of the famous 666 in 13:18, "Nero Caesar" fits the bill extremely well. This is not only because of the numerical value of the name within the familiar gematria. The number possesses other properties that would make it all the more clear what the church was up against. The repeated "six" is not only a parody of 777, a number of utter perfection, but also more particularly of the hyper-perfect numerical value of the name "Jesus Christ," which is 888. The beast, supported by the dragon and operating through the "beast from the land," and thus standing at the center of the unholy trinity, is a parody of Jesus at several levels, not least the refrain that "he was, and is not, and is to come." The reality is that the living Creator God wills to rule his world through Jesus the Messiah and his people. The parody is that the dragon rules the world through the beast and his henchmen, notably the second beast.

But if Nero is identified, at least in a preliminary way, with the beast from the Sea, where do we go from there? Two questions in particular: first, can we then locate the book's date precisely enough to figure out who all the other characters are? And second, does this mean that the book possessed great meaning for that generation but none, except distant historical reminiscence, for any other generation, our own included? These are major questions and deserve some care.

First, as to the date. A majority of biblical scholars today agrees with Irenaeus in dating the book in the reign of Domitian, toward the end of the first century. I have no a priori reason against this, except that there is less evidence than used to be thought for a serious Domitianic persecution. Like a great deal in ancient history, that does not mean that nothing was going on. The reference to Nero would then be explained by the widespread myth of Nero *redivivus*—either that Nero did not actually die, had gone to the East, and would return to take vengeance on the Rome that had rejected him, or that he had indeed died but would revive and, once again, take vengeance. There are plenty of signs of this legend in chapters 12–18. But I am not entirely convinced that an earlier date, perhaps in late 68 or early 69, has to be ruled out. I have long thought that if Saint Paul had lived to see what we call "the year of the four emperors," that is, 69, with Rome threatening to implode once more into the chaos from which Augustus claimed to have rescued it a century earlier, and then Jerusalem falling at the climax of it all, he might well have reckoned that this was the "day of the Lord" of which he had warned, the day when the propagandists of "peace and security" would be overtaken by sudden destruction (1 Thess 5:3). And there is no reason to suppose that John, on Patmos, would have as good information as we do about the quick post-Nero succession of Galba, Otho, Vitellius, and Vespasian. The numbered schemes in 17:9-13 may thus be strictly inaccurate yet sufficient to summon up the sense of a quick succession of rulers.

But equally, second, I believe this part of Revelation, though to be sure carrying very specific historical reference, is written in such a way as to open up a window on a much larger issue even than Rome and Nero. The model for Revelation 13 is of course Daniel 7, but it is noticeable that whereas Daniel has four beasts emerging from the sea, Revelation only has one—but it resembles three different animals, a leopard, a bear, and a lion (13:2). Could it be that the writer is signaling that the real problem is not Nero himself but that which Nero, for the moment, embodies and expresses—something that will emerge in different guises at different times? This has of course been a popular route in exegesis, and the thing that Nero embodies is often labeled simply "empire." This points toward

a route, as well, through the fascinating but difficult chapter 17, where the
Great Whore, Babylon, is of course Rome itself, sustained by its sequence
of emperors of whom the beast is one. (There is virtually no doubt about
this identification. I say "virtually" because one or two scholars have tried
to make out that the great city that is destroyed is Jerusalem in 70 C.E.,
making way for the "New Jerusalem." This has the considerable apparent
merit that it draws Revelation much closer to the so-called "little Apocalypse" in Mark 13 and parallels, which is undoubtedly about the fall of
Jerusalem, and uses similar sources, from Jeremiah and elsewhere, to talk
about it. If Revelation were written in 69 or 70, the sight of a city in smok-
ing ruin would be spot-on. But in Revelation this is more or less insup-
portable. The great trading city at whose fall merchants from around the
world wail for their loss [18:11-19] cannot be other than Rome.)

But if we make this identification, we have three routes then open
to us. First, we could say that the writer believed that the fall of Rome
and the ushering in of the complete new age was imminent, and he was
wrong. (Unless you say that 69 C.E. was enough of a "fall" to be going on
with, which seems straining it more than a little.) Or we could say, with
the dispensationalists, that though Rome may have been John's model
he was in fact writing history in advance—the history, in fact, of our own
day. The fact that this has been tried unsuccessfully again and again for
a thousand years is of course not of itself enough to disprove it. False
dawns do not mean that no such thing as a dawn exists. No: the main
argument against the dispensationalists is their failure to take seriously
the nature of John's symbolism. Or we could say that his prophecies
are consistent with the fall of Rome, which happened some four hundred years after his day, in which case he was right—but we would still
be left with a large hermeneutical gap, the one between his writing and
that event, and then the larger one between the event and everything
that has happened subsequently. Or we could say that, though John certainly envisaged Rome's fall, he saw it as encapsulating and embodying
the disastrous and self-destructive way of life of all human empires, or all
human empires of a certain type. This is the power of using "Babylon" as
symbol, rather than merely as code—a key hermeneutical point in several
parts of the book. The Cain-and-Babel narrative, in which humans grasp
at the eschatological city-gift but inevitably corrupt it and use it as an
instrument of their own self-aggrandizing power, reaches various climactic moments, of which Rome is the obvious foreground for John. That is
the interpretative route to which I am drawn.

This is not to make Rome a mere example of a larger general truth.
Just as Jesus and his death and resurrection are not mere examples of the

larger truth of God's powerful redemptive love but are actually the mid-point of history, the point at which the ancient door of God's purposes swings open at last to reveal the new world that lies ahead, so Rome—the great power that at that unique moment summed up arrogant human rebellion—will fall. That will be the sign that Jesus has won the decisive victory, however many new Babylons, new Romes, appear between that time and the eventual consummation.

Two main features of the rule of the beast are of particular concern to John. The first is idolatrous worship; the second is aggressive economic exploitation. On the first: it is now well known that the imperial cult was the fastest growing religion in first-century Asia Minor. Detailed studies, which could really have been undertaken since Deissmann but which had to wait for the failure of the Bultmann school before, like the horsemen of chapter 4, they could be unleashed, have now charged out, showing the way in which the worship of Rome itself, and of the emperor and his family, increasingly dominated city life not only in Ephesus, though that great city remained central, but throughout the province. We remind ourselves, of course, that religion and politics have hardly ever been separable throughout human history, as they still are not for most of the world, and that they were completely intermingled in the first-century Roman world. Ultimately, power was what counted, and power came from the gods. Worship that power and some of it rubs off on you. The dragon who has been thrown down from heaven—chapter 12 is John's reworking of the "fall from heaven" taunt in Isaiah 14 and Ezekiel 28—retains the power that is his as a former member of the heavenly court. We should not be surprised that, just as in those chapters an earlier myth of Lucifer's fall is being reworked in terms of oracles against Babylon and Tyre respectively, so here the dragon who has fallen gives his power to a beast who later on supports the woman in whom Rome's seductive power is symbolized. Beast and dragon together appear to present an all-powerful combination. The second beast—now regularly understood to be composed of the local officials who eagerly promote the imperial cult—acts as might dragons in lambs' clothing (13:11), insisting, on pain of death, that the beast be worshiped.

This power is then worked out, particularly through the second beast in 13:16-17, in economic exploitation. To buy or sell, one must have the mark of the beast. Iron control of economic life, justified by the apparently overwhelming evidence for the beast's supernatural power (13:11-15), is one of the signs of the dragon's power. The kings of the earth have "committed fornication" with Babylon. This metaphor develops powerfully through chapters 17 and 18, and forms another parody, this time

between Babylon as the Great Whore and the church as the bride of the
Lamb. In 18:3 we see the unholy combination of money, sex, and power,
used nakedly and for their own sake instead of for the good of humans
and creation, and to God's glory. And, though the last generation of
commentators has been quick to insist that "fornication" is here simply
a metaphor for power and money, the regular condemnation of idolatry,
and its coupling with fornication in, for example, 2:14, 20, and the final
condemnation of it in 21:8 and 22:15, seem to indicate that illicit sexual
practices were one of many signs of the same overall bestial and dragon-
inspired way of life that John is naming and shaming. The downgrading
of responsibility into power for its own sake, of resources into money for
its own sake, and of relationships into sex for its own sake, and the multiple combinations of all three, seem to lie at the heart of the critique of the
Babylonian empire. At this point the "masters of suspicion" (Nietzsche,
Marx, and Freud) seem to be spot-on.

Here we must face the problem that the word "empire," like the word
"apocalyptic," has had a checkered career over recent years. How fashions
change. Twenty years ago one heard almost nothing of "empire" in New
Testament studies; now it is omnipresent. The reasons for this have to do
particularly with the shift away from existentialist interpretations to political ones, which itself has to do with the shift away from divinity schools
to departments of religion. It also has to do with a rapidly rising awareness that today's world, following the collapse of the earlier European
and Russian empires, has entered a new mode characterized by dangerous
and unstable post-imperial societies on the one hand and by the rise of a
different sort of empire, largely controlled by American interests, on the
other. Since my topic here also includes the political "implications" of
Revelation, one can hardly omit this consideration, difficult though it is
for a British citizen to tell his American cousins how not to organize their
tea party. All this, as you know, came out sharply in the varied reactions
after 9/11, with some, including some Americans, placing part of the
blame on American imperialism, and others reacting with vitriolic anger
to such a suggestion.

Part of our problem, I suggest, is that our mental grid for understanding power, and hence politics, is very different from that of a first-century
Jew or Christian—and it is of course the latter grid that should control
our reading of Revelation. Ever since the two great revolutions (American
and French) of the late eighteenth century, European and American politics have increasingly seen themselves on a left-right spectrum (this was
an invention of the French revolutionaries), with the central problem of
organizing a society, that of avoiding chaos on the one hand and tyranny

on the other, sloping off to the left among those who regard tyranny as the greater evil, and to the right among those who fear chaos most. The tyrannies of the twentieth century have pushed all our spectrums further to the left, with the exaltation of freedom over order, liberty over constraint. This works through contemporary western society in ways, and with multiple and sometimes paradoxical complexities and reactions, far too numerous even to list here.

But the result, especially among liberation theologians and those most aware of the postcolonial imperatives, has been that we have perhaps smiled our approval a bit too easily at the unmasking of the demonic and bestial regimes of Revelation 13 and 17. Again and again one meets the familiar antithesis between Revelation 13 and Romans 13, with the assumption that Revelation 13 is supporting our kind of left-wing politics and that Romans 13 is in favor of our kind of right-wing politics. Quite apart from considerations of canonical readings, and of the old but difficult rule of interpreting Scripture by Scripture, this simply fails, in both its parts, as a first-century Jewish or Christian reading. They simply did not see things as we do.

Part of the problem, of course, is that various recent regimes and programs have indeed appealed to these passages in support of nakedly left- or right-wing regimes. I think particularly of the almost obscene misuse of Romans 13 by the *apartheid* regime in South Africa, but also of the over-eager appropriation of Revelation 13 on the part of those with a rather obvious contemporary left-wing agenda. Another part of the problem is that exegetes have for years simply not been trained in the political thinking of the ancient world, so that just as we have exported sixteenth-century theology back into ancient Galatia and made Paul's letter address our post-Reformation concerns in their own terms, we have exported modern political assumptions back into ancient Asia Minor and made Revelation, and Paul too for that matter, address our political anxieties in their own terms.

The full antidote to this, and the proper ground plan for a fresh appraisal, would of course be a detailed analysis of the larger world of ancient political thought and philosophy. There being no time (or, in my case, expertise) for such a thing, we may simply note the assumption that obtains right through Israel's Scriptures, and on into the New Testament and early Christianity: that a proper, wise, and effective ordering of society is one aspect of creational monotheism itself. In other words, the Creator God wants humans to run his world, to make the wilderness flourish and to build wise and healthy cities and run them humanely. But, from the Cain-and-Babel story onward, it was recognized that the humans upon whom this responsibility falls will abuse it for their own ends—again, power, money, and sex. The people of God, from Abraham onwards, are therefore constantly called to articulate and embody the God-given critique of this abuse of human responsibility; and, where such abuse occurs within God's people themselves, to address it prophetically by critique from within. Even the prophetic critique then needs critique: the distinction between false and true prophecy, so important for ancient Israel as for John the Seer, is the final layer in the multiply-structured critique of power. But all this critique happens, not because power is bad in itself, but because it is abused. As with gardens and cities, so with power: the nostalgic or romantic longing for a world without power is a desire to return to the nursery. Joseph, the archetypal wise ancient Israelite, becomes second-in-command to Pharaoh—a kind of long-range paradoxical fulfillment of the place of human beings in Genesis 1 and 2. Daniel and his friends, having launched their highly daring critique of Babylonian power and come out smiling, resume their top jobs in the civil service. Paul, on trial in Acts, will respect the office while sharply criticizing the behavior of its present holder. Polycarp, having declared roundly that he is not going to worship Caesar's image, knowing perfectly well where that will lead, agrees to civilized discussion with the Roman tribune on the grounds that the Christian Scriptures teach him to respect those in authority. And Jesus himself, astonishingly, declares to Pilate that he could have no power over him were it not given him from above—meaning that the chief priests, who handed him over, had the greater sin. That Johannine theme is one of the sharpest and starkest: "the ruler of this world" is cast out, overthrown, defeated—but he still rules by God's appointment. Part of the mystery of the cross itself, in John, lies exactly there. Tyranny is horrible; it is defeated by the cross. But the beasts that tyrannize the world in Daniel, and the great beast of Revelation 13, emerge from the sea. They are actually chaos-bringers. Their enforced and dehumanizing "order" will in fact result in destruction, devastation, and chaos come again.

It will not do, then, to read Revelation 12–19 with the kind of satisfied glow that comes from having all our nice liberal prejudices so easily confirmed. That does not imply, of course, that conservative prejudices are thereby confirmed instead; to imagine that would be simply to return to our normal and highly misleading left–right spectrum. Rather, we are called, I believe, to recognize the way in which bestial regimes rise, gain power, deceive many with their apparent success, attain economic supremacy, and then traffic so readily in all sorts of commodities including, as in 18:13, human beings. We are called to recognize that this happens and will happen, not because we should be aiming at a world without structures of power but because power corrupts and the church must bear witness against that corruption, by critique, by non-collaboration, by witness, and if need be by martyrdom. If the world were to listen to the church—and twice in my lifetime it has done so, in South Africa and in eastern Europe—the result should not be, though sadly it has sometimes been, a post-tyrannical chaos, but a fresh order, this time humanizing, this time striving afresh toward the garden city. As we all now know, and should have known long since, it will not do to assume that to overthrow a tyranny will result in the spontaneous growth of a healthy liberal democracy.

Of course it will not do, either, to assume that what we think of as healthy modern western democracies are themselves the ultimate and eternal answer to the problems of Revelation 12–18. That is part of the eighteenth-century lie. In fact, the very separation of religion and politics that was so vital a part of that essentially Deistic settlement on both sides of the Atlantic has resulted in regimes that, claiming their power gave them the right, acted in ways far more like the beasts than like the church. Pushing God out of the equation, politically in the *vox populi, vox Dei* theory, scientifically with the neo-Epicureanism that created the context for the appropriation and exploitation of Darwin, economically with the "invisible hand" of the market, and ethically with the post-Freudian assumption that sex will do what it will do—all this has the mark of the beast about it. These questions need to be worked out in other contexts, but it would be unwise to leave the central chapters of Revelation with the impression that bestial regimes are only and always non-democratic tyrannies. They may be closer to home than we like to think. Perhaps this is why the western church, so comfortable now within its present world, is not persecuted.

The vision of hope, then, confronts the regimes of the dragon and the beasts. And the church, caught up within and bearing witness to that hope, must constantly be refreshed in worship of the true God, the real Trinity, and so learn to avoid collusion with the beast in a way that will be much more demanding than any easy-going, one-size-fits-all solution would allow. The church is to live as the alternative *polis*, not by separating itself into sectarian isolation but by bearing witness, like Daniel and his friends, before kings and rulers. The aim is not to damn, but to redeem; the leaves on the tree are for the healing of the nations, and the gates stand open for the kings of the earth to bring their treasures. Only if we keep that goal before us will we avoid the isolation that is the mirror image of collusion.

Revelation in Canon and Tradition

I have said enough, I hope, to give an overall picture of Revelation with particular reference to hope on the one hand and political implications on the other. I conclude with some reflections on the place of this book within the canon of Christian Scripture—and on the puzzling relation between canon, itself an early part of tradition, and the larger tradition itself.

We have seen again and again, and could have developed much more, the ways in which Revelation continually draws upon and develops many great themes and insights from the Old Testament prophets. This is not, we should stress, because Scripture is simply a bran-tub out of which one might scoop enough, now and then, to make into a fresh meal. It is because Revelation, like all the New Testament, sees the Old Testament in terms of a great, complex, multifaceted *narrative* that came to its climax in Jesus the Lion of Judah and has now generated a new narrative that is demonstrably the fulfillment of that ancient story but also in a significantly new mode. The fact that one could say just the same thing about Matthew or Paul or John or Hebrews makes the point. Revelation is, in Richard Bauckham's phrase, "the climax of prophecy." It seems that the writer is aware of this.

In particular, the story Revelation tells is the same story that all four Gospels tell, though the church, which has done its best to hush up this fact about the Gospels, has not usually recognized the similarity. The four canonical Gospels (unlike the so-called gnostic "gospels"!) tell the story of *how Jesus of Nazareth, Israel's Messiah, conquered the power of evil through his death and became the lord of the world.* They are not about how Jesus revealed that he was divine and then died so that we could go to heaven. They are about how Jesus acted as the embodiment of Israel's God to overthrow the usurping forces of evil and to establish, through his death, resurrection, and ascension, God's kingdom on earth as in heaven. We see this strikingly, for instance, in Mark 10:35-45, where Jesus, faced with the foolish request of James and John, insists on a radical redefinition of power itself, and indicates that his forthcoming saving death will be the means of instantiating that radical redefinition. But the point is perhaps clearest in John, in the passages already alluded to: the ruler of this world is cast out, is coming to get Jesus, has been condemned (12:31; 14:30; 16:11). This sequence leads the eye up to the final clash between Jesus and Pilate, where Jesus points out that his kingdom, which is not "from" this world but is emphatically *for* this world, must be of a different sort than Caesar's, since if it were the normal kind his followers would fight. The attentive reader is left to ponder John's meaning, that somehow the crucifixion that follows is the means by which all this is accomplished. The famous *tetelestai* (John 19:30) means more (though not less) than "he has dealt with our sins."

The same is true, though again often ignored, in Paul. By common consent, Romans 8 expresses something like the very heart of Paul, and here we have themes familiar now from a new angle in Revelation: abolition of accusation and condemnation, suffering as the prelude to glory, and particularly the new creation, born from the womb of the old. But then in the glorious coda to that chapter we have, in Pauline language and idiom, the theology of Revelation in a nutshell: God justifies, so no one can condemn; Jesus died, so all will be well; suffering of every kind will not separate us from his love; and then, particularly, in all these things *we are more than conquerors* through him who loved us. It is not accidental that that Pauline phrase was used as the title for a famous commentary on Revelation: the theme of conquest, the unique victory of Jesus but also the consequent victory of his followers, is foundational for both writers. And, once we understand Revelation and, for that matter, the gospels, we can see that the great poem that Paul has placed at the heart of Philippians 2 is a more exact summary of their combined message than we might have imagined.

What does all this say about the tradition of the church? Sadly, it reveals the extent to which the tradition has got it both right and wrong. Of course, many Christian theologians and exegetes have glimpsed and expressed these themes, often far better than we can. But, equally, many have found them strange and off-putting, and have opted instead to place their emphasis on themes that, though themselves important, do not have the same high profile and urgent insistence in the New Testament itself. In particular, and speaking as one who has lived and worked in an established church, I believe that ever since the fourth century, but particularly in the medieval west, the great church has become increasingly alienated from the vision of God and God's kingdom that we find right across the New Testament, and by way of displacement has highlighted themes that, though themselves important, are not the urgent and driving heart of the canon itself. The radical misunderstandings of the dispensationalists are simply one recent outgrowth of this phenomenon. Far more dangerous, I think, are the more deep-rooted misunderstandings that have construed the Christian hope as simply "going to heaven for ever," which have invoked the divinity of Jesus and his saving death in the service of that vision rather than in the service of the overthrow of the powers and the establishment of God's kingdom, and which have apparently abandoned politics as a dirty, bestial game and then have ended up colluding with the deeper structures of abuse. Revelation shows us, in and through all its puzzling and arcane imagery, a vision of the Creator God reclaiming sovereignty over the whole world through the slaughtering of the Lamb, and entrusting to the present worshipping church the responsibility to bear witness to Jesus as the world's true lord, and to his way of victory as the power that is greater than the power of Babylon. That is the ground of Christian hope. That is the foundation of a Christian vision of the *polis*, in the present as much as in the ultimate future.

7

Witness or Warrior?

How the Book of Revelation Can Help Christians Live
Their Political Lives

Stefan Alkier

Introduction

Readers in different times and cultures have read the book of Revelation not as an autonomous piece of literature and not as a book of mere intertextual relations but rather as a book of extratextual references in need of decoding. Reading this way, they have actualized certain signs, symbols, and actors in the book of Revelation. The book itself seems to teach readers to do that. For example, when we read Revelation 13:18—"This calls for wisdom: let anyone with understanding calculate the number of the beast, for it is the number of a person. Its number is six hundred sixty-six"—this verse demands an allegorical interpretation in which one sign in the text is to be replaced by either another sign or extratextual entity. One has to know the right code to find the intended solution. There are some cases, in which the text itself may be our guide and explain the allegorical images it uses, as for example in Revelation 1:20: "As for the mystery of the seven stars that you saw in my right hand, and the seven golden lampstands: the seven stars are the angels of the seven churches, and the seven lampstands are the seven churches." But without this guidance and without the right code, the intended solution cannot be found.

The method of allegorical interpretation is customarily used by readers who connect their own individual, religious, and political experiences directly to the book of Revelation. For example, consider the very important commentary of Joachim of Fiore, who died in 1202. He identifies the first beast in chapter 13 with Mohammedanism and its mortal wound with the Crusades.[1]

It is the same allegorical reading strategy that many Christians of
today employ. But we find such allegorical readings in contemporary New
Testament exegesis as well. Thomas Witulski reads "the beast rising out of
the sea" in Revelation 13:1 as an allegory for Hadrian, who loved to travel,
and on that basis he dates the production of the book of Revelation to the
time of Hadrian.[2]

Indeed, in order to date a book that does not say when it was written,
we must always relate some parts of the text to extratextual phenomena.
And a reading of a biblical book that wants not only to engage religious
or cultural history but also theology has to relate its reading not only to
present but also future life. As Paul de Man understands it, every interpretation is an allegorical reading.[3] However, while extratextual allegorical
readings seem to be the most useful for Christian life, they are at the same
time the most dangerous readings because they always stand at the edge
of the exegetical abyss, running the risk of having the text say whatever the
reader wants to hear.

Critical exegetes should always bind all extratextual relations back to
intratextual and intertextual studies to employ criteria for relating the text
to extratextual experiences, hopes, and desires. Therefore, with regard to
Joachim's allegorical reading connecting this biblical book with the Crusades of the Middle Ages, and with regard to Christian fundamentalists
of today who connect the book of Revelation with their desires to fight
against Islamic societies, we must say that these are misreadings because
no part of the book of Revelation motivates the true witnesses of God's
grace, justice, and power to become warriors who have to fight against
other people.

On the other hand, and in reaction to those who want to take Revelation as an exhortation to battle, a humanistically enlightened Christianity
wishes that this book, with its horrifying, violent visions, had never been
included in the canon.[4] The use made of Revelation by potentially violent
fundamentalists (and the churches they inhabit) who have divided the
world into an empire of evil and an empire of good, and who have thus
even justified war and torture, unfortunately blocks access to the cosmological Christology and soteriology of the Revelation to John for many
contemporary peace-loving men and women.

Additionally, the interest of the Enlightenment in rational, proposi-
tional truths contributed mightily to the increasing sidelining of Revelation in academic theology, but two other factors also played a decisive
role. On one hand, it was with the images of the Revelation to John that
the church spread fear and fright and thus maintained its social power.
On the other hand, many opposition movements likewise legitimated
their own violent rebellions with the Revelation to John.

In spite of the outstanding works of Wilhelm Bousset[5] and Adolf von Harnack,[6] the Enlightenment tendency to marginalize the Revelation to John continued. The cosmological visions of the book did not fit well with the individualizing existential theology of the Bultmannian school, whose demythologizing endeavors increased after the Second World War in part as a reaction to the horrors of Nazi ideology, pervaded as it was with numerous mythologems. This may also have contributed to the separation of the Revelation to John from the other Johannine writings on the part of the majority of exegetes.[7]

That one encounters scenes of horror following upon scenes of horror, gruesome images of dreadful wars, natural disasters, and hellish judgments of punishment in Revelation has clouded the vision of the prophetic power of this book in view of concrete experiences of injustice, oppression, war, and natural disasters. The religious fiction of Revelation is highly realistic.

The Revelation to John is not a depressing book singing the downfall of the world. It longs much more for and expects a new heaven and a new earth in the face of the experience of the structures of power. It draws its counterfactual hope from the paradigm of witness, Jesus Christ, the resurrected and exalted Crucified.

The prophetic visions of the book set up the powers of evil in a scene like a radio play. It allows the audience to feel their aggressive wishes about revenge, but the recipients of the book are not to become aggressive warriors fighting against the human enemies of the churches. Rather, they are to become trusting witnesses of the witness of God, aware of the cosmic power of evil and the greater power of God.

My thesis, then, is that Revelation's pragmatic model of *Zeugenschaft* (witness) could be a political model for Christian life today, but only if we find a non-fundamentalist way of talking about the power of the evil and the greater power of God. The theology of the book of Revelation may help us to create a biblical theology of power from the center of the cross if we do not isolate the visions, symbols, and signs of the book and relate them to our enemies, and if we read the book intratextually as a whole, paying attention also to its intertextual relations.

Therefore, in the bulk of what follows I try to show through an intratextual reading that the book of Revelation wants to enable its readers to become and to stay witnesses and not warriors. Then I want to work out this pragmatic thesis with some intertextual remarks. A short theological reflection on the question of God's power will be my last point.

The Book of Revelation as a Complete
and Coherent Whole

Interpreters of any sign-complex should always ask first if it is possible to read the given signs as a whole, because the meaning of a sign depends on its relations to other signs. A group of signs only gives the impression of being a text when verbal signs have been organized or can be organized syntactically, semantically, and pragmatically, thus producing meaning. János Petöfi writes:

> For us textuality is not an inherent quality of verbal objects. A producer or recipient considers a verbal object a text when he/she believes that this verbal object is a complete and coherent whole, which corresponds to a real or assumed situation of communication. A text is . . . a complex verbal sign (or a verbal sign complex), which corresponds to the given expectation of textuality.[8]

In my view, the book of Revelation is a well organized text that plays with different genres.[9] At first glance, it is an open letter to the churches in Asia Minor. In 1:4-6 we find a proemium, whose structure is close to the Pauline formula. And corresponding to this proemium we find the end of the letter in 22:20. But this letter breaks the rhetorical rules of a letter. Its composition is too complicated and the letter is much too long. But using the letter form, the writer evokes the effects of communication between an addresser and an addressee given with the form of a letter. And with the breaking of the formal rules of letter writing, he communicates that what he is writing does not fit into the borders of any genre.

Although Martin Karrer[10] and Elisabeth Schüssler Fiorenza[11] have shown in different ways that it makes sense to read Revelation as a letter, I propose that a game is being played that at the same time uses particular rhetorical features and breaks genre rules as a rhetorical strategy in itself. One very important effect of this rhetoric is to show that human language is not able to speak adequately about the almighty power of God and his Son. Another result is that the text can produce different effects of meaning from different genres simultaneously.

Revelation narrates a story. I do not mean that Revelation *is* a novel in terms of genre, and not a letter, but rather that it is both and more than these two possibilities. And this could be a good explanation for different readers' feelings that the signs of Revelation are, as Petöfi claims, "a complete and coherent whole," even though they do not find agreement about Revelation's genre and meaning.

My feeling as a reader leading me to read Revelation as a well-organized text depends on a very simple macro-structure that we can describe with the categories of a *generative poetics* (Erhardt Güttgemanns)[12] as the transformation of a situation of *lack* to a situation in which lack has been removed (*lack liquidated*) by the narration of significant action (*transformation*).

The Macrostructure of the Revelation to John

PART I (1:1-8)
Instructions to the reader/hearer
>1:1-3: Comprehensive instructions for all readers of all times
>1:4-8: Situational instructions for the explicit reader (proemium)

Part II (1:9–3:22)
Depiction of the situation of deprivation that motivates the action (lack)
>1:9-20: Commissioning vision
>2:1–3:22: Open letters to the seven churches of Asia Minor

PART III (4:1–20:15)
Depiction of the actions that dispel the deprivation (transformation)
>4–13: Judgment is prepared
>4:1–6:1: Necessary preparations in heaven (throne vision)
>4: God as source of power
>5: The commissioning of the protagonist: the handover of the sealed book and the enthronement of Christ
>6–11: Omens of the coming judgment: 7 seals and 7 trumpets
>6:1-17: The first six seals
>7: Sealing of the tribes of Israel
>8:1-5: The seventh seal
>8:6–9:21: The first six trumpets
>10: The angel and the little book
>11:1-2: The measuring of the temple
>11:3-14: The two witnesses
>11:15-19: The seventh trumpet
>12–13: Peripeteia: the casting of Satan from heaven and his limited effects upon the earth
>14–20: Judgment is executed: 7 bowls of wrath
>14: The opening of the judgment
>15–18: Execution of the judgment through the bowls of wrath and the annihilation of Babylon
>19:1-10: Wedding feast of the Lamb
>19:11-21: Victory over the beast (Satan) and his worshippers
>20: Millennial kingdom, ultimate annihilation of Satan, final judgment, book of life

Part IV (21:1–22:5)
Depiction of new life free of deprivation (lack liquidated)
New heaven, new earth, new Jerusalem with the throne of God and the Lamb, seeing the face of God, tree of life for the healing of the nations, reign of the servants of God

PART V (22:6-21)
Instructions to the reader
22:6-17: Conclusion of the commissioning vision
22:18-19: Comprehensive instructions to the reader taken up again
22:20: Authorial congruence as guarantee of truth for that which is read
22:21 Conclusion to the letter including all readers

I organize my reading of the book of Revelation in five parts. These parts interact in a high degree.[13]

The first part gives instructions to the readers and hearers. This part does not only say, as the text wants to be read, but also installs in terms of text pragmatics the most important relation between Jesus, John, and the readers/hearers in terms of being witnesses.

Verses 4-8 of chapter 1 are not only a formal proemium to the letter to the seven churches, but they introduce the book's universe of discourse—a universe that the reader must always keep in mind in order to make sense of the text. These verses name the theological, christological, cosmological, and soteriological presuppositions of the argumentation of the book; and so to become a reader of this book that is *makarios* (in the sense of 1:3) means to agree with these principles and to live as a witness of these convictions.

The term "words of prophecy" (1:3) opens the universe of discourse of Revelation to the prophecy of the Holy Scriptures of Israel and installs the intertextual relation to the books of Moses and all the other prophets such as Isaiah, Ezekiel, Daniel, Joel, and so on. With 1:7 the universe of discourse is connected to the gospel story of Jesus Christ, for it is only by knowing the story of Jesus Christ that this verse can be understood.[14]

Part II—chapters 1:9–3:22—generates the situation of lack. Not only John on Patmos but all churches in Asia live in troubles.

Part III—chapters 4–20—narrates the actions that change the situation of lack (transformation). This section is the *book of visions* and it is very simply structured in terms of an action story. However, at the beginning of every action story, whether it is about Rambo or the Ram of Revelation,[15] the text must show the reader which forces the hero has to engage in order to win his difficult fight, so chapters 4 and 5 reveal the center of power and how the ram got the power of the almighty God. Then, because it is a universal war that is to be fought (of the scale, say, of either World War I or II), the transformation takes time and proceeds through several different episodes. The opening of the seven seals and the seven trumpets must be understood as signals that the last judgment comes now, but they are not the last judgment. The last judgment is the seven bowls.

Chapters 12 and 13 are, in terms of Aristotelian poetics, the peripeteia, and in 12:7 we read what it is: a πόλεμος ἐν τῷ οὐρανῷ, a war in heaven. So, after Satan has lost this war and has been thrown down on earth, the last judgment starts with the first bowl.

This situation is the link to the present time of the writer and first addressees of the book. John understands his times as the time when Satan is fighting on earth and is responsible for all troubles. Thus, in 2:10 we read: "Do not fear what you are about to suffer. Behold, the devil is about to throw some of you into prison, that you may be tested, and for ten days you will have tribulation." The devil works on earth now to enact evil, but he has only a limited time to do so.

Part IV—chapters 21:1–22:5—shows the new situation, where the lack is liquidated.

In Part V—chapter 22:6-21—we encounter again pragmatic instructions for building a contract between text and reader.

It is not possible here to go into every detail of the whole text; therefore, in what follows I shall analyze particular parts of the text in order to examine if the book of Revelation wants us to be witnesses or warriors.

1:4-8: Situational Instructions for the Explicit Reader (Proemium)

The proemium (Rev 1:4-8) of the introductory letter (1:4-20), directed to the seven churches in Asia Minor, outlines in a compressed manner the connections among the theology, pneumatology, Christology, cosmology, and soteriology of the Revelation to John, and thus designates the cornerstones that lend plausibility to the argumentation, visions, and stories of the book.

After John identified himself as the sender of the letter in a most modest manner, without any title or further designation but only with his proper name, and also after he very soberly named his addressees solely as "the seven churches that are in Asia" (Rev 1:4), without any *captatio benevolentiae*, the accompanying wish of grace and peace designates God, "the seven spirits," and Jesus Christ as the givers of grace and peace.

In an instance of syntax that ruptures grammatical rules, God is designated first and foremost as the one "who is and who was and who is to come," the Word "God" lacking explicit mention (Rev 1:4c).[16] The syntagm that is repeated in Revelation 1:8 and introduced with the phrase, "'I am the Alpha and the Omega, says the Lord God,'" refers to the creative power of God, encompassing all time, who then at the end of verse 8 is also titled comprehensively as the ruler of all (*Pantokrator*).

The God of the Revelation to John is, then, the powerful Creator God, who encompasses all time and rules everything (cf. Rev 1:8; 4:11). His power is limitless and precisely therein is founded the hope for the ultimate victory over the limited but nevertheless dreadful havoc-wreaking power of evil. The God of the Revelation to John is a cosmological *Pantokrator* whose power knows no bounds. The plausibility of the talk of the resurrection in the Revelation to John lies grounded in this unlimited power of the Creator, to whom the final writing of the New Testament permits no deity to be compared and permits not even one opponent to stand aside independent of him, in spite of the numerous powers of evil that Revelation depicts in drastic visions. This *Pantokrator* allows no dualistic theology, as some gnostic systems would have it. Even the destroyers ultimately receive their power from God (e.g., cf. 13:15).

The *Pantokrator* is, however, none other than the wonderfully creative Creator God of Israel (cf. Rev 4:11), whose works of creation in 15:3 are sung with the "song of Moses," which is at the same time the "song of the Ram." Although the Revelation to John employs no direct citations of the Holy Scriptures of Israel, it is intertextually and inseparably bound up with them.[17]

The "seven spirits who are before his throne" (Rev 1:4d) are closely connected through their ordering with God and his witness Jesus Christ. In the throne vision in chapter 4 they are depicted as the seven "torches" burning before the throne of God (cf. 4:5) and in 3:1 the seven spirits belong to the exalted Christ.[18]

The christological expressions in Revelation 1:5-6 are also inscribed in the soteriological connection of creation and new creation. Jesus Christ is designated first and foremost as "the faithful witness" (ὁ μάρτυς, ὁ πιστός at 1:5). Thus the "testimony (μαρτυρία) of Jesus Christ" in 1:2 is taken up again and strengthened. Jesus Christ is *the* witness of God par excellence. His witness was and is without limit and no power could and can hinder him from laying aside the absolutely valid and therefore convincing testimony about God, the Creator and ruler of all. His true and effective witness, in which he took upon himself suffering to the point of death on a cross (cf. 1:7b; 11:8b), is the paradigm for all who like John make themselves servants of the resurrected Crucified in his domain and thus become witnesses themselves (cf. 1:2).

However, this witness does not protect one from suffering and death. Jesus Christ, the "faithful and true witness" (Rev 3:14b), was cruelly killed (cf. 1:7b). But the power of the violence directed at him did not have the final word. The "pierced" witness (cf. 1:7b), the "Ram who was slain" (cf. 5:6), received from God, the *Pantokrator*, new life given by God's creative Spirit and also power that overcomes all earthly rulers. As the resurrected one, he who was killed by earthly kingdoms is established "the ruler of the kings of the earth" (1:5).

Because the witness who was killed, Jesus Christ, is the "firstborn of the dead" (Rev 1:5), he is at the same time himself the testimony to God's unlimited creative power, which gives all following witnesses confidence, that their testimony, even when it leads to death, is true and the witnesses themselves are not ultimately devoured by the power of death, but rather receive new life through the Spirit of God (cf. 11:11). The proemium presents Jesus Christ as God's Witness who was killed, raised, and exalted, as the paradigm for all witnesses who follow him, and through this complex of death, resurrection, and power, it offers effective consolation as well as the hermeneutical key for the interpretation of the suffering of those who have given themselves over to discipleship but who in that discipleship also experience violence and disaster. In being a disciple of Jesus Christ, the complex of witness, suffering, and participation in the power of God becomes a model for everyone's world- and self-understanding.

Because this salvific complex has come about with the fate of Jesus, which can be communicated through the witness of this complex, his death has redemptive power. The witness to God, which Jesus Christ himself has provided with his life and death, becomes a witness to the resurrection and exaltation of faithful and true witnesses, a witness to which his followers testify.

What Paul expresses with the syntagm ὁ λόγος ὁ τοῦ σταυροῦ (Word of the cross, 1 Cor 1:18), the Revelation to John designates as τὴν μαρτυρίαν Ἰησοῦ Χριστοῦ (the witness of Jesus Christ, cf. Rev 1:2, 9) or τὸν λόγον τῆς μαρτυρίας αὐτῶν (the word of their witness, Rev 12:11). In spite of the diversity of theological approaches and ways of thinking, the phrases come together in this: the eschatological complex of the events of Jesus' death, resurrection, and exaltation, which lays a new foundation, unfolds its soteriological power through the Word, which testifies spiritually to this event.[19]

At the time of the composition of the Revelation to John, however, the crucified, resurrected, and exalted witness to God has not yet become visible to all. The "kings of the earth" still exercise their violence, but he will come soon (cf. Rev 1:7). The time of composition is a paradoxical

in-between time. The resurrected Crucified is already ruler over the kings
of the earth, but they still exercise their dominion of violence. Those who
bear witness to Jesus Christ are already "kings and priests before God"
(1:6), but they still endure the violence of the "kings of the earth" (1:5).
God, the ruler of all, himself guarantees that the hope for the speedy coming of Jesus Christ and the concomitant hope for the end of injustice and
the beginning of the indestructible new life is no cheap, empty promise
but rather God's potent comfort: "'I am the Alpha and the Omega,' says
the Lord God, who is and who was and who is to come, the Almighty"
(1:8).

1:9-20: Commissioning Vision

The Greek word θλῖψις used in 1:9 marks in John's wide range of meaning
the situation of lack. Despite being kings and priests of God, as we read
in 1:6, John and the seven churches are brothers in "trouble." The witness of John, already introduced in Revelation 1:2 as an essential identity
marker, is made concrete in 1:9. John finds himself in trouble (*thlipsis*) on
the island of Patmos "because of the word of God and the testimony of
Jesus" (1:9). We are not told what trouble John had to suffer on Patmos;
the semantic indeterminacy permits its identification with every sort of
suffering. What is more, all other readers who are brought into the reader-
ship through the prophetic words of the proemium in 1:1-3 can also feel
integrated into the community of oppressed witnesses and, similarly, with
those who have a share in the kingdom of God.

But trouble is not the only characteristic of John's situation. He is
at the same time much more a member in the kingdom of God and in
"endurance in Jesus." He characterizes himself in this way when writing to
the "brothers" in Asia Minor. Their communal sharing in the kingdom of
God does not protect them from their troubles. They can only persevere
in this paradoxical situation "in the endurance of Jesus." This endurance
of Jesus is, however, nothing other than the persistence with which Jesus
went his way of witness to the cross, as the Gospel of John tells it. In the
same way God has answered the faithfulness and perseverance of his witness Jesus with his resurrection from the dead, so can Jesus' followers in
their witness also hope in confidence that they will receive new life as a
gift from God. The resurrection of the Crucified is a paradigm for them
and a hermeneutical key for the meaning of their own experiences of
troubles and for their bearing up under the terrors caused thereby.

The particular self-presentation of the resurrected and exalted Crucified found preceding the individual letters is the same as John's self-
presentation found in his vision, which in the introductory letter John

imparts to all the churches to which he writes: "Do not be afraid; I am the first and the last, and the living one. I was dead, and see, I am alive forever and ever; and I have the keys of Death and of Hades" (Rev 1:17b-18). The vision of the mighty resurrected Jesus dovetails with the seven letters to the churches and is motivated by the problems of the churches in Asia Minor and is at the same time the answer to all problems.

Through the power of his resurrection from the dead, the resurrected Crucified receives a share in the eternal life of God and now in a transformed way can refer the self-predication of God as the Alpha and the Omega (Rev 1:8) to himself. His essential identity marker is therefore the expression, "I was dead, and see, I am alive forever and ever." With the help of the aorist the state of death is marked as a closed act lying in the past. Jesus was dead (*lack*), but he did not remain in this death. He became living in a way that in the breaching of the temporal earthly order shows him to be living forever and ever (*lack liquidated*). He was thus not made alive again simply within the timeline of earthly time in order to die again according to the laws of earthly time, but rather he was gifted with a life that endures forever and ever. This life, however, is the life of God alone, God the Creator, the *Pantokrator*, who introduced himself in 1:8. Jesus was resurrected into the eternal life of God and was at the same time endowed with cosmic power (*transformation*; cf. 1:6).

To that also corresponds his fear-inspiring form, which is barely recognizable as human, and his unconquerable strength, which is visualized with "eyes . . . like a flame of fire," "feet . . . like burnished bronze, refined as in a furnace," and a "face . . . like the sun shining with full force" (Rev 1:14b-16b). Thus John says of the effect this terror-inducing form had upon him: "When I saw him, I fell at his feet as though dead" (1:17). This form fits perfectly with the cosmological war that the visions in chapter 6 to 20 set in scene.

An essential component of this power consists in the giving of the "keys of Death and of Hades" (1:18b). The resurrected Crucified, endowed with power, is deemed judge of death and life, of heaven and hell. He assumes God's eschatological office of judge. Even the churches, symbolized by the seven lampstands, are subject to his judicial office, symbolized by the two-edged sword in his mouth (cf. 1:16, 20). But if the churches—and with them all readers of the book of Revelation—live their lives as witnesses of the witness, they do not have to fear either the cosmological powers of evil or the last judgment. Their deprivation will be removed as well and they will live forever in communion with God and Jesus Christ.

The letters to the seven churches provide insight into a number of different troubling situations: some are problems in the church, some are problems with false apostles from outside, some are problems with Jews, and some are problems with the government. As a result they are in danger of being arrested or even killed, like Antipas the "faithful witness" of Jesus (cf. 2:13). The main issue is that the churches cannot live their new life in freedom and peace but in troubles. But it is precisely the end of all troubles that is prophesied in the sayings of the Spirit and these sayings relate the present situation of *lack* to the coming situation of *lack liquidated* in the New Jerusalem described in chapters 21:1–22:5. I only want to give one example of that: the Spirit says to the church in 2:7b, "To everyone who conquers, I will give permission to eat from the tree of life that is in the paradise of God." This tree the reader of the book of Revelation finds in 22:2: "the tree of life with its twelve kinds of fruit, producing its fruit each month; and the leaves of the tree are for the healing of the nations." A very important rhetorical strategy of the book of Revelation is its use of many of those prolepses and analepses to generate a coherent text. The war the witnesses have to fight is to stay witnesses. They are not told to become physical warriors, but they have to win the fight against all challenges that could lead them away from being witnesses (cf. 2:7, 11, 17, 26; 3:5, 12, 21).

Together the letters in Revelation 1:9–3:22 show that the resurrected and exalted Crucified communicates with his churches through the Spirit and reveals to them his own fate as the hermeneutical key to their own situations. Just as he lived his witness to God, accepted the consequence of suffering violent death, and lived out his unlimited faithfulness to God therein, so also should the churches persevere in their witness to Jesus Christ, even if they must suffer violence. Just as the murdered Jesus was repaid for his faithfulness with new, eternal life and with a share in the cosmic power of God, so also can those who stand in discipleship to Jesus Christ be assured that violence and physical death will not have the last word. Even more, their patient abiding in witness to Jesus Christ leads to eternal life in communion with Jesus Christ, the "firstborn of the dead" (1:5) and with God, the cosmic Creator God, who is able to give the dead the gift of new life.

Chapters 12–13 (the Peripeteia) and the Beginning of Chapter 14

Chapter 12 narrates Satan being thrown down to earth and chapter 13 narrates the wicked deeds of the two beasts on earth. Revelation 13:9-10 links this with an important analepsis to the situation of the seven churches of chapters 2 and 3: "Let anyone who has an ear listen: If you are to be taken captive, into captivity you go; if you kill with the sword, with the sword you must be killed."

When one observes that Jesus has through his death on the cross effected the battle against the adversary as *pars pro toto* for all powers opposed to God, and that the witnesses to Jesus also contribute through the "word of their testimony," three things become clear: (1) the times and worlds are compressed together; (2) therefore, the futuristic eschatology already affects the present; and (3) the present also influences the future:

> Now have come the salvation and the power and the kingdom of our God and the authority of his Messiah, for the accuser of our comrades has been thrown down, who accuses them day and night before our God. But they have conquered him by the blood of the Ram and by the word of their testimony, for they did not cling to life even in the face of death. (12:10-11)

The witnesses, comprising both the churches addressed in Asia Minor as well as all readers of the Revelation to John who, according to the reading compact of 1:1-3, commit themselves to their words and align themselves with them in their lives, are not merely a football in a cosmic match. Rather, their faithfulness to the word of testimony is demonstrated in the way in which they as witnesses participate in the struggle on the battlefield of the earth.

And this battle is hard. Because the devil knows that his time is short, he lashes out mercilessly (Rev 12:12). But this means that although evil will end, the lives of the witnesses will not because they will be transformed like the crucified witness into everlasting life with God.

Chapter 14:1-6 provides another break before the last judgment starts with its annunciation by three angels. The first one proclaims: "Fear God and give him glory, for the hour of his judgment has come; and worship him who made heaven and earth, the sea and the springs of water" (14:7). The seven bowls of God's wrath are the beginning of the last judgment. Faithfulness to the word of testimony does not shield one from the violence of the adversary and those who stand in league with him, consciously or unconsciously. Even witnesses suffer death. But they can be certain that they will receive new life from God, the wonderful ruler of all, who accomplishes his justice: "'Blessed are the dead who from now on die in the Lord.' 'Yes,' says the Spirit, 'they will rest from their labors, for their deeds follow them'" (14:13). The living, however, receive a challenge: "Fear God and give him glory, for the hour of his judgment has come; and worship him who made heaven and earth, the sea and the springs of water" (14:7).

In the midst of the cosmic battle, the events of which play out on earth, we find those holy ones who "die in the Lord," who do not take up weapons in gross impatience or who do not go over to the side of earthly perpetrators of violence: "Here is a call for the endurance of the saints, those who keep the commandments of God and hold fast to the faith of Jesus" (Rev 14:12). The battle of the witnesses at all places and at all times, who will be rewarded with the "first resurrection" (cf. 20:5), consists in three things: (1) to live in trust in the Jesus-Christ-Story, which reveals Jesus as God's outstanding witness, in whose destiny one's own destiny can be read; (2) to remain firm against the fact of injustice and violence themselves in the solidarity of creaturely life; and (3) to give God honor thereby, that he might be praised as the Creator of all life and that earthly life might be shaped in recognition of the way which God's commands prescribe. That means to be witness and not warrior.

Reading Intertextually

Texts are relational objects composed of signs. No text is produced and received in isolation from other texts. Therefore, the concept of intertextuality involves the task of investigating the relationships that a text can have with other texts and understanding the hermeneutical consequences of this insight: that the unavoidable intertextual composition of every text consists of the decentering and pluralizing of textual meaning, and that texts have no meaning but rather enable the production of meaning in the act of reading. The generation of meaning is always codetermined—intended or not, consciously or unconsciously—through the actualization of potential relationships of the text in question to other texts.

Intertextual investigation concerns itself with the effects of meaning that emerge from the references of a given text to other texts. We should only speak of intertextuality when we are interested in exploring the effects of meaning that emerge from relating at least two texts together and that neither of the texts considered alone can produce. We must also remember that within the paradigm of intertextuality, intertextual generation of meaning proceeds in both directions: the meaning potential of both texts is altered through the intertextual reference itself. Since a text can be brought into relationship not only with one but also with many other texts, intertextuality involves the exploration of the decentralization of meaning through references to other texts.[20]

The relationships to the Holy Scriptures of Israel that have been read in Christian services are most important to have in view when interpreting the book of Revelation. In the contract with the readers in Revelation 1:3, the text labels itself as "words of prophecy"—a description that can signal associations with other Jewish and Christian prophetic texts. Thus, from this perspective it makes sense to look for more concrete *intertextual dispositions* in the book of Revelation with prophetic texts, and we do indeed find a lot of them: for example, the throne-visions of Isaiah and Ezekiel in Revelation 4.

However, returning to the question of what it means to be a witness and not a warrior, let me choose another text. In the fifth trumpet we read about horrible locusts that are described as follows:

> In appearance the locusts were like horses equipped for battle. On their heads were what looked like crowns of gold; their faces were like human faces, their hair like women's hair, and their teeth like lions' teeth; they had scales like iron breastplates, and the noise of their wings was like the noise of many chariots with horses rushing into battle. They have tails like scorpions, with stingers, and in their tails is their power to harm people for five months. They have as king over them the angel of the bottomless pit; his name in Hebrew is Abaddon, and in Greek he is called Apollyon. (Rev 9:7-11)

And in the book of Joel these horrible locusts are also found: "What the cutting locust left, the swarming locust has eaten. What the swarming locust left, the hopping locust has eaten, and what the hopping locust left, the destroying locust has eaten. . . . For a nation has invaded my land, powerful and innumerable, its teeth are lions' teeth, and it has the fangs of a lioness" (Joel 1:4, 6). There are more passages that we can identify as quotations in the fifth trumpet of the book of Revelation, but there is more to say here, for we find the trumpet itself in the same eschatological context in Joel 2:1: "Blow the trumpet in Zion; sound the alarm on my holy mountain! Let all the inhabitants of the land tremble, for the day of the Lord is coming; it is near—a day of clouds and thick darkness!" (2:1-2a). With Joel we identify the seven trumpets in the book of Revelation as alarms, as signals for the nearness of God's coming day. Therefore if the locusts in Joel work as metaphors for a powerful army that will destroy Jerusalem, the creatures in the book of Revelation can be understood as war metaphors. When we read Joel from the perspective of the book of Revelation, we will identify the horrible army of the enemies as connected with a cosmic evil.

If we compare the macrostructure of Joel with that of the book of Revelation, we in fact find a similar structure. A situation of deprivation (the enemies want to destroy Jerusalem, Rev 1:1–2:10), a transformation sequence starting with the introduction of the Lord in 2:10 and ending with the Lord's Judgment of the Nations (3:16), and the description of the new situation where the deprivation is removed (3:17-21).

However, if we compare both books and look for significant differences, we find one with regard to the question of violence: in the book of Revelation, God and his heavenly agents destroy the powers of the evil and no human witness on earth takes part in that horrible war. The book of Joel also produces God as the destroyer of the enemies, but his people seem to be involved when God says, "Put in the sickle, for the harvest is ripe" (3:13a). If we take John and Joel at their words we find a real dialogue with different positions, and this intertextual dialogue lets us see both positions as positions, and we, the readers, have to decide what we want to do with the problems of violence in our lives and societies. Do we find the courage to have visions of God's justice and peace? Do we dream dreams about justice and peace for everyone? Perhaps Joel motivated John to prophesy and I hope the spirit of their Scriptures will motivate Christians today to find the courage to have good visions for the future of mankind (cf. 3:28-29).

Testimony (*Zeugenschaft*) and the Question of Power

The different images of the Revelation to John prevent one from exchanging their depicted signs for that which is signified by them. The visions do not depict, but rather symbolize, that which will happen and that which happens now. They are borne by the confidence that the death and resurrection of Jesus Christ do not form a special eschatological case, but rather represent the model and ground of the destiny of those who are convinced of the truth of the Jesus Christ Story, in spite of their experience of catastrophe, and who orient their lives accordingly, even if that brings with it violent death. In this situation, be it under Nero, Domitian, Nerva, Trajan, or Hadrian, the violent vision relocates the desire for revenge to the God who judges and his Christ. The Revelation to John thus legitimates feelings of aggression and the desire for revenge, but it pleads that these destructive feelings not be given leave to take charge. Rather, one should hold fast to the commands of God and to faith in his resurrected witness Jesus Christ, even if the believer is put at a disadvantage. Vengeance should be left to God and to his mighty Ram. The believers did not themselves become mighty, but rather God will demand his justice with the assistance of Jesus Christ, and all who decide against God and his creatures, even indeed inflicting immeasurable suffering on them, will be held accountable. Faithfulness, however, will be repaid with the first resurrection, which already leads ultimately to eternal life with God and Christ. The powers and violence opposed to God and his creatures will not be annihilated in one stroke but rather will first be imprisoned for a thousand years and only then ultimately deprived of power.

The Revelation to John shows that the resurrection of the dead, wholly bound up with the conviction of the resurrection and exaltation of Jesus Christ, is woven inseparably into the hope for the end of injustice. In uncomfortable and therefore precisely unavoidable ways the Revelation to John brings to expression that the question of power and the concomitant question of God's justice are posed with the question about the resurrection of the Crucified and the resurrection of the dead. The question is, however, which power effects and determines the destiny of this world and those who live on and from it? The answer of the Revelation to John is shockingly clear. It is the power of the almighty Creator God, of whom also the Holy Scriptures of Israel rightly speak.

The Revelation to John does not ultimately shy away from the consequences of speaking the theological language of the Creator God as the ruler of all, which involves understanding that the destructive violence in the cosmos and thus also such violence on earth is at least tolerated by God for a determined time. Note well: tolerated, not willed. God permits his creatures the choice and in this granted freedom lies the ground of the possibility and the reality of all injustice and of every lapse from the life willed by God lived in solidarity with his creatures. God himself is thus ensnared in sin. His eschatological judgment is necessary to render his justice ultimate and eternal. Therefore the eschatological resurrection of the dead is not an act of mercy of an uninvolved deity, but rather the pledge (*Erweis*) of theodicy, of the justice of God. Christians should live their political lives based on the eschatological hope of God's justice, and if they do that, they themselves become witnesses of God's love, power, and justice, signs of his truth. And that will make a difference now.

The Revelation to John makes this connection more clearly than any other writing of the New Testament and therefore it must remain in the canon as an uncomfortable book, in order to keep Christian thinking alert.

8
The Apocalypse in the Framework of the Canon

Tobias Nicklas

Introduction

While some readers of the Christian Bible may view it as a unified whole, it is a unified whole that nevertheless consists of a "library" of different books coming from different times and contexts and uttering "God's Word" in very different and human voices. It is a "choir" of assorted voices, but a choir that should not be seen too quickly as being "in harmony" or easily "harmonizable." This presents challenges. First, any fundamentalist interpretation that sees the words of the Bible too plainly and directly as God's immutable word thus becomes inappropriate. Second, the rationale for the relevance of any particular set of biblical writings becomes subject to question. This is certainly true of the book of Revelation.

The last book of the New Testament plays a special role within the Christian Bible, and some years ago Thomas Hieke and I tried to show that this epilogue could be understood as a kind of "keystone" or "cornerstone" that closes the "literary building" of the Christian Bible.[1] However, understanding the role of Revelation in the framework of an already existing canon does present challenges and also raises important questions. Therefore, here I would like to explore the following: What is the import of Revelation's voice in the "choir" of voices we hear in the canon of the Christian Bible? What would be missing if the Apocalypse did not stand at the end of the canon of Old and New Testaments?

However, before I begin to answer these questions, it might be helpful to survey some issues that are of importance but on which I shall not dwell.

First, Revelation's *historical* route into the canon of the New Testament was, as is well-known, extremely problematic.[2] Partly due to Dionysios of Alexandria's critical evaluation of the text, many important authors of the east did not accept it,[3] and the canon of the Peshitta, the classical Syriac version of the Bible, still does not contain the Apocalypse. Even if it surely makes sense to look again at the different steps of the Apocalypse's route into what we call "the New Testament," and to reevaluate some of the relevant sources, I do not think that this approach would be fully appropriate to our topic, given that I wish to try to understand the role of the Apocalypse as part of the canon.

Second, more than any other early Christian writing, Revelation makes claims of authority. In its "prescript" it describes itself as the "Revelation of Jesus Christ" going back to God's word.[4] The text wants to be understood as a "prophecy," whose words have to be read (aloud during Christian "liturgies") and have to be heard and kept because they are relevant for salvation (Rev 1:3). In turn, Revelation 22:18-19 uses a "canon formula" (or better, *integrity formula*) as we find it in the book of Deuteronomy, where it ensures the immovable authority of the Torah. Because I have elsewhere tried to describe the different literary techniques used by Revelation to assure its authority, I shall not go over old ground here.[5]

A third approach to my topic could be to ask how the book of Revelation treats the many different (mainly Old Testament) intertexts it uses and how it creates links to other biblical texts. Taking this route, we would get to know the Seer of Patmos as a "new Ezekiel" and would learn how he reinterprets Old Testament books such as Isaiah, Daniel, Zechariah, Exodus, and others.[6] However, while I will surely not turn a blind eye to this dimension of my question, I would note that other chapters of this book concentrate on exactly these issues.[7]

Apocalypse, World, and Time

The different early Christian writings show different relationships to "time." Several passages of the authentic Pauline letters show how much Paul, but also his communities, were expecting Christ's *Parousia* in their nearest future. One of the clearest examples can be found in 1 Thessalonians 4, which describes the community's hope to participate in Christ's *Parousia* within their own lifetimes. During his first mission in Thessalonica, Paul seems not even to have addressed a topic that is nowadays regarded as the center of the Christian message: the connection between the resurrection of the crucified Jesus of Nazareth and the eschatological resurrection of all dead (see, however, his 1 Cor 15). Obviously, the Apostle had not yet seen the problem that members of the newly founded communities could die before Christ's (more or less) immediate *Parousia*. Paul only reacts after this happened. In 1 Thessalonians 4:15 he writes: "For this we declare to you by the word of the Lord, that we who are alive, who are left until the coming of the Lord, will by no means precede those who have died." The deceased will resurrect when Christ descends from heaven (4:16), and they will be gathered with the living ones into eternal community with Christ, the Lord (4:17).

Many early Christian writings of the third (and later) Christian generations, however, testify to the enormous crisis that occurred with the failure of this expectation. The impact of this situation cannot be overestimated and I would regard it as one of the greatest accomplishments of Christian history that this crisis was overcome. One of the main challenges of the situation was to create a new idea of the "time of the church" now living within world and society. The church had not only to survive a little while, but was more and more forced to understand itself as part of "world," "society," and "history." While Paul was still creating ad hoc solutions to concrete problems, the church now had to develop "theories" and had to arrange its affairs for a longer period of living in this world.

That is why different texts created different ideas of how to deal with the non-appearance of the *Parousia*. While its author's opponents claimed that "the day of the Lord is already here" (2 Thess 2:2), the pseudepigraphical 2 Thessalonians[8] developed a complex plan of the events to be expected before the end of times, including the motifs of the mysterious "katechon" and the revelation of the "antichrist."[9] In this way, the text does not only safeguarded Paul's authority, which seems to have been endangered by his opponents' ideas, but also "created time" wherein the church could arrange itself.

An even later text is 2 Peter,[10] which seems to have faced a similar crisis: while its use of the motif of "memory" tries to keep a certain continuity with apostolic times, the text tries to cope with the extension of time by an exegesis of Psalm 90:4: "with the Lord one day is like a thousand years, and a thousand years are like one day" (2 Pet 3:8).[11]

Of course, early Christian communities' changing relation to "time" had a great impact on their relation to "world" and "society." This can even be seen in the development of images of the church as a kind of ancient *oikos* (i.e., "house"), as we find them in the Pastoral Epistles (which I would date at the end of the first century C.E.).[12] The church began to arrange itself as part of world and society, and stood, more and more, under the influence of its surroundings (the development of the role of women being but one example). As theological problems in more than one passage of the Pastoral Epistles show us, the church has always been in danger of being too much a part of "this world" and its establishment.[13]

The book of Revelation can be understood as a powerful voice against all these tendencies. One of the decisive questions of this text seems to be the problem of how far Christian communities should become part of their surrounding world and how far their own system of values can more or less coincide with the world's views. The Seer's opponents, partly represented by the seer Jezebel (Rev 2:20) in Thyatira, seem to have been much more open—should we call it "tolerant"?—to the surrounding world. The Apocalypse is much more radical and shows a high measure of aggressiveness against them.[14] It warns against making too many compromises, being too much "just" another part of the world, not focusing on what really counts. One of the text's sharpest criticisms is directed against the community of Laodicea, which is warned by the risen Christ: "'I know your works; you are neither cold nor hot. I wish that you were either cold or hot. So, because you are lukewarm, and neither cold nor hot, I am about to spit you out of my mouth. For you say, "I am rich, I have prospered, and I need nothing." You do not realize that you are wretched, pitiable, poor, blind, and naked'" (3:15-17).

As other third-generation Christian texts,[15] the book of Revelation creates "time"—just think of the many events that have to happen before the final judgment—but this time is always related to this final judgment, the "end of times" that is "coming soon" (2:16; 3:11; 22:7, 12, 20). It warns the communities to take God's and Christ's (i.e., the Lamb's) part radically and not settle for wrong compromises. The danger of being too unconcerned with the requirements of a Christian life *in this world* is met with the admonition that *this whole world*—as God's creation—will be reckoned in God's final judgment.

Apocalypse and State/Society

My second point is closely connected to the first: as a young movement worshipping a crucified criminal, early Christianity had to face dangerous prejudices, criticisms, and sometimes even persecution. In this context, therefore, it was vitally important to show solidarity with the powerful Empire and its representatives. A good example of this attitude can be seen in Tertullian's *Apologetics* from the end of the second century C.E. According to Tertullian, Christian solidarity with the Empire is shown by the fact that Christians were praying for the Roman Emperor (*Apol.* 31). Tertullian bases this practice not on a single quotation from Scripture, but gives a resumé of the Christian attitude to the Roman state by creating a text inspired by several scriptural passages: Romans 13:1; 1 Timothy 2:2; Titus 3:1; and 1 Peter 2:13.

Such a—surely comprehensible—defensive attitude of early Christian communities against state and Empire is probably also mirrored in the Gospels' descriptions of Pontius Pilate—although the New Testament Pilate remains admittedly a somewhat ambivalent figure, but compared with the deeply negative images we find in Philo of Alexandria and Josephus, this Pilate is depicted as extremely positive.

While Jesus' response to the question as to whether it is allowable to pay taxes to the emperor (Mark 12:13-17 par.) surely shows some critical awareness of the political situation, and other texts such as the healing of the demoniac from Gerasa (Mark 5:1-20 par.) can be understood as a kind of "underground" criticism of the *de facto* political situation, for centuries many Christians used Romans 13:1-7 (and its receptions in the Pastoral Epistles) when it came to the question of Christian relationship to state and society.[16]

However, all of us know from history—and here I refer only to the context of twentieth-century totalitarian dictatorships—this kind of attitude against a state can become extremely problematic, if not dangerous. Interestingly, in a certain sense Revelation seems to be more sensitive toward these problems. We might say that it understands the Roman state as a kind of "totalitarian dictatorship" or—in the book's own terms—as being led by satanic powers, the great dragon and his forces (see, e.g., Rev 12–13 and 17).[17] According to the Seer, becoming involved with this power and its representatives is a dangerous compromise, a compromise that means turning away from God, the "Pantokrator," and taking the side of evil.

Of course, we cannot simply appropriate Revelation's "mythological" language and apply it to modern (sometimes more or less secular) systems of state and society, but wherever state and/or (strands of) society show totalitarian claims on human beings and arise as quasi-godly, life-destroying powers, the Seer's message can be of enormous relevance. In a post-twentieth-century world, the voice of the Apocalypse could at the very least be a necessary corrective to other New Testament voices.

The God of the Apocalypse

Since Marcion's time the question of whether Old and New Testament are speaking about two different deities has remained open. Does the Old Testament portray a more or less jealous and vindictive tribal God of Israel, while the New Testament portrays Jesus of Nazareth's God, the "God of pure love"?[18]

Perhaps the most well-known dictum for such thoughts can be found in Adolf von Harnack's well-known monograph on Marcion:

To reject the Old Testament in the second century was a mistake which the Church rightly repudiated; to retain it in the sixteenth century was a fate which the Reformation could not yet avoid; but to continue to keep it in Protestantism as a canonical document after the nineteenth century is the consequence of religious and ecclesiastical paralysis.[19]

Harnack's statement is now more than a hundred years old, but in fact comparable ideas are evident even today, and are found wherever Jesus of Nazareth is cut off from his Jewish roots.

While in contemporary scholarly debates Jesus' Jewishness is at least commonly acknowledged, many western Christians without theological education are in danger of understanding the New Testament God as just "dear daddy," and they are at the same time losing touch with the great variety of experiences of God that we find in the Old Testament. In this context the voice of Revelation with its image of a very transcendent God who remains a (sometimes even terrifying, seemingly threatening) *mysterium*, a *mysterium tremendum*, can be of importance.

The book of Revelation connects the ideas of God as the eternal Creator[20] who is standing outside of time, but accomplishing actions that reach into time, with the image of the impenetrable "Pantokrator" sitting on his heavenly throne.[21] Of course, these images are closely connected to comparable ideas in other Old and New Testament texts. However, the fact that Revelation as the *last book* of the Christian Bible again speaks about God as Creator of the world overarches the whole of the Bible, which from its very first chapters deals with God's creation of the cosmos. Revelation, however, adds new perspectives to the biblical theology of creation. By saying that God has created the world "by his will" (cf. Rev 4:11), Revelation rejects the possible idea that God could be more or less a kind of craftsman, a *demiurge*. It emphasizes the idea of God's continuous creative activity until the events of the end of times, when a new heaven and a new earth will be created (Rev 20:5). And it is in this way the theology of creation and eschatology become closely connected. Seen as such a Lord of the whole of creation, the God of Revelation is the only sovereign, the only one to be worshipped; in this way the book unmasks any kind of ideological claims against humanity.

Nevertheless the God of the Apocalypse still remains the great *mystery*. The great vision of chapter 4, where the Seer is entering the heavenly throneroom, can be understood as a kind of *relecture* of Ezekiel's vision of God's throne,[22] but it is remarkable that John—contrary to Ezekiel 1:26-27—does not even try to describe God's outward appearance: God is only the one who is sitting on the throne (Rev 4:2 and elsewhere). While the text offers quite a detailed depiction of the throne room, the reader does not get a description of the one sitting on the throne. The Seer tries to avoid any image of God.

Another scene demonstrates the Pantokrator's removed stance in an even sharper way. After the opening of the fifth seal, an altar of sacrifice is seen in the heavenly throne room. Under the altar, obviously at the very place where usually the blood of the sacrificial animals flows, the Seer recognizes the "souls" of the ones "who had been slaughtered for the word of God and for the testimony they had given" (Rev 6:9). In their mouths we hear the great question of a suffering humanity in despair: "'Sovereign Lord, holy and true, how long will it be before you judge and avenge our blood on the inhabitants of the earth?'" (Rev 6:9b).

In this way Revelation asks the question of all humanity—the question of God's righteousness—and puts it in the mouths of the ones who have even given their lives for God.[23] This is not just another way of uttering the question of theodicy as we find it—starting with Job—many times in the Bible. In fact it is an even more radical way to pose it: the one who is sitting on the throne *does not respond*—at least he does *not yet respond in the expected way*. Even if the crying ones receive "white robes" according to Revelation 6:11, this is no real response to their question. God remains distanced. In fact, we could understand the whole of Revelation as a response to the question asked in Rev 6:9b,[24] but, within the book, we have to wait until the very end. As far as I understand the text, God's final response does not come before Revelation 21:5, the only passage where the text tells us that the one sitting on the throne is talking: "See, I am making all things new."

This statement, however, does not occur until after the new heaven and the new earth appear, when the threatening power of the sea has been removed (Rev 21:1), and when the Holy City, the New Jerusalem, has descended from heaven (Rev 21:2). It is surely not by chance that this passage takes up central promises from Israel's Scriptures again. From now on God will no longer be the more or less inaccessible one, but "he will dwell with them; they will be his peoples, and God himself will be with them" (Rev 21:3). This also means that all kinds of suffering and even death will come to an end: "he will wipe every tear from their eyes. Death will be no more; mourning and crying and pain will be no more, for the first things have passed away" (Rev 21:4; cf. Isa 25:8).[25] Revelation 21:5 makes clear that all this—promised already by the Scriptures of Israel, but as yet unfulfilled—is not forgotten but will be encompassed through God Himself, the One who is sitting on the throne.

What does this mean for the role of Revelation in the canon of Old and New Testaments? By making clear that the decisive promises of the

Old Covenant—the annihilation of death and suffering—are not yet perceptible even after the Christ-event, the Apocalypse offers an important counterargument to any naive ideas about the relation between Old and New Testaments: the Old Testament should not be purely understood as "promise," and the New Testament is in no way only its "fulfillment." From earliest times Christians have been reading Israel's Scriptures from a christocentric perspective, that is, differently from Jews who do not believe in Christ. Revelation with its sharp focus on the problem of theodicy, even after the Christ-event, and its recapitulation of central Old Testament prophecies clearly shows that reading the Old Testament must be more than understanding it as foreshadowing Christ.

Insisting on God's open promises to Israel and the world, Revelation impedes any kind of a Christian theology that could be in danger of overlooking the suffering of the just and innocent after the Christ-event. In this way the text gives a voice to the continuing human cry for justice.

But even if Revelation describes God as the transcendent sovereign ruler of the world, although a ruler removed from human sight, he is always seen as the one who is already acting as he has always done before. The God of Revelation is remaining the *Handlungssouverän*, the one who leads the world to a good end.

This can be shown for example in the text's reception of the exodus plagues in the vision cycles. Read without its Old Testament background, these texts seem only to describe the horrors of eschatological times, and the intertextual relation between the four horsemen and the visions of Zechariah shows that this interpretation is not totally wrong. However, the fact that many of the images used here can be related to the plagues of the exodus shows us that the coming events are not directed against God's people, but must be interpreted as signs that God is already taking sides with his Elect, and that the God of Revelation is exactly the one who had—beginning with the exodus event—always been on the side of his people. Additionally, the idea of a covenant between God and his people makes clear that the exodus event describes not only a singular event, but an event that becomes the basis of God's relation to his people once and forever.

Standing at the very end of the Christian Bible, Revelation not only takes over this idea, but puts it into cosmic dimensions, showing that God's "historical actions" should not be misunderstood as more or less "singular" events of the past. The Apocalypse relates these events to the eternal, to God's all-embracing mysterious acting in world and time, which is leading the whole of his creation to its final destiny.

Conclusion

In the consciousness of western European churches, Revelation plays a more or less marginal role. Many Christians of our times would even prefer to ban this book from the canon of the Christian Bible: its message seems to be too difficult and its text too full of violent, dark images. But already the three lines of argumentation above show that the Christian Bible would lose a decisive dimension without Revelation:[26]

First, in many ways Revelation is embedded in the Christian Bible's witness about God and his relation to humanity expressed in his covenant with his chosen people Israel and the Christ event. Revelation takes over many important lines and develops them even further. God is the Creator of the world, the "Pantokrator," and he will lead this world to its final destiny. Over the course of history he proves to be just and faithful. But at the same time he remains distanced and ultimately inaccessible, even where he reveals himself. Revelation combines specific aspects of this image of God and confronts it with the human cry for justice. However, it does not simply give a plain answer to the theodicy quest, but takes up God's promises to Israel. Finally, Revelation describes the image of a relation between God, Christ, and man, where everything human can find its final destiny in an untroubled relation with God and the Lamb.

Second, the book of Revelation is an important counter-voice to voices within the canon that can be problematic, if not dangerous, if they are overemphasized. Revelation creates the image of a church, which—contrary to the earliest Pauline communities—can see itself as part of time and history, but which also—contrary to the communities of the Pastorals—is not in danger of being *just* a part of this world. In this way Revelation radically questions any kind of "totalitarian" claims of state and society against human beings. And ultimately, Revelation proclaims the God of Abraham, Isaac, and Jacob, the God of Israel, who is also the God of Jesus Christ. Against all modern tendencies to understand this God as a cozy father figure and see his love as warm and fuzzy, the last book of the Bible presents the image of the transcendent "Pantokrator" who rules the world and leads it to its final destiny, but who sometimes seems to keep silent when we would like him to "speak."

While the above ideas attempt to give at least a partial answer to the question of what would be lacking in the Christian Bible without the book of Revelation, it is also important to invert this question and ask what is lacking in the book of Revelation and why it needs the canon.

First, the book of Revelation is a witness of a deeply Jewish Christianity; its ideas find their roots in the Scriptures of Israel, the images and thoughts of which are mirrored in almost every single sentence. Its description of the church in time and end time are developed from Old Testament images of God's chosen people; its depiction of eschatological salvation in a New Jerusalem descending from heaven, a city whose gates bear the names of the twelve tribes of Israel (Rev 21:12), cannot be understood without the idea of God's covenant with Israel. But even with these points in mind the book's relation to Jews is not without problems. Its passages about the "synagogue of Satan" (Rev 2:9 and 3:9) surely belong to the very New Testament texts with the clearest anti-Jewish potential.[27] What can be seen as a kind of inner-Jewish conflict on a historical level became even more problematic after the so-called "parting of the ways," when Jews and Christians first belonged to separate religions. Moreover, Revelation does not offer a positive idea of the fate and theological impact of the parts of Israel that did not come to believe in Christ. Here Revelation needs correction through voices of other biblical texts: one of the decisive ones surely being found in Paul's Letter to the Romans (see Rom 11:25-36).

A second point must be added: asked by Pharisees and scribes which of the commandments of the Torah is the most important one, Jesus responds with a combination of Deuteronomy 6:4-5 and Leviticus 19:18, a combination of the commandments of an all-embracing human love of God and a love of one's neighbor (cf. Mark 12:18-31 par. Matt 22:34-40 and Luke 10:25-28, where the teacher of the Torah gives the decisive response). It is this combination of love of God and love of one's neighbor that is understood as the center of God's will.

Even in his letter to the Galatians, where Paul preaches a radically changed understanding of the Torah, he sees the love commandment as a center of the Torah that still has to be observed. According to Galatians 5:13-14, the whole of the Law can be summarized in one command: "For you were called to freedom, brothers and sisters; only do not use your freedom as an opportunity for self-indulgence, but through love become slaves to one another. For the whole law is summed up in a single commandment, 'You shall love your neighbor as yourself.'"

Already the first words of the Decalogue make clear that this command is not just a demand, but that it is part of a living relationship where God is acting first, creating salvation and loving without precondition. It is surely not by chance that God introduces himself as the one who has led Israel "out of Egypt, the house of slavery" (Exod 20:1 par. Deut 6:5). The Johannine community understood the Christ event as another, decisive sign of this love—and is drawing the radical conclusion: "God is love, and those who abide in love abide in God, and God abides in them" (1 John 4:16b).

Thoughts like these apparently play only a minor role in the book of Revelation. Even if the book does not proclaim a God without love, the motifs of "love" and "loving" occur only rarely, as can be seen in the text's vocabulary.[28] Particularly the letters to the communities of Asia show a high level of aggressiveness against opponents and people of different opinions. These tendencies can become dangerous if overemphasized. Just one example of such an interpretation of Revelation was its reading by the Nazi ideologist Joseph Goebbels, who in his younger years was inspired by the text's statements about the destruction of God's enemies (which he of course understood as the Jews) by a messianic figure of the end times.[29] In fact, the Nazi idea of creating a kind of "messianic Millennium" found its background in apocalyptic thinking (see Rev 20:4-6).

The correcting voices of the canon, together with a clearly reflected hermeneutics of the canon, will always be necessary to ensure that the "words of the prophecy of this book," claiming to go back to God's word itself, are not turned into dead (or even deathly) letters.

9

Reading What Is Written in the Book of Life

Theological Interpretation of the Book of Revelation Today

Marianne Meye Thompson

Perhaps no book of the Bible has as many monographs, articles, websites, and lecture series devoted to its interpretation as does the Revelation of John, perhaps because no book of the Bible needs them more. One finds Revelation deciphered, decoded, unlocked, introduced, explained, interpreted, understood, and revealed. For some, the keys to reading Revelation lie in the future; for others, in the past. Thus, on the one hand, there are interpreters who read the Apocalypse of John as predicting a future scenario that includes the—often imminent—return of Christ and the battle of Armageddon, and the code of Revelation can be cracked by correlating the various prophecies of the Bible with each other in a narrative of the events of these "end times." But for other interpreters, especially those in the scholarly academy, the keys to unlocking the book of Revelation lie in its apocalyptic genre, historical circumstances, symbolic universe, rhetorical conventions, literary structure, and so on. In order to understand Revelation we must give attention not to the future but to the past, to the rhetoric and symbolism employed by first-century apocalyptic literature, and to the social, political, and economic practices of the Roman Empire, especially in the closing decades of the first century.

These are two radically different ways of reading the last book of the New Testament. If the "futurist" interpreters consign the book to an unknown time in the future, making it essentially irrelevant for all generations of readers until the end, the historically oriented academic interpreters often consign the book to the past. Assuming that the mysterious beast whose number is 666 can be explained by a knowledge of the Hebrew alphabet and myths about the imminent return of Nero, or that "Babylon" is actually a cryptogram for ancient Rome, scholars can "explain" how the book would have been heard by its first-century readers. But an explanation of the book is not identical with an interpretation of it, let alone with a theological interpretation of it.

It is in fact arguable that one particular manifestation of futurist interpretation, namely, the dispensationalist school of interpretation[1] of the book of Revelation—responsible for spawning so much popular American literature, including *The Late Great Planet Earth* and the *Left Behind* series[2]—might well be called a theological interpretation of the book. Indeed, this approach articulates a vision of God's sovereignty and ultimate victory, and finds it narrated, even if obliquely, in the Scriptures. It can explain both the whole of Revelation and each constituent part of it. No doubt that constitutes a large part of its mass appeal at the popular level.

If the strength of the dispensationalist system lies in its own peculiar style of theological interpretation, its chief weakness can be found in the way that it employs such theological interpretation. One can object to any particular theological conviction and the way in which it shapes exegesis, indeed, the way that it has usurped exegesis. For example, in its understanding of the authority of Scripture, classic dispensationalism insists that prophecies recorded in the Old Testament must be fulfilled exactly as they were originally given. If an Old Testament text promises the restoration of the Davidic kingship and a rebuilt temple, then both must be realized. Since those promises were originally given to the Jewish people, they must and will be fulfilled for the Jewish people, and Jerusalem will be the site of their fulfillment. New Testament texts that reread these Old Testament promises—perhaps promising a different kind of temple, or a different sort of royal restoration—are "applications" of these Old Testament passages, but bear little on how one understands the ongoing significance of these Old Testament texts. One may well take issue with this particular way of interpreting the Old Testament. Indeed, a different understanding of how the New Testament reads the Old Testament or, in particular, how the book of Revelation appropriates the Old Testament, would yield a different understanding of Revelation's promises and challenges. In other words, the way in which one construes the intertextuality of Revelation matters greatly in its theological interpretation.

Second, classic dispensationalism—or at least its popularizers—paid little heed to the fruits of academic study of apocalyptic literature, its genre and literary conventions, or the first-century context in which Revelation was composed. Indeed, the results of historical criticism were often greeted with alarm and hostility, as they seemed so often to vitiate any claim to Scripture's authority.[3] The upshot is a way of reading the text that does not acknowledge its social, cultural, and political contexts nor bring any such data to bear on its interpretation. One could easily add the objection that much futurist interpretation pays little attention to the history of the interpretation of the text, learning little from repeated failed attempts—including, ironically, its own—to derive a timetable of the events of the end from Revelation. In other words, the problem with this interpretive approach is not that its fails to be theological, but that its theological convictions produce certain readings of biblical texts that do not take its historical and literary contexts, including the history of interpretation of the book, seriously. By cutting itself off from the realities of the first century and the likely actual readers of the text, by neglecting the original context into which this prophetic word was given, and by ignoring the history of the book's interpretation, such interpretation isolates itself from the larger community of interpretation. It also forfeits its ability to offer a compelling vision for Christian faith and hope that may appeal to any other than those already committed to its theological system, because it depends upon its theological underpinnings for exegetical analysis.

What, then, of ways of reading the text that take seriously its context, both in the first century and throughout the centuries? Studies of the first-century context, including the apocalyptic genre, literary and rhetorical conventions, and the social, political, and cultural situation of the Roman Empire at the end of the first century,[4] have shed light on virtually every aspect of Revelation, even if disagreements remain about various details, such as the date of the book. But the often unintentional result of reading Revelation with a primary focus on its past is that it remains an artifact of the past. Indeed, historical criticism has often been practiced by those in the academy who have little or no interest in these texts as Scripture and for whom historical approaches are ways of holding ancient texts at arm's length without having to attend to any claims regarding their authority or canonicity. For those interpreters who employ historical methods, but who also receive the Revelation of John as part of their Scripture, it is then a second and optional step to ask how they ought to receive the Revelation of John, what it might be heard to say to the contemporary world, or how it serves in the Christian formation of its readers.

This brings us, then, to the task of theological interpretation. As the preceding brief sketch of two approaches to interpretation has suggested, even if an approach to the book of Revelation has been deeply shaped by theological convictions, that alone cannot commend it, particularly if it remains uninformed by historical analysis. Similarly, however, interpretative practices sensitive and attuned to historical concerns, while crucial

for responsible interpretation, cannot by themselves produce readings
whose results are immediately transparent to at least one of the aims of
theological interpretation, namely, the Christian formation of its readers.
We may ask whether such theological interpretation *from the very outset*
reads the book of Revelation differently, or whether it uses the same methods as, say, historical criticism, but then, only as a second (and secondary)
step, inquires after its theological character or substance. To ask it differently, what distinguishes "theological interpretation" as *theological?* Is
there anything intrinsic in the way in which the text is read, the questions
or the sensitivities that are brought to it, or the convictions underlying
interpretation of it, that shape the way in which the book is interpreted?
Is there something intrinsic in this way of reading the text that makes it
"theological" and, if so, what difference does it make in reading the book
of Revelation? We turn, then, to some brief comments on the aims and
practice of theological interpretation.

A Brief Description of Theological Interpretation

In spite of the fact that, in the past few decades, "theological interpretation" of Scripture has been a burgeoning field of study, there is little
agreement about what it is or how one undertakes a "theological reading"
of a text. This scarcely makes theological interpretation unique in biblical studies. But since there is no single "method" of theological interpretation, those persons who understand themselves to be engaged in the
enterprise in one way or another often come at the task differently. Even
given the differences, theological interpretation does rest on the (theological) conviction that the Bible is sacred Scripture; that is to say, it has its
"origin, subject matter, and purpose in God."[5] Faithful interpretation of
scriptural texts will pay attention not only to various historical and literary
features of the texts, but will also take account of and elucidate the text
as from, about, and leading to God. Ultimately, then, the aims of such
interpretation are not only increased knowledge or understanding, but
the shaping of individuals and communities to be obedient to and to live
in communion with the God who is the giver and subject of Scripture.

For a theological interpretation is above all interpretation of *Scripture*,
and theological interpretation of Scripture will have as its ultimate goal
the formation of its readers and their allegiances, convictions, and practices. This is not to say that such interpretation is uncomplicated, straightforward, transparent, or immediate, but that reading the Scriptures for
such formation is not a secondary aim of their interpretation. Theological
interpretation thus takes its place among the practices of reading that
dominated prior to the modern period of study of the text, practices that

either assumed[6] or aimed at the formation of those who read these texts.[7] While theological interpretation may include, it will not be limited to, an understanding of the events that generated the text, nor will "meaning" be vested solely in the originating moment of that text.

Second, if theological interpretation has certain ends (formation) because it reads certain kinds of texts (Scripture), it is also located in a certain context, and that is the ecclesial context. However much the books of the Bible may be regarded today as literary and cultural artifacts of significance, they were originally written out of and for an ecclesial context; they have been preserved, read, studied, and proclaimed by the church; they have formed the church's theology and shaped its liturgy; and they continue to challenge and nourish the church today. But those who acknowledge themselves part of the church are not the only students, or the only apt students, of these texts. Theological interpretation, done by and for the church, must guard against cutting itself off from important conversations *extra ecclesiam* and of being done by an ingrown and self-contained circle of interpreters (again, scarcely unique to theological interpretation!). Such conversations can be found in the academy, among professional biblical scholars who do not profess Christian faith or practice theological interpretation, among archaeologists and historians and exegetes; they are also going on among those outside of the academy or the church who yearn for hope, seek a sense of their place in a troubled world, or worry about the degradation of the earth's resources, and fear the approach of an Armageddon such as nuclear war could unleash. While theological interpretation has become a label for certain kinds of biblical interpretation, by its very nature it demands engagement with a wide variety of interpretative practices and communities.

Our task may be illuminated if the adjective "theological" is understood to modify "text" rather than "interpretation." What we are interested in is interpretation of certain kinds of texts, namely, theologically interested texts. If the texts themselves treat of such properly theological matters as the character and identity of God, and the purposes and people of God, and if ultimately the aim of the texts themselves is the formation of its readers, then "theological" interpretation must attend to these concerns, whether by describing what is expressed in the texts themselves or by delineating the apparent function of these texts in their contexts. Indeed, one can fairly claim that *any* act of interpretation will be incomplete unless it attends seriously to the theological interests of these texts and the ways in which they were intended to address and shape their readers.[8]

But this is really to say only that interpretation of any text, in order to properly honor that text, must take that text seriously in its specificity.

Hence, interpretation of the book of Revelation needs to pay attention to its genre, its historical setting in the first-century Roman Empire, the literary features of the text, and the like. To be sure, not every instance of theological interpretation—be it sermon, liturgy, written commentary, or lived practice—needs to rehearse every aspect of such historical interpretation. But the overall enterprise of theological interpretation need not be less interested in matters traditionally allotted to historical or literary criticism, although it will assume that such investigations are always only partial investigations of the text and that they ultimately serve another purpose. As already noted, theological interpretation insists on attention to the explicitly theological subject matter of the text, and to the formative aims of the text as read and heard in its ecclesial contexts. These features, too, are part of the specificity of the texts.

But, having said all that, at least two problems remain. First, it is easy to speak of theological interpretation when we are speaking of certain kinds of passages; namely, and not surprisingly, those that are explicitly theological. These passages might include the blessings and benedictions of Revelation; its scenes of heavenly worship; the grand hymns sung by the heavenly choirs; and the final vision of the heavenly Jerusalem. These scenes foster Trinitarian readings; have the crucified and risen Lord at their center; speak of the vocation of the church; and are replete with theological convictions about God and the Lamb. No doubt about it: not only are these scenes crucial to the structure and theology of the book of Revelation, they cry out for theological readings—for readings that shape the imagination, discipleship, and worship, for this is surely how they were intended to function in their original context and have often functioned for Christians throughout the centuries. At once the height of the theological rhetoric of the book, such passages are also in many ways the low-hanging fruit for theological interpretation.

Second, and closely related to the previous point, it is much easier to read the whole of Revelation theologically than to read some of it theologically. Sometimes this may be due to the opaqueness of the imagery; but sometimes, and more problematically, to the troubling character of the material itself. One can celebrate the "great supper of God" (Rev 19:17), until one reads the menu: "the flesh of kings, the flesh of captains, the flesh of the mighty, the flesh of horses and their riders—flesh of all, both free and slave, both small and great" (19:18). There are other passages that seem to celebrate the violence wrought or allowed by God or by the Lamb on the earth and its inhabitants (9:4-6, 13-19).[9] Is it enough to say that Revelation depicts a God who is ultimately sovereign and who will win the victory over evil, if that victory seems to be won by means of, or attained only after, such great violence and destruction? Or how does one read the little vision of Revelation 14:1-5 "theologically"? Whoever the 144,000 in this vision may represent, they are all male and are characterized as those "who have not defiled themselves with women" (14:4), thus seeming to privilege men and to denigrate women and/or sexual relations. What would it mean to read such a text "theologically"? In what follows, I do not propose to answer all these difficult questions. But I would like to suggest how we might allow the book of Revelation itself to shape our understanding of theological interpretation.

Theological Interpretation
of the Book of Revelation

In what follows, I offer five theses about some underlying assumptions and aims of theological interpretation, and suggest how they are both prompted by Revelation itself and how, in turn, they underlie the theological interpretation of Revelation. These theses do not intend to offer guidelines for how a particular text should be interpreted, but rather to offer an overarching framework of the kinds of concerns and interests that shape theological interpretation of the book of Revelation. Not all theses are likely to be represented in every instantiation of a theological interpretation—be that a hymn, sermon, or essay—but theological interpretation, as I envision it, will be marked by these commitments. For example, the fifth thesis reads, *Theological interpretation of Scripture reads Scriptural texts within the context of the canon.* While one can easily imagine a particular theological interpretation that does not pay explicit attention to Revelation's place in the canon, it would be much more difficult to entertain a theological interpretation that explicitly or implicitly denied the place of Revelation in the canon of Scripture. Exactly how interpretation proceeds with an eye toward the canonical role and status of any given text cannot be determined ahead of time, since interpretation always works with specific texts and endeavors to hear not only their distinctive voices but the larger choir of voices of which they are a part.

The church today hears the book of Revelation addressed to it because there is only one church.

The conviction that Christ's church is one church undergirds theological interpretation because it forbids contemporary readers from dismissing Scripture out of hand as "irrelevant" for modern readers. The conviction of the oneness of Christ's church, if carried through, would also mean that the contemporary members of Christ's church reading the book of Revelation—or any book of Scripture—ought more readily to open or expose themselves to the text, and allow more vigorous scrutiny of themselves in its light.

The letters to the seven churches at the outset of this book are addressed to actual churches known to the Seer, John, and these churches are in need of both exhortation and encouragement. Their chief problems vary: some congregations are dealing with hostility (Rev 2:8-11; 3:7-13); others have compromised with or assimilated to local civic and religious practices and customs (2:14-15; 2:20); and still others are complacent or self-sufficient (2:4; 3:1-3; 3:15-18). When Christians today read these letters as addressed to them, they do so in part because the letters have timely warnings and because they are heard or read as Scripture. But these letters speak to the church today not just because they are Scripture but because the church they address today is one with the church they addressed in the past. While the seven churches of Revelation were undoubtedly historical congregations, there were more than these seven churches in the province of Asia. But since seven is a number of fullness, the enumeration of seven churches points to the entire church. And even though the letters are contextually targeted messages to local congregations, the letter to each church can be "overheard" by all of the others. The individualized word that targets each church may also be directed to anyone who has ears to listen, whoever they may be and wherever and whenever they may live.

Second, if the book of Revelation is to have the capacity to speak to and against the church, as these seven letters indicate that it was intended to have, then theological interpretation of Scripture today will allow Scripture to tell us something that we would not otherwise believe—about ourselves, our church, our world, and the decisions and judgments that we make. Theological interpretation cannot simply be the elucidation or reaffirmation of the theological convictions of the church, or of our own predilections and sensitivities, but must serve to call the church to account, as the letters of the book of Revelation sought to call these first-century churches to account. Indeed, theological interpretation may well catalyze a critical reading of the church's convictions and practices. Put differently, because theological interpretation attends to *theology* proper, it must assume that its task is to allow the divine voice—sometimes an alien voice—to be heard through the text. God may speak in the tongues of mortals, but in Scripture God does not always say what mortals want to hear. So it is with the opening epistles of the book of Revelation; and theological interpretation must not only describe the contents of God's judgments and exhortations, but serve to call the church to faith and obedience as these letters did. The words of the book are to be kept (Rev 1:3; cf. 3:8; 12:17; 14:12; 22:9).

Third, theological interpretation of Scripture will recognize that although the church is one church, it does not always share a common mind. While each of the letters to the seven churches is addressed to the "angel" of the church, at times "some" are singled out for commendation or warning; "some" may be implicated in the exhortations to the whole church (e.g., "some," 2:14, 15; "the rest of you," 2:24). Even the repeated exhortation, "Let anyone who has an ear listen" implies that not all are expected to listen. Theological interpretation of the book of Revelation should empower and equip the church to speak to and against others in the church in order to encourage and exhort each other to "follow the Lamb wherever he goes." The church is called to bear faithful witness not only to the world outside but to the church; however, the task requires discernment. The churches are called to remember, to listen, and to repent. The capacity to speak the truth of God requires the capacity to hear that truth and to live it.

Theological interpretation takes the historical particularities of the text seriously because it acknowledges that God spoke and still speaks through human agents who wrote and who read these particular texts.

In order for Scripture to speak to and against the church, the text must always be treated empathetically as a "subject" to be heard and not just an "object" to be studied. Empathetic listening calls for close and careful listening, and attention to detail and nuance, and this is why historical, literary, and grammatical study are crucial. In his commentary on the book of Revelation, Robert Mounce notes, "It is difficult to say what anything means until one has decided in a sense what everything means," and in order to know "what everything means," one needs "an informed sensitivity to the thought forms and vocabulary of apocalyptic [that] is the *sine qua non* of satisfactory exegesis."[10] He is not alone in voicing such sentiments.

But it is also typically the case that as soon as one speaks of Revelation as an early Christian apocalypse, one must hasten to enumerate the ways in which Revelation departs from other apocalypses.[11] Even if Revelation were a perfect specimen of an apocalypse, theological interpretation would remain uneasy with the assertion that "thought forms and vocabulary" could be the sine qua non of satisfactory exegesis. Indeed, from study of the book itself, it becomes apparent that its structure, plot, imagery, themes, exhortations, and promises are determined not by the book's genre, but by the convictions held by the author and that he, presumably, assumed his readers would or should also share. That is to say, theological interpretation requires "an informed sensitivity" to the theological convictions latent within the text, convictions that are also part of the historical particularities of that text. These theological convictions have to do with the sovereignty, justice, and mercy of God, supremely manifested in the life, death, and resurrection of Jesus, through which God has begun to achieve and will finally achieve victory over evil.

The mistake that so much "futurist" interpretation has made is that precisely by ignoring the generic features of apocalyptic literature, it has confused the imagery of the book with its substance, thus making the imagery its central message and point. Attention to early Jewish and Christian apocalypses would have helped to provide important sensitivities to reading the book and perhaps fostered closer attention to its subject matter. But at the same time, paying close attention to the subject matter of the text might have served to forestall a fixation with deconstructing the symbolic universe of the text, whether that deconstructionist project were to be undertaken by "futurist" or "historicist" interpreters.

If the function of Scripture is the "renewing of our minds," then the book of Revelation ought to be read and interpreted in ways that serve that end.

To say this is not to impose an alien agenda upon the text, for arguably the book of Revelation, both a highly imaginative and yet simultaneously carefully crafted literary work, has as its aims the reshaping of the mind so that it may see and grasp what cannot be seen and grasped simply by looking at an object. And there is much to be seen in the pages of Revelation: fantastic creatures, including heavenly beings who are "full of eyes in front and behind, each with six wings" and a red dragon with seven heads, ten horns, and seven crowns; a world where things are described in vivid colors including green, purple, blue, and gold, as well as white and black; and where the cities, buildings, and furniture in them are made of precious jewels and metals, including sapphires, amethysts, emeralds, pearls, gold, and bronze. The various scenes in the book are also characterized by virtually constant noise: unceasing singing, including choruses of praise, laments, and dirges; blowing of trumpets; crashes of thunder loud cries; and constant prayers. In short, the Revelation is intended to be *seen* and *heard*.

Not surprisingly, readers are repeatedly invited to "look" or "see" (Rev 1:7; 1:18; 3:8, 5:5; 16:15; 21:3; 21:5; 22:7; 22:12) and to "listen" (2:7, 11, 17, 29; 3:6, 13, 20, 22; 13:9); and John, the prophet who "sees" the vision, repeatedly describes what he saw (e.g., 1:2, 12, 13, 17; 5:1, 2, 6; 6:1, 9; 7:1, 2; 8:2, etc.) and heard (1:10; 4:1; 5:11, 13; 6:1, 3, 5, etc.). The point is not only to see *what* John sees or to hear *what* he heard, but also to see *as* John sees, and to hear *as* John hears. To put it differently, John calls not for sight but for insight, not just for hearing but for understanding. Such insight and understanding are not simply the result of knowledge gained through ordinary human study and experience, but require the words of God (1:8) or of the Son of Man (1:11-19); the assistance of an interpreting angel (1:1; 22:6, 8-9) or of a heavenly creature or elder (5:5; 7:13-14). Indeed, the voice of God, the guidance of the heavenly interpreters, and the use of the Old Testament indicate that John wants his readers not only to see and hear what and as he sees and hears, but to see the world as God sees it, to say no to what God says no to, including economic exploitation, political domination and injustice, religious idolatry, religious persecution, and every kind of immorality.

In one of the more memorable "visions" of the book (Rev 17–18), the Seer "sees" the judgment of "a great whore" seated simultaneously on "many waters," and on a "scarlet beast that was full of blasphemous names . . . [that] had seven heads and ten horns" (17:1-3). On her forehead was the name "Babylon," and she was "drunk with the blood of the saints" (17:6). She is the "mother of whores," with whom "the kings of the earth have committed fornication, and with the wine of whose fornication the inhabitants of the earth have become drunk" (17:2). As various interpreters have argued, the woman is presented as *Dea Roma*, who was depicted seated sedately on the seven hills of Rome.[12] But her identity as "Babylon," the "great whore" comes from the prophetic oracles of the Old Testament. So, for example, in Jeremiah 28:7 LXX (Matt 51:7), Babylon makes the whole world drunk. And the church would know, from its Scriptures and from recent events, that it was Babylon that destroyed the first temple, and a second "Babylon" (Rome) that destroyed the second temple. Furthermore, the pages of Scripture often picture Israel itself as guilty of adultery, as playing the whore, in its abandonment of the sole worship of YHWH and in its practices of idolatry. The image applied in Scripture to Israel is here applied to Rome. By exercising the imagination, one can picture or "see" the woman of Revelation 17 as described by John; and then, by bringing together knowledge of Roman myths, various Old Testament texts, and recent events, one can "see" Rome as a whore guilty of fornication or idolatry, who drinks the blood of the saints of God.

But one does not see Rome as immoral, idolatrous, exploitative, corrupt, and corrupting merely by "looking." To hear the Emperor Augustus tell it, one could look around and see the Roman Empire as a great accomplishment. How could one miss seeing "the sums of money he spent upon the Republic and the Roman People," the "liberty" he brought to the Republic, aqueducts restored and improved, buildings erected, the sea cleared from pirates, and entertainments offered for people to enjoy?[13] Of course, one might also see masses of people enslaved and killed in war, but these are part of the price to be paid for making Rome supreme over all and enjoying the benefits to be reaped from such victory. To hear Jose-phus tell it, God was on the side of the Romans, "for it is impossible that so vast an empire should be established without God's providence" (*J.W.* 2.390). Thus Josephus warns his countrymen that they are fighting "not only against the Romans, but against God himself" (5.378).

But to hear John the Seer tell it, Rome is not a great accomplishment, but a great whore. And, according to John, to see Rome this way is to see it as God does. For God sees Rome very differently, and thus when "God remembered great Babylon" (Rev 16:19), and her iniquities (18:5), the result was the fall of "Babylon the great" (18:2). Often in the Bible the assertion that "God remembered" someone or something portends God's imminent salvation and mercy: God remembered Noah (Gen 8:1); Rachel (Gen 30:22); his covenant with Abraham, Isaac, and Jacob (Exod 2:24); or his steadfast love for Israel (Ps 98:3). But God does not see as human beings see, so that when God "remembers" Babylon, God "sees" an economically exploitative and dangerously seductive empire (Rev 18:3, 7, 9, 11-17, 23-24).

The question that Revelation poses to its readers is whether they will see the world from the vantage point of John or of Augustus or, to put it more sharply, of God or of Rome. Posed that way, the question is too easy, for few would claim that they want to see things from Rome's perspective and most would claim that they already see with God's. And that claim must be challenged. The exaggerated images of the book—its vivid colors, cacophony of sounds and voices, fantastic symbols, and grim tableaus of death and destruction—are all enlisted to make the point: the world is not as you see it, and in order to see it as God does, all its features must be exaggerated. Rome is not *Dea* (Goddess) sitting on seven hills offering the benefits of the *Pax Romana*, but a whore seated on a seven-headed mon-ster, beguiling and corrupting the inhabitants of the earth.

The imagery of Revelation presents Rome in extraordinary terms, and as extraordinarily and obviously wicked, but in many ways Rome itself is simply an ordinary empire and, like all empires, needs wealth, power, territory, inhabitants, and allies to support itself.[14] Revelation functions most like a political cartoon that makes readers see what they might not have seen before; namely, that Rome and Roman power are not benign. Its persecution of the saints of God will make that obvious. Those who are blind need to see (Rev 3:17); and the blind church needs to see the great whore as the antithesis to the woman clothed with the sun (12:1-6); the city of Babylon as the antithesis of the heavenly Jerusalem, the city of

God (21). The church must be taught to see, and the book of Revelation is part of the curriculum.

Scripture serves to orient its readers to worship and serve God alone, and theological interpretation of Scripture will impel its readers toward those same ends.

If Revelation were a sermon, then the biblical text it expounds would not be a prophetic prediction, but the first commandment: "You shall have no other gods before me." Or, in the words of the angel of God with the "eternal gospel to proclaim to those who live on the earth": "Fear God and give him glory, for the hour of his judgment has come; and worship him who made heaven and earth, the sea and the springs of water" (Rev. 14:7). Revelation depicts worship in numerous scenes (4–5; 7:9-12; 8:3-4; 11:15-19; 14:2-5; 15:2-4; 16:5-7; 19:1-8; 22:1-5) and calls its readers to worship (19:10; 22:9). The temple dominates as an image for the saints (3:12; 11:1-3) and as a symbol of God's presence (15:5-8; 16:17), until its absence (22:22) in the New Jerusalem signifies the final and full fellowship of God with the people of God. And the faithful saints are "priests" to their God (1:6; 5:10; 20:6), and because they are priests, they are holy ("saints"), and everything that they wear (3:4; 7:14; 15:6; 19:8, 13-14; 22:14), practice (9:21; 21:8, 27; 22:15), and inhabit (18:4-5; 21:21; 22:3, 13-15) must also be holy.

It is in this context that we may interpret the two brief passages about the 144,000 (7:4-8; 14:1-3). The 144,000 are characterized, first, as belonging to those who have "washed their robes and made them white in the blood of the Lamb" (7:14) and, second, as maintaining the highest standards of ritual purity (14:4). Because sexual intercourse was ritually defiling it needed to be followed by ritual purification. But the 144,000 have "never defiled themselves," that is, they have never been subject to such ritual impurity at all. Even as the features of the woman in chapters 17–18 are exaggerated in order to portray her immorality and uncleanness, so the first fruits of the holy people of God have exceeded the standards of purity, and have apparently done so because they have washed their robes in the blood of the Lamb. Commentators debate whether they are portrayed as warriors preparing for holy war, or as priests preparing themselves for temple service. But the distinction may be moot, since it is precisely as priests who offer pure worship to a holy God, rather than polluted worship to the demonic beast, that they engage in "holy war." This is a "war" not for territory, but for the allegiance of the inhabitants of the earth.[15]

There are also numerous hymns or parts of hymns within Revelation that proclaim that God's sovereign purposes for the world will be accomplished (4:8-11; 5:9-14; 7:9-12; 11:15-18; 12:10-12; 15:3-4; 16:5-7; 19:1-8). At this point, the twin scenes of worship in chapters 4 and 5 are surely the most important, not only in terms of their position in the structure of the book, but in terms of characterizing the one who is worshiped. In a nutshell, these chapters together portray worship of the thrice-holy Creator God, on whom all things in heaven and on earth depend (4:11), and of the Lamb who was slaughtered, and who thus "ransomed for God saints from every tribe and language and people and nation" (5:9).

If these two chapters could be extracted from the rest of the book and read on their own, a major contemporary objection to the Revelation might well fall by the way; namely, that both God and the Lamb, who are here worshiped by the heavenly hosts, are sometimes portrayed in Revelation as acting remarkably like the beast who destroys and devours. In the end, God simply overpowers the beast, but all the trappings of empire, including the use of brutal force against one's enemies to secure one's position and enforce worship, remain in place. When God's wrath is poured out on the earth, there is unspeakable bloodshed (14:20), while the Lamb apparently watches the torments of the wicked (14:10).

But the imagery of the text should not be taken "literally" here anymore than it is elsewhere in Revelation. Even as Rome is caricatured as a corrupt and corrupting prostitute, so the victory of God is also portrayed in overblown martial rhetoric throughout the book. As Ian Boxall puts it:

> In the Apocalypse's cyclic pattern, the battle against the forces of evil and chaos is viewed from every conceivable angle, and exploited for every conceivable effect. But it is not a new battle: it is essentially the battle fought and won on the cross, replayed with shocking mythological vividness.[16]

Revelation thus depicts in vivid and concrete detail what can be, and is, said in other ways in Scripture. The book's imagery of "holy war," outdoing any such descriptions in the Old Testament, can be construed as an intensely graphic way of depicting "spiritual warfare" (Eph 6:10-18; 1 Thess 5:8-9; Isa 59:17-18). The letters to the seven churches urge love, faith, service, patient endurance, repentance, and hatred of evil in order to "conquer" and receive the victor's reward of a crown, authority, and rule over the nations, a share of the heavenly throne, and a place in the heavenly city. But while the virtues and practices urged there are scarcely the weapons of ordinary military conflict, they are the means by which the churches combat the threats to the exercise of their vocation.

Although the struggle which John describes is real, it is not military; it has to do with faith and obedience. Not surprisingly, Revelation is replete with exhortations to faithfulness, obedience, and endurance, as exemplified in the following admonition: "Here is a call for the endurance of the saints, those who keep the commandments of God and hold fast to the faith of Jesus" (e.g., Rev 1:9; 2:2-3, 13, 19; 3:10; 13:10; 14:12).

Revelation could also be read as a graphic apocalyptic version of the exhortations of Romans 12. Called to true worship of God, the saints of Revelation discover that they may be called to present their bodies—their lives—as bloody sacrifices. They are not to be conformed to this world, but are to hate what is evil (Rom 12:9), be patient in suffering while persevering in prayer (Rom 12:12), blessing those who persecute them, without repaying evil for evil (Rom 12:17), and finally, leaving all vengeance to God (Rom 12:19; Deut 32:35; Isa 59:17-18). Indeed, in the book of Revelation, Rome drinks the blood of the saints of God, and the saints cry out for God to act. They themselves actually wage no warfare, leaving God to avenge their deaths (Rev 6:10). But this means that some will suffer and die (6:11), even as the Lamb himself has suffered and died at the whim of the Empire. Mysteriously, even as God's victory is won through the death of the Lamb, so the saints participate in that victory through their deaths as well, as they fill up the sufferings of the Messiah (Col 1:24).

Theological interpretation of Scripture reads Scriptural texts within the context of the canon.

To read Revelation canonically includes reading it in light of the Old Testament, to which it so frequently alludes, with respect to other books in the New Testament, and as the final book of the entire canon. But while Revelation draws extensively on biblical imagery, it never quotes the Old Testament. Especially missing is anything akin to Matthew's "formula quotations," or Paul's extensive and complex exegetical rereadings of Old Testament texts. Moreover, the primary way in which Revelation appropriates the Old Testament is by a creative reworking of its imagery of judgment and salvation, so that the continuity and consummation of God's purposes are disclosed.

So, for example, the openings words of the book of the "revelation of Jesus Christ" speak of what "must soon take place" (ἃ δεῖ γενέσθαι ἐν τάχει) even as Daniel disclosed to the King of Babylon "what must happen at the end of days" (Dan 2:28; ἃ δεῖ γενέσθαι ἐπ᾽ ἐσχάτων τῶν ἡμερῶν). Traces of Psalm 2 appear in the Seer's visions: the nations rage, but God's wrath will come upon them (Rev 11:19); the male child born from the woman "clothed with the sun" will rule the nations with a rod of iron (12:5);

and the Lamb, the Lion of the tribe of Judah, will stand on Mount Zion (14:1). As G. B. Caird notes, John engages in an exposition of Psalm 2 as Christian Scripture, by reading the text through the Christological lens, because the warrior king expected in the Psalm is Jesus, the Lamb who was slain.[17]

Or, again, the 144,000 who have on their foreheads the twin names of the Lamb and his Father (Rev 7:2-3; 14:1) calls to mind a similar scene in Ezekiel 9. There the inhabitants of Jerusalem who "groan over all the abominations that are committed in it" are marked on their foreheads so that they will be protected. Here, too, Ezekiel 9 is reread christologically; the faithful who are protected from God's wrath are those who, like their counterparts, abhorred the abominations done in the city—whether Jerusalem or Rome—but now are also followers of the Lamb. The great beast with seven heads and ten horns (Rev 13:1), who mirrors the satanic seven-headed and ten-horned dragon (12:3-9), is itself a composite of four beasts—lion, leopard, bear, and a ten-horned beast—of the vision of Daniel 7:1-7. As a composite, this great beast is both Rome[18] and every empire: all will fail, and all will ultimately be put under the dominion of the Lord's Messiah, who will reign "forever and ever" (Rev 11:15). All these biblical texts, and so many more, are appropriated not for their predictions of the coming of the Messiah, but as testifying that God's purposes, prefigured in the Scriptures, are brought to fruition in the unexpected appearance of the Lion of Judah as the Lamb who was slain but who does and will reign forever and ever.

Further, theological interpretation will locate Revelation within the context of the New Testament's witness to the crucified and risen Jesus as fulfilling God's purposes for his people and for the world. In this regard, it is striking that the one certainly identifiable historical event in the book is the crucifixion of Jesus under the auspices of the Roman Empire. In this particular concrete historical event, one finds the revelation of the character of the one who is worshiped; the purposes of history; the vocation of the church; and the plot of the book of Revelation. As argued earlier, Revelation can often be read as the "apocalyptic illustration" of material contained elsewhere in the New Testament. The visions of Revelation 4 and 5 reveal that the world is not under the control of human or demonic powers, but that it is ruled by God. If the delay in justice allows the saints to suffer, the conclusion is not that there has been a lapse in God's purposes, any more than the death of Jesus indicated such a lapse. Jesus' death within the providential purposes of God becomes the polestar of reading the events of history. Nor is the ultimate question of Revelation, who reigns supreme? Indeed, there is no real contest in

Revelation between God and the unholy triad of the whore, the beast, and the dragon. God is not contending for the heavenly throne; God now rules from it.[19] What is at issue, however, is how God's sovereignty manifests itself, and whether God's purposes for the world are manifested and accomplished through the life, death, and resurrection of Jesus and his followers, or whether they are accomplished through the power and might of Rome and Rome's adherents.

Finally, then, reading Revelation canonically and theologically entails a recognition of its position as the last book of the Christian canon. Obviously this is due to its subject matter: it speaks of the obliteration of the old world of injustice and evil, and the coming of the "new heaven and new earth." It brings the story of God with his people and the world to its grand finale, while at the same time opening up an entirely new creation. The book of Revelation indicates that the biblical story is yet unfinished: it anticipates a great ending, a world in which the leaves of the trees are for the healing of the nations, where God wipes away every tear from every eye, where human beings dwell together in harmony with each other and with their God, worshiping God alone. Insofar as theological interpretation takes its cue from the book of Revelation, it resists closure until such time when God proclaims that "it is done" (21:6).

Abbreviations

AJEC   Arbeiten zur Geschichte des antiken Judentums und des Urchristentums

BETL   Bibliotheca ephemeridum theologicarum lovaniensium

BIBInt   *Biblical Interpretation*

BibS[N]   Biblisch-Theologische Studien

BNTC   Black's New Testament Commentary

BT   *The Bible Translator*

BTHSt   Biblische-Theologische Studien

BZ   *Biblische Zeitschrift*

BZNW   Beihefte zur Zeitschrift für die neutestamentliche Wissenschaft

CBQ   *Catholic Biblical Quarterly*

CTM   Calwer Theologische Monographien

DCLY   Deuterocanonical and Cognate Literature Yearbook

EdF   Erträge der Forschung

EKK   Evangelisch-katholischer Kommentar

FRLANT   Forschungen zur Religion und Literatur des Alten und Neuen Testaments

HAR   Hebrew Annual Review

HNTC   Harper's New Testament Commentaries

JBTh   *Jahrbuch für Biblische Theologie*

JSJSup   Journal for the Study of Judaism Supplemental Series

JSNT   *Journal for the Study of the New Testament*

JSNTSup   Journal for the Study of the New Testament: Supplemental Series

JSNTSymS   Journal for the Study of the New Testament: Symposium Series

JSOT   *Journal for the Study of the Old Testament*

KEK	Kritisch-exegetischer Kommentar über das Neue Testament
LNTS	Library of New Testament Studies
Neot	*Neotestamentica*
NICNT	New International Commentary on the New Testament
NIGTC	New International Greek Testament Commentary
NovT	*Novum Testatmentum*
NovTSup	Novum Testamentum Supplements
NTAbh	Neutestamentliche Abhandlungen
NTOA	Novum Testamentum et Orbus et Antiquus
NTS	*New Testament Studies*
OTL	Old Testament Library
RAC	*Realexikon für Antike und Christentum.*
SBB	Stuttgarter biblische Beiträge
SBLSymS	Society of Biblical Literature Symposium Series
SJT	*Scottish Journal of Theology*
SNTSMS	Society for New Testament Studies Monograph Series
TThZ	*Trierer theologische Zeitschrift*
TU	Texte und Untersuchungen
VCSup	*Vigiliae christianae Supplements*
VTSup	Vetus Testamentum Supplements
WBC	Word Biblical Commentary
WUNT	Wissenschaftliche Untersuchungen zum Neuen Testament
ZAW	*Zeitschrift für die alttestamentliche Wissenschaft*
ZKG	*Zeitschrift für Kirchengeschichte*
ZRGG	*Zeitschrift für Religions- und Geistesgeschichte*

Notes

Introduction

1   For an overview of the historical setting of Revelation's composition, see the introduction in David E. Aune, *Revelation 1–5* (WBC 52A; Dallas: Word Books, 1997), xlvii–lxx; also, Ian Boxall, *The Revelation of St. John* (BNTC 19; London: Continuum, 2006), 5–15.

2   This view is epitomized in the oft-cited quip of the famous nineteenth-century evangelist D. L. Moody, "You don't polish the brass on a sinking ship." (This was Moody's opinion regarding Christians' involvement in various social issues—he wanted to focus solely on evangelism, i.e., "saving souls"—and it became a very prominent view among those who followed him, especially in dispensational-premillennialist circles, throughout the twentieth century.)

3   Tim LaHaye and Jerry B. Jenkins, *Left Behind: A Novel of the Earth's Last Days* (Carol Stream, Ill.: Tyndale House, 1995); Hal Lindsey, *The Late Great Planet Earth* (Grand Rapids: Zondervan, 1970).

4   Friedrich Nietzsche, *The Birth of Tragedy and the Genealogy of Morals* (trans. Francis Golffing; Garden City, N.Y.: Doubleday, 1956 [1887]), 185.

5   For an overview of past and current historical readings of Revelation, see Jörg Frey, "The Relevance of the Roman Imperial Cult for the Book of Revelation: Exegetical and Hermeneutical Reflections on the Relation between the Seven Letters and the Visionary Main Part of the Book," in *The New Testament and Early Christian Literature in Greco-Roman Context: Studies in Honor of David E. Aune* (ed. John Fotopoulos; NovTSup 122; Leiden: Brill, 2006), 233–36; see also, Steven J. Friesen, *Imperial Cults and the Apocalypse of John: Reading Revelation in the Ruins* (Oxford: Oxford University Press, 2001); Aune, *Revelation 1–5*, lvi–xc.

6   Friesen, *Imperial Cults*; Frey, "The Relevance of the Roman Imperial Cult."

7   See, e.g., John J. Collins, *The Apocalyptic Imagination: An Introduction to the Jewish Matrix of Christianity* (New York: Crossroads, 1984); Richard A. Horsley, *Revolt of the Scribes: Resistance and Apocalyptic Origins* (Minneapolis: Fortress, 2010); Anathea Portier-Young, *Apocalypse Against Empire: Theologies of Resistance in Early Judaism* (Grand Rapids: Eerdmans, 2011).

8   For helpful overviews of the literature and worldview of the Qumran community, see James C. VanderKam, *The Dead Sea Scrolls Today* (rev. ed.; Grand Rapids: Eerdmans, 2010); George W. Nickelsburg, *Jewish Literature Between the Bible and the Mishnah* (2nd ed.; Minneapolis: Fortress, 2005), 119–90; also, John J. Collins, *Apocalypticism and the Dead Sea Scrolls* (London: Routledge, 1997).

9   Douglas Harink, *Paul among the Postliberals: Pauline Theology beyond Christendom and Modernity* (Grand Rapids: Brazos, 2003); Joseph L. Mangina, *Revelation* (Brazos Theological Commentary on the Bible; Grand Rapids: Brazos, 2010); Walter Lowe, "Why We Need Apocalyptic," *SJT* 63.1 (2010): 41–53. In his contribution to the present volume, N. T. Wright expresses critical skepticism toward the use of "apocalyptic" as a theological category in the work of Käsemann, Beker, and Martyn. Clearly, this is a matter requiring ongoing critical reflection.

10 See, e.g., Richard A. Horsley, *Jesus and Empire: The Kingdom of God and the New World Disorder* (Minneapolis: Fortress, 2003); Neil Elliott, *The Arrogance of Nations: Reading Romans in the Shadow of Empire* (Paul in Critical Contexts; Minneapolis: Fortress, 2008); Warren Carter, *Matthew and Empire: Initial Explorations* (Harrisburg, Pa.: Trinity Press International, 2001); also, see N. T. Wright's essay in the present volume. For a recent study that helpfully poses similar questions about the Acts of the Apostles, see C. Kavin Rowe, *World Upside Down: Reading Acts in the Graeco-Roman Age* (Oxford: Oxford University Press, 2009).

11 The ground-breaking work of scholars such as Brevard Childs and James Sanders on the hermeneutical role of the canon has continued to influence many biblical scholars seeking to recapture the theological and ecclesiological import of biblical interpretation. See, e.g., Craig G. Bartholomew, et al., eds., *Canon and Biblical Interpretation* (Scripture and Hermeneutics Series 7; Grand Rapids: Zondervan, 2006). For a concise statement of some issues pertaining to the hermeneutical significance of the canon, see Stefan Alkier and Richard B. Hays, eds., *Kanon und Intertextualität* (Kleine Schriften des Fachbereichs Evangelische Theologie der Goethe-Universität Frankfurt/ Main, Nr. 1; Frankfurt am Main: Lembeck, 2010).

12 See especially Stefan Alkier and Richard B. Hays, eds., *Die Bibel im Dialog der Schriften: Konzepte intertextueller Bibellektüre* (Tübingen: Francke, 2005), and the literature cited there. This book, with the addition of some supplemental material, is now available in English translation: Richard B. Hays, Stefan Alkier, and Leroy Huizenga, eds., *Reading the Bible Intertextually* (Waco, Tex.: Baylor University Press, 2009).

13 The conference was conceived as a sequel to an earlier conference in 2004 at Johann Wolfgang Goethe Universität, Frankfurt am Main, Germany, on the topic of intertextuality. The essays from that conference were published in the book cited in n. 12 above.

Chapter 1: Gorman

1   Luther once said, "The Epistle to the Galatians is my dear epistle. I have put my confidence in it. It is my Katy von Bora" (referring to his wife Katherine) (*Luther's Works: Table Talk* [vol. 54; ed. Theodore G. Tappet; Philadelphia: Fortress, 1967], 20).

2   G. K. Chesterton, *Orthodoxy* (centennial ed.; Nashville: Sam Torode Book Arts, 2009 [1908]), 13.

3   Martin Luther, "Preface to the Revelation of St. John [II]," in *Luther's Works: Word and Sacrament* (vol. 35; ed. E. Theodore Bachmann; Philadelphia: Fortress, 1960), 400.

4   M. Eugene Boring, *Revelation* (Interpretation: A Bible Commentary for Teaching and Preaching; Louisville, Ky.: John Knox, 1989), 4.

5   Luke Timothy Johnson, *The Writings of the New Testament* (3rd ed.; Minneapolis: Fortress, 2010), 507.

6   Loren L. Johns, *The Lamb Christology of the Apocalypse of John: An Investigation into Its Origins and Rhetorical Force* (WUNT 2.167; Tübingen: Mohr Siebeck, 2003), 187.

7   Judith L. Kovacs, "The Revelation to John: Lessons from the History of the Book's Reception," *Word and World* 25.3 (2005): 255, 257.

8   Bernard McGinn, *Antichrist: Two Thousand Years of the Human Fascination with Evil* (San Francisco: HarperSanFrancisco, 1994).

9   Ulrich Luz, "The Contribution of Reception History to a Theology of the New Testament," in *The Nature of New Testament Theology: Essays in Honour of Robert Morgan* (ed. Christopher Rowland and Christopher Tuckett; Oxford: Blackwell, 2006), 123.

10 In this paper, for my own account of things, I will use "reception history" when stressing the audience and "impact history" when stressing the text, with an occasional combination of the two ("reception/impact history).This is not to say that these terms are universally understood in this manner.

11 Luz, "Contribution," 123–34. Luz insists (124) that *Wirkungsgeschichte*, which he translates as "effective history" or "history of effects," is not the same as reception history. He seems to think that "reception history" is the more objective, distanced study of the history of interpretation, while "effective history," or a consciousness of effective history, implies a more participatory (and thus, for Christians, more theological) engagement with the reception history in which interpreters recognize that their own identity is caught up in the reception of the text over time. (In my specific references to Luz's work, I will use the term "reception history" because he does.) Markus Bockmuehl (*Seeing the Word: Refocusing New Testament Study* [Studies in Theological Interpretation; Grand Rapids: Baker Academic, 2006]), who refers to

both *Wirkungsgeschichte* and "effective history," concurs nonetheless with my main point when he asks rhetorically, "[A]re not the 'effects' of the text much bigger than its conscious 'reception' . . . ?" (166), and when he claims, "Rightly understood as the history of the text's effects, *Wirkungsgeschichte* speaks of how Scripture has interpreted *us*, the readers" (164–65; emphasis in original).

12   See also 1 Cor 10:11 and especially other texts from New Testament writers besides Paul, though the same principle implicitly operates in all biblical writers who re-appropriate biblical texts and themes such as creation and exodus.

13   Luz, "Contribution," 124. See also Bockmuehl, *Seeing the Word*.

14   See Joel B. Green, *Seized by Truth: Reading the Bible as Scripture* (Nashville: Abingdon, 2007), 18, 51, 103.

15   Bockmuehl, *Seeing the Word*, 65.

16   Luz, "Contribution," 125.

17   Luz, "Contribution," 125–26.

18   Luz, "Contribution," 126–28.

19   Luz, "Contribution," 126.

20   Luz, "Contribution," 128–29.

21   Luz, "Contribution," 129.

22   Luz, "Contribution," 129–30.

23   Luz, "Contribution," 130.

24   Luz, "Contribution," 130–32.

25   Luz, "Contribution," 132–33.

26   Space does not permit additional consideration of the importance of effective history. Of particular importance on this subject is Bockmuehl's *Seeing the Word*, where he shows not only the theological and hermeneutical significance of *Wirkungsgeschichte*, but also its exegetical potential (esp. in chap. 4).

27   Arthur W. Wainwright, *Mysterious Apocalypse: Interpreting the Book of Revelation* (Nashville: Abingdon, 1993); Judith Kovacs and Christopher Rowland. *Revelation: The Apocalypse of Jesus Christ* (Blackwell Bible Commentaries; Malden, Mass.: Blackwell, 2004).

28   For a rather comprehensive survey, see Rowland's introduction to his commentary on Revelation: Christopher C. Rowland, "The Book of Revelation: Introduction, Commentary, and Reflections," in *The New Interpreter's Bible* (vol. 12; ed. Fred B. Craddock, et al.; Nashville: Abingdon, 1998), 12:501–736, esp. 528–56. For recent briefer overviews, see Kovacs and Rowland, *Revelation*, 14–38; Kovacs, "Lessons"; and Craig R. Koester, "On the Verge of the Millennium: A History of the Interpretation of Revelation," *Word and World* 15.2 (1995): 128–36.

29   Kovacs and Rowland, *Revelation*, 7–11. They also further subdivide these two basic types. The following discussion draws heavily on my *Reading Revelation Responsibly: Uncivil Worship and Witness: Following the Lamb into the New Creation* (Eugene, Ore.: Cascade Books, 2011), chap. 4.

30   Kovacs and Rowland, *Revelation*, 8.

31 In her article on Revelation's reception history, Kovacs refers to "decoding" and "metaphorical" readings as the two types ("Lessons," 256).

32 I have adapted this graphic from several similar graphics presented by Rowland in various lectures and publications, including Kovacs and Rowland, *Revelation*, 8. (Kovacs and Rowland, however, do not use the phrase "text as lens/mirror.") The graphic appears also in my *Reading Revelation Responsibly*, 64.

33 Richard B. Hays, *The Moral Vision of the New Testament: A Contemporary Introduction to New Testament Ethics* (San Francisco: HarperCollins, 1996), 170–73.

34 Hays, *Moral Vision*, 173.

35 Koester, "On the Verge," 128–29. I suspect that Koester omits the "historical" approach noted by Hays because it has not been commonly practiced, at least not in its pure form, outside certain forms of modernist biblical scholarship.

36 Koester, "On the Verge," 129.

37 M. H. Abrams, ed., *The Norton Anthology of English Literature* (3rd ed.; 2 vols.; New York: W. W. Norton, 1974), 2:663n1.

38 Gregory L. Linton, "Reading the Apocalypse as Apocalypse: The Limits of Genre," in *The Reality of Apocalypse: Rhetoric and Politics in the Book of Revelation* (ed. David L. Barr; Atlanta: SBL, 2004), 13.

39 Richard Bauckham, *The Theology of the Book of Revelation* (Cambridge: Cambridge University Press, 1993), 2.

40 Linton, "Reading the Apocalypse as Apocalypse," 18.

41 Linton, "Reading the Apocalypse as Apocalypse," 18–19.

42 Linton, "Reading the Apocalypse as Apocalypse," 18–19.

43 Linton, "Reading the Apocalypse as Apocalypse," 23.

44 Linton, "Reading the Apocalypse as Apocalypse," 22.

45 Linton, "Reading the Apocalypse as Apocalypse," 22. In conversation at the conference, Stefan Alkier commented that humans can receive several generic signals simultaneously. While this is correct, I would contend that we still tend to foreground one or another genre and that we cannot simultaneously receive and process a large quantity of different generic signals.

46 Linton, "Reading the Apocalypse as Apocalypse," 20–21.

47 Linton, "Reading the Apocalypse as Apocalypse," 25.

48 Linton, "Reading the Apocalypse as Apocalypse," 25.

49 Linton, "Reading the Apocalypse as Apocalypse," 28–41.

50 On the inherently participatory nature of biblical interpretation, see Matthew Levering, *Participatory Biblical Exegesis: A Theology of Biblical Interpretation* (Notre Dame, Ind.: University of Notre Dame Press, 2008)

51 Luz, "Contribution," 126.

52 David Rhoads, ed., *From Every People and Nation: The Book of Revelation in Intercultural Perspective* (Minneapolis: Fortress, 2005). See also Luz, "Contribution," 127–28. Bockmuehl (*Seeing the Word*, 36) rightly observes that "[i]n an age of globalization, it seems increasingly imperative for the health of this discipline [New Testament studies] that its investigations take account, however modestly or indeed critically, of where the New Testament in fact resides in the continuous history of its reception."

53 See, e.g., J. Nelson Kraybill, "Apocalypse Now," *Christianity Today*, October 25, 1999, 30–40; David A. deSilva, *Seeing Things John's Way: The Rhetoric of the Book of Revelation* (Louisville, Ky.: Westminster John Knox, 2009), 337–38.

54 In conference conversation, Tobias Nicklas reminded us of some of the misreadings of Revelation during the Nazi era.

55 Ellen T. Charry, "'A Sharp Two-Edged Sword': Pastoral Implications of Apocalyptic," in *Character and Scripture: Moral Formation, Community, and Biblical Interpretation* (ed. William P. Brown; Grand Rapids: Eerdmans, 2002), 344–60.

56 Thus another scriptural motto for interpreters of Revelation may need to be, "Father, forgive them (and us), for they (and we) do not know what they (and we) are doing."

57 Stephen E. Fowl, *Engaging Scripture: A Model for Theological Interpretation* (Malden, Mass.: Blackwell, 1998), 32–61, esp. 56–61; J. Todd Billings, *The Word of God for the People of God: An Entryway to the Theological Interpretation of Scripture* (Grand Rapids: Eerdmans, 2010); Michael J. Gorman, *Elements of Biblical Exegesis: A Basic Guide for Students and Ministers* (rev. and exp. ed.; Peabody, Mass.: Hendrickson, 2009), 135.

58 A ruled reading is one that is guided by the core beliefs and practices of the reading community.

59 Billings, *The Word of God*, 124.

60 See Heikki Räisänen, "Revelation, Violence, and War: Glimpses of a Dark Side," in *The Way the World Ends? The Apocalypse of John in Culture and Ideology* (ed. William John Lyons and Jorunn Økland; Sheffield: Sheffield Phoenix, 2009), 151–65. Räisänen appreciates the work of Kovacs and Rowland in the Blackwell commentary but rightly notes that they over-emphasize the positive, inspiring interpretations and under-emphasize the "dark side."

61 Edith M. Humphrey, "Firing the Imagination: Visions with Embedded Propositions," in *And I Turned to See the Voice: The Rhetoric of Vision in the New Testament* (Grand Rapids: Baker Academic, 2007), 151–94.

62 Robert M. Royalty, Jr. makes this point forcefully—perhaps too forcefully—in "The Dangers of the Apocalypse," *Word and World* 25.3 (2005): 283–93.

63 Kovacs and Rowland (*Revelation*, 249) rule out interpretations leading to "revolutionary violence, naïve complacency or self-congratulatory celebration . . . [or] 'baptiz[ing]' the status quo."

64 Kovacs and Rowland, *Revelation*, 248.

65 So also Kovacs and Rowland, *Revelation*, 248–49.

66 *Reading Revelation Responsibly*, chap. 6. I would argue that this is the case for at least two reasons: (1) the rhetorical role of Revelation 4–5 in the book as a whole, and (2) the prominence of the Lamb image throughout the book, including the symbolic significance of its being used 28 times (7 × 4, signifying universal perfection and rule) to identify Jesus. For an incisive summary of Revelation's Christology, see the essay by Richard Hays in this volume.

67 Rowland, "The Book of Revelation," 544. See also Kovacs and Rowland, *Revelation*, 248–49.

68 Richard B. Hays, *The Conversion of the Imagination: Paul as Interpreter of Israel's Scripture* (Grand Rapids: Eerdmans, 2005).

69 Bruce M. Metzger, *Breaking the Code: Understanding the Book of Revelation* (Nashville: Abingdon, 1993), 11. I think that Metzger wrongly says, however, that Revelation is unique in the Bible in this regard. On Revelation and imagination, see also Rowland, "The Book of Revelation," 503–13.

70 Bauckham, *Theology*, 159.

71 Rowland, "The Book of Revelation," 556.

72 Kovacs and Rowland, *Revelation*, 13.

73 Allan A. Boesak, *Comfort and Protest: The Apocalypse from a South African Perspective* (Philadelphia: Westminster, 1987). Also see, e.g., the essays in Rhoads, *From Every People and Nation*.

74 Koester (*Revelation and the End of All Things*, 31–37) suggests that "mainline" Christians know Revelation primarily through music.

75 A. K. M. Adam, "Poaching on Zion: Biblical Theology as Signifying Practice," in *Reading Scripture with the Church: Toward a Hermeneutic for Theological Interpretation* (ed. A. K. M. Adam et al.; Grand Rapids: Baker Academic, 2006), 27.

76 Adam, "Poaching on Zion," 27.

77 This last phrase is borrowed from the title of a course created by my former colleague Corbin Eddy: "Word Beyond Words: The Arts and the Christian Imagination."

78 See especially the work of Jeremy Begbie, beginning with *Voicing Creation's Praise: Towards a Theology of the Arts* (London: T&T Clark, 1991), particularly part III.

79 Udo Schnelle, *Theology of the New Testament* (trans. M. Eugene Boring; Grand Rapids: Baker Academic, 2009), 771.

80 Kovacs, "Lessons," 263.

81 In using the phrase "coherency and contingency," as well as "word-on-target" below, I am indebted to my late teacher, J. Christiaan Beker.

82 Rowland's conclusion to his survey of the history of Revelation's interpretation includes these words: "[T]he differences of the contemporizing approach [i.e., interpretive differences among those who have related Revelation's images to their own contemporary realities] suggest that the impact of the images has as much to do with the complex preferences and interests of the readers as it does with what the text demands" ("The Book of Revelation," 555).

83 Kovacs and Rowland, *Revelation*, 11.

84 In her formal conference response to my paper, Sujin Pak asked whether a hermeneutic of correspondence can be faithful and, if not, on what hermeneutical and theological grounds. It seems to me that generic and historical considerations permit a cautious correspondence mode for the original, literal meaning of the text (e.g., "the beast from the sea likely signified X for the original author and audience") on the assumption that this was in some important sense either the primary intent of the author and/or the expected

understanding of a contemporary model reader/hearer. For later appropriation, which moves beyond the original, literal sense, the earlier mode of
cautious correspondence should rather naturally (and thus faithfully, hermeneutically speaking) give way to cautious analogy (e.g., "X is analogous to the
beast from the sea"). That said, not every analogy-driven interpretation of
Revelation has been theologically excellent, and not every correspondence-
driven interpretation of Revelation has been theologically disastrous. We
should probably speak of greater and lesser degrees of both hermeneutical
and theological appropriateness/faithfulness.

85   Wright calls it a "fourfold reading of scripture." See N. T. Wright, "The
Fourfold Amor Dei and the Word of God," at http://www.ntwrightpage
.com/Wright_Vatican_Amor_Dei.htm. The text was his invited address to
the international Synod of Roman Catholic Bishops in October 2008.

86   *Reading Revelation Responsibly*, xi–xiii.

87   See Koester, "On the Verge," 131–33. Independently, I have attempted to
capture this dynamic in the subtitle and contents of my book on Revelation:
*Reading Revelation Responsibly: Uncivil Worship and Witness: Following the Lamb
into the New Creation.*

88   I am grateful to Richard Hays and Stefan Alkier for the invitation to participate in the conference for which this paper was prepared. I am also grateful
to Richard, Stefan, and all the other conference participants for simulating
conversation and work together; to Sujin Pak for the formal response to my
paper; and to Al McDonald and the McDonald Agape Foundation for funding the conference.

Chapter 2: Moyise

1   George Aichele, "Canon as Intertext: Restraint or Liberation," in *Reading
the Bible Intertextually* (ed. Richard B. Hays, Stefan Alkier, and Leroy A. Huizenga; Waco, Tex.: Baylor University Press, 2009), 146.

2   Julia Kristeva, "Word, Dialogue and Novel," in *The Kristeva Reader* (ed. Toril
Moi; New York: Columbia University Press, 1986), 34, developing the ideas
of Mikhael Bakhtin.

3   Pride of place undoubtedly goes to Richard B. Hays, *Echoes of Scripture in the
Letters of Paul* (New Haven: Yale University Press, 1989).

4   Anthony C. Thiselton, *New Horizons in Hermeneutics: The Theory and Practice
of Transforming Biblical Reading* (London: HarperCollins, 1992), 506 (emphasis in original).

5   For previous explorations of such "models," see Steve Moyise, "Intertextuality and the Study of the Old Testament in the New Testament," in *The Old
Testament in the New Testament: Essays in Honour of J. L. North* (ed. Steve Moyise; JSNTSup 189; Sheffield: Sheffield Academic, 2000), 14–41; "Intertextuality and Biblical Studies: A Review," *Verbum et Ecclesia* 23 (2002): 418–31.

6   Meir Sternberg, "Proteus in Quotation-Land: Mimesis and the Forms of
Reported Discourse," *Poetics Today* 3 (1982): 108.

7   Gregory K. Beale, *The Book of Revelation: A Commentary on the Greek Text*

(NIGTC; Grand Rapids: Eerdmans, 1999), 182; see also 152–70. Key to this interpretation is that the phrase "what must soon take place" (*ha dei genesthai*) occurs three other times in Revelation (1:19; 4:1; 22:16), all at significant transition points in the text.

8   See the application of relevance theory to the book of Revelation in Stephen Pattemore, *The People of God in the Apocalypse: Discourse, Structure and Exegesis* (SNTSMS 128; Cambridge: Cambridge University Press, 2004).

9   George B. Caird, *A Commentary on the Revelation of St John the Divine* (2nd ed.; London: A&C Black, 1984), 74

10   Caird, *Commentary on Revelation*, 75.

11   Caird, *Commentary on Revelation*, 74.

12   Caird, *Commentary on Revelation*, 194.

13   Caird, *Commentary on Revelation*, 194.

14   Caird, *Commentary on Revelation*, 242.

15   Caird, *Commentary on Revelation*, 243.

16   Caird, *Commentary on Revelation*, 244.

17   Caird, *Commentary on Revelation*, 247.

18   Thomas M. Greene, *The Light in Troy: Imitation and Discovery in Renaissance Poetry* (New Haven: Yale University Press, 1982), 40.

19   The reality is more complex, with some texts being used more than once. See Beate Kowalski, *Die Rezeption des Propheten Ezechiel in der Offenbarung des Johannes* (SBB 52; Stuttgart: Katholisches Bibelwek, 2004), who discusses John's use of Ezekiel in seven sections: (1) Ezek 1:1-3, 15, 16-21; 33:1-9 in Rev 1:9-20; 4:1-5, 14; 10:1-11; (2) Ezek 9:1-11 in Rev 7:1-8; (3) Ezek 40:3–42:20; 43:13-17 in Rev 11:1-14; (4) Ezek 26:1–28:19 in Rev 17:1-18; 18:9-24; (5) Ezek 37:1-14 in Rev 11:3-14; 20:4-6; (6) Ezek 38–39 in Rev 16:13-16; 19:11-21; 20:7-10; (7) Ezek 40–48 in Rev 21:1–22:5. See also Thomas Hieke, "Der Seher Johannes als neuer Ezechiel. Die Offenbarung des Johannes vom Ezechielbuch her gelesen," in *Das Ezechielbuch in der Johannesoffenbarung* (ed. Dieter Sänger et al.; BTHSt 76; Neukirchen-Vluyn: Neukirchener, 2004), 1–30.

20   There is in fact some doubt about the plural reading. The majority of manuscripts have the singular and the plural could be seen as an attempt to conform to the preceding "they" (*autoi*). On the other hand, it is supported by Sinaiticus and Alexandrinus, and it is possible that later scribes conformed it to Ezekiel 37:27 (or Jer 31:33; Zech 8:8).

21   Jeffrey M. Vogelgesang, "The Interpretation of Ezekiel in the Book of Revelation" (Ph.D. diss., Harvard University, 1985), 77.

22   For a discussion of the language of John's allusions, see Steve Moyise, "The Language of the Old Testament in the Apocalypse," *JSNT* 76 (2000): 97–113.

23   Alison M. Jack, *Texts Reading Texts, Sacred and Secular: Two Postmodern Perspectives* (JSNTSup 179; Sheffield: Sheffield Academic, 1999), 76, citing Jacob Neusner, *What Is Midrash?* (Philadelphia: Fortress, 1987), 103.

24   Jack, *Texts Reading Texts*, 124.

25   Robert M. Royalty, "Don't Touch This Book!: Revelation 22:18-19 and the Rhetoric of Reading (in) the Apocalypse of John," *BibInt* 12 (2004): 298–99.

26 Royalty, "Don't Touch This Book," 294.

27 Beale, *Book of Revelation*, 770.

28 Beale, *Book of Revelation*, 963.

29 Gregory K. Beale, *John's Use of the Old Testament in Revelation* (JSNTSup 166; Sheffield: Sheffield Academic, 1998), 46.

30 Frederick J. Murphy, *Fallen Is Babylon: The Revelation to John* (Harrisburg, Pa.: Trinity Press International, 1998), 193.

31 Murphy, *Fallen Is Babylon*, 193.

32 Richard Bauckham, *The Climax of Prophecy: Studies on the Book of Revelation* (Edinburgh: T&T Clark, 1993), 233.

33 Bauckham, *Climax of Prophecy*, 230.

34 David E. Aune, *Revelation 6–16* (WBC 52B; Nashville: Thomas Nelson, 1998), 874.

35 God's mighty act of judgment results in deliverance (Exod 15:1-10, 12), it demonstrates his incomparable superiority to the pagan gods (15:11), it fills the pagan nations with fear (15:14-16), brings his people into his temple (15:13, 17) and ends with the refrain: "The Lord shall reign forever and ever" (15:18).

36 The origins of a "tree of life" are obscure. In the *Epic of Gilgamesh*, we hear of a "plant held in secret by the gods that grants life to the one who grasps hold of its fruit," but this is referring to rejuvenation rather than immortality. Trees with magical powers are sometimes mentioned in Akkadian literature and appear on monuments, stelae, and cylinder seals. And in a Mari wall-painting from the eighteenth century B.C.E., four streams with fish are depicted as emerging from a tree or plant held by two goddesses. See G. Luttikhuizen, ed., *Paradise Interpreted: Interpretations of Biblical Paradise in Judaism and Christianity* (Leiden: Brill, 1999).

37 Claus Westermann, *Genesis 1–11: A Commentary* (London: SPCK, 1984), 271–78. He also challenges the translation "eternal life," which suggests the Greek idea of immortality as a different mode of existence. The text simply means "living on."

38 Gerhard Von Rad, *Genesis: A Commentary* (OTL; London: SCM, 1972), 97. More positive still are the comments of Bruce C. Birch, et al. in *A Theological Introduction to the Old Testament* (Nashville: Abingdon, 1999), 97: "The humans leave the garden with integrity, and are not described in degrading terms; they are still charged with caring for the earth."

39 This is the most straightforward punctuation and followed by most modern translations. The alternative is to take the clause "through the middle of the street of the city" as the start of the next sentence (so KJV).

40 Beale, *Book of Revelation*, 1106.

41 There is debate as to whether this fall from heaven is offered as an explanation for the presence of the serpent in paradise or for the current persecution of Christians. In the former, the dragon/serpent is cast out of heaven prior to creation (*1 En.* 1-6; *2 En.* 29; *Life of Adam and Eve* 13) and this is alluded to in texts such as Ps 74:14 and Isa 27:1. For the latter, the close

connection with the child being snatched up to heaven suggests the "fall" is a result of Christ's victory and thus offers no explanation for the origin of the dragon/serpent, only its ultimate defeat.

42   George Aichele, "Canon as Intertext," 146.

43   Paul B. Decock, "The Scriptures in the Book of Revelation," *Neot* 33 (1999): 403-4.

44   Aichele, "Canon as Intertext," 148.

45   David L. Barr, "The Lamb Looks Like a Dragon," in *The Reality of Apocalypse: Rhetoric and Politics in the Book of Revelation* (ed. David L. Barr; Atlanta: SBL, 2006), 220. He says, "John's divine warrior is not some evil twin of the savior Jesus who conquered by his own death. He is the same person, and the battle has already been won. We have all the paraphernalia of Holy War, but no war" (215).

46   Murphy, *Fallen Is Babylon*, 193 (emphasis added).

47   Thus, although the Sermon on the Mount (Matthew 5–7) speaks of judgment, such verses only constitute about eleven percent of the discourse. The figure rises to twenty-five percent in Matthew 23–25 but this still means that seventy-five percent is *not* about judgment.

48   Aichele, "Canon as Intertext," 143.

49   Jacques Derrida, *Dessemination* (Chicago: Chicago University Press, 1981), 63.

Chapter 3: Hieke

1   See, e.g., Yarbro Collins, "Influence," 112; Beale, *John's Use*, 61.

2   As Gregory K. Beale, *The Use of Daniel in Jewish Apocalyptic Literature and in the Revelation of St. John* (Lanham, Md.: University Press of America, 1984), 306, correctly points out, it is very difficult to achieve a probable judgment whether or not "intention" is present. Often one is not able to determine whether an apocalyptic author is consciously alluding to an Old Testament text, is making an unconscious reference via his "learned past," is merely using stock apocalyptic phraseology, or is referring to an actual experience that has parallels with an Old Testament text.

3   See Konrad Huber, *Einer gleich einem Menschensohn: Die Christusvisionen in Offb 1,9–20 und Offb 14,14–20 und die Christologie der Johannesoffenbarung* (NTAbh 51; Münster: Aschendorff, 2007), 126. For the context of Daniel 7, see John E. Goldingay, *Daniel* (WBC; Dallas: Word Books, 1989), 158–59.

4   See John J. Collins, *Daniel: A Commentary on the Book of Daniel* (Hermeneia; Minneapolis: Augsburg Fortress, 1993), 277, 323; Paul R. Raabe, "Daniel 7: Its Structure and Role in the Book," *HAR* 9 (1986): 272-73.

5   See, e.g., Norman W. Porteous, *Das Buch Daniel* (Das Alte Testament Deutsch 23; Göttingen: Vandenhoeck & Ruprecht, 1985), 95.

6   "Pious Jews," according to Maurice Casey in "The Corporate Interpretation of 'One Like a Son of Man' (Dan. VII 13) at the Time of Jesus," *NovT* 18.3 (1976): 167; see also Casey, *The Solution to the 'Son of Man' Problem* (LNTS 343; London: T&T Clark, 2007), 85-87.

7   Alexander A. Di Lella, "The One in Human Likeness and the Holy Ones of the Most High in Daniel 7," *CBQ* 39 (1977): 19 (emphasis in original).

8   Casey, *Solution*, 85; see also Alfons Deissler, "Der 'Menschensohn' und 'das Volk der Heiligen des Höchsten' in Dan 7," in *Jesus und der Menschensohn: Festschrift für Anton Vögtle*, (ed. Rudolf Pesch and Rudolf Schackenburg; Freiburg: Herder, 1975), 91; Porteous, *Daniel*, 92; G. R. Beasley-Murray, "The Interpretation of Daniel 7," *CBQ* 45 (1983): 55; Othmar Keel, "Die Tiere und der Mensch in Daniel 7," in *Europa, Tausendjähriges Reich und Neue Welt: Zwei Jahrtausende Geschichte und Utopie in der Rezeption des Danielbuches* (ed. Mariano Delgado and Klaus Koch; Studien zur christlichen Religions- und Kulturgeschichte 1; Stuttgart: Kohlhammer, 2003), 55; Heinz Giesen, *Die Offenbarung des Johannes* (Regensburg: Pustet, 1997), 336.

9   See Beasley-Murray, "Interpretation," 56; Collins, *Daniel*, 324. Collins also points out that the chapter assimilated a historical situation to a mythic pattern and hence it served as a paradigm for other events down through history. The chapter plays an important role for Jewish and Christian eschatology from *4 Ezra* 12–13 to the Revelation of John and from Early Judaism and Christianity to the Middle Ages.

10   For details see, e.g., Huber, *Menschensohn*, 135–43; Thomas B. Slater, "One Like a Son of Man in First-Century CE Judaism," *NTS* 41.2 (1995): 193–98; Slater, "Homoion huion anthropou in Rev 1.13 and 14.14," *BT* 44 (1993): 349–50; Slater, "More on Revelation 1.13 and 14.14," *BT* 47 (1996): 146–49; John J. Collins, "The Son of Man in First-Century Judaism," *NTS* 38 (1992): 451–64; Adela Yarbro Collins and John J. Collins, *King and Messiah as Son of God: Divine, Human, and Angelic Messianic Figures in Biblical and Related Literature* (Grand Rapids: Eerdmans, 2008), 75–100; Ulrich B. Müller, "Jesus als 'der Menschensohn,'" in *Gottessohn und Menschensohn: Exegetische Studien zu zwei Paradigmen biblischer Intertextualität* (ed. Dieter Sänger; BibS[N] 67; Neukirchen-Vluyn: Neukirchener, 2004), 94–99; Benjamin E. Reynolds, *The Apocalyptic Son of Man in the Gospel of John* (WUNT 2.249; Tübingen: Mohr Siebeck 2008), 41–64.

11   See especially Gabriele Boccaccini, ed., *Enoch and the Messiah Son of Man: Revisiting the Book of Parables* (Grand Rapids: Eerdmans, 2007); James C. VanderKam, "Daniel 7 in the Similitudes of Enoch (1 Enoch 37–71)," in *Biblical Traditions in Transmission: Essays in Honour of Michael A. Knibb* (ed. Charlotte Hempel and Judith M. Lieu; JSJSup 111; Leiden: Brill, 2006), 291–307; Casey, *Solution*, 91–111.

12   For the use of Daniel 7 in *1 En.* 69:26–71:17 see, e.g., Beale, *Use of Daniel*, 108–12.

13   For the use of Daniel 7 in *4 Ezra* 11–13 see, e.g., Beale, *Use of Daniel*, 112–44. Casey, *Solution*, 112, points out that the term "Son of Man" probably was not used in the original text of *4 Ezra* 13.

14   See Collins, "Son of Man," 464–66.

15   See Karl A. Kuhn, "The 'One Like a Son of Man' Becomes the 'Son of God,'" *CBQ* 69.1 (2007): 22–42, for details.

16 Casey, "Corporate Interpretation," 167–80, presents two passages of rabbinical literature in which the original corporate interpretation (the "one like a son of man" as a symbol for the pious Jews of the time of the author) has been preserved (Mid. *Tehillim*/Ps 21:5; Tanchuma Toledot 20). He also points to the commentaries on Daniel by Rashi and Ibn Ezra, who both identify the son of man with Israel. See also Casey's comprehensive treatment of the issue in *Solution*.

17 For the Old Testament background of Revelation see (among others): Beale, *Use of Daniel*; Beale, *John's Use*; Jan Fekkes, *Isaiah and Prophetic Traditions in the Book of Revelation: Visionary Antecedents and Their Development* (JSNTSup 93; Sheffield: Sheffield Academic, 1994); Steve Moyise, *The Old Testament in the Book of Revelation* (JSNTSymS 115; Sheffield: Sheffield Academic, 1995); Steve Moyise, "Language of the Old Testament," 97–113; Steve Moyise, "The Psalms in the Book of Revelation," in *The Psalms in the New Testament* (ed. Steve Moyise and Maarten J. J. Menken; London: T&T Clark, 2004), 231–46; Jon Paulien, "Dreading the Whirlwind: Intertextuality and the Use of the Old Testament in Revelation," *Andrews University Seminary Studies* 39 (2001): 5–22 (which also mentions further scholarly literature); Marko Jauhiainen, *The Use of Zechariah in Revelation* (WUNT 199; Tübingen: Mohr Siebeck, 2005); Kowalski, *Rezeption des Propheten Ezechiel*; Sänger, ed., *Das Ezechielbuch*.

18 See Yarbro Collins, "Influence," 107.

19 See, e.g., Giesen, *Offenbarung*, 254.

20 For the birth myth of Artemis and Apollon as the closest Hellenistic background of Rev 12, see Akira Satake, *Die Offenbarung des Johannes* (KEK 16; Göttingen: Vandenhoeck & Ruprecht, 2008), 279–80. See also Giesen, who points to the Egyptian myth of Hathor/Isis and Horus vs. Seth-Typhon (*Offenbarung*, 295–99).

21 See Satake, *Offenbarung des Johannes*, 283; Giesen, *Offenbarung*, 280.

22 Collins, *Daniel*, 320–21, suggests for Dan 7:24 a list of seven Seleucid kings and then speculates about the remaining three kings. He also states, "The number ten may well be a round, schematic number. Division of history or a period thereof into ten periods is a common device in apocalyptic and oracular literature" (see, e.g., the Apocalypse of Weeks, the *Sib. Or.* 1, 2, and 4; 11QMelch). See also Louis F. Hartman, *The Book of Daniel (Daniel 1–9)* (The Anchor Bible; New York: Doubleday, 1977), 214.

23 See Yarbro Collins, "Influence," 108.

24 See Giesen, *Offenbarung*, 300–304.

25 Rev 13:6 appears as a summary of Dan 8:10-14 with the following elements: an attack on heavenly beings, a rebellion against God, an attack on the temple, and an indication of how long this situation will continue. See Yarbro Collins, "Influence," 108; Beale, *Use of Daniel*, 233–34.

26 Yarbro Collins, "Influence," 109.

27 Yarbro Collins, "Influence," 108. On the legend of Nero *redivivus*, see Giesen, *Offenbarung*, 304–5, 387–89.

28 Beale, *Use of Daniel*, 243.

29 For an overview of scholarly approaches to the Christology of the book of Revelation, see Huber, *Menschensohn*, 16–73.

30 Collins, *Daniel*, 304–5.

31 See Collins, *Daniel*, 305. Another occurrence can be noted in Dan 10:16: The human-likeness of the angelic figure is expressed by the phrase בְּנֵי אָדָם בִּדְמוּת, in the Old Greek ὡς ὁμοίωσις χειρὸς ἀνθρώπου, in proto-Theodotion ὡς ὁμοίωσις υἱοῦ ἀνθρώπου. See also Huber, *Menschensohn*, 124.

32 See e.g., Yarbro Collins, "Influence," 96–102; Müller, "Jesus als 'der Menschensohn,'" 92; Slater, "More," 148. Interestingly, there are three passages in Revelation that are obviously variants of sayings in the Synoptic tradition that refer to the Son of Man: Rev 3:3 and 16:15 are related to Matt 24:43-44 par. Luke 12:39-40; Rev 3:5 is related to Matt 10:32 par. Luke 12:8. Only the Lukan verses contain the phrase "Son of Man." Huber, *Menschensohn*, 125, states that the author of Revelation deliberately refrained from using the phrase "Son of Man" as a title; however, the readers of the text necessarily infer this to be a title for Jesus Christ and tend to identify the visionary figure with Jesus Christ. By avoiding the titular use, Revelation stresses the connection with the Old Testament background, especially Daniel 7.

33 One has to note a text-critical issue here: while the majority of manuscripts read μετὰ τῶν νεφελῶν "with the clouds" (like in the proto-Theodotion version of Dan 7:13), there are a few witnesses (C, 2053 and others) who have the preposition ἐπὶ τῶν νεφελῶν "on the clouds" according to the OG of Dan 7:13.

34 See, e.g., Yarbro Collins, "Influence," 102.

35 For the Canaanite background of the "Rider of the Clouds," see, e.g., Collins, *Daniel*, 286–94. For general remarks about the Canaanite influence, see André Lacocque, "Allusions to Creation in Daniel 7," in *The Book of Daniel: Composition & Reception* (ed. John J. Collins and Peter W. Flint; VTSup; Leiden: Brill 2001), 2:114–31.

36 The use of ὅμοιον instead of ὡς, which is attested to in OG *and* prTH may indicate that the text regards ὅμοιον as a translation of כְּ in the Aramaic text of Dan 7:13. The text uses ὅμοιος similarly to ὡς both in meaning and construction (see Yarbro Collins, "Influence," 104–5).

37 Yarbro Collins, "Influence," 105.

38 To be more exact, in Dan 7:9 (MT) the clothing of the Ancient One is white as snow, and the hair of his head like pure wool; Rev 1:14 mixes the attributes and reads "His head and his hair were white as white wool, white as snow." See Yarbro Collins, "Influence," 102–3. Yarbro Collins also discusses the possibility that the Ancient One is not actually God but a distinguishable manifestation of God as a high angel. Then the text of Revelation 1 identifies the two figures of Daniel 7 as Christ exalted to the status of the principal angel.

39 See, e.g., Giesen, *Offenbarung*, 87–88.

40 The OG reading of Dan 7:13 in papyrus 967, minuscule 88, and the Syro-Hexapla, namely ὡς παλαιὸς ἡμερῶν ("as the Ancient of Days") for ἕως τοῦ παλαιοῦ ἡμερῶν ("to the Ancient of Days") goes obviously back to an error. However, once it was in circulation, it might have been an inspiration for the writer of Rev 1:13-14 to see the two figures of Dan 7:13 as hypostatic manifestations of God in anthropomorphic form as a high angel. From this viewpoint, one can explain the conflation of images from Dan 7:9 and 7:13 (see Yarbro Collins, "Influence," 103; Andreas Vonach, "Der Hochbetagte und sein Umfeld. Von prophetischen Theophanien zu christologischen Epiphanien," in *Im Geist und in der Wahrheit: Studien zum Johannesevangelium und zur Offenbarung des Johannes sowie andere Beiträge: Festschrift für Martin Hasitschka SJ zum 65* (ed. Konrad Huber and Boris Repschinski Geburtstag; NTAbh 52; Münster: Aschendorff Verlag, 2008), 328; Huber, *Menschensohn*, 146, 153).

41 Huber, *Menschensohn*, 146-70.

42 See, e.g., Otfried Hofius, "Der Septuaginta-Text von Daniel 7,13-14: Erwägungen zu seiner Gestalt und seiner Aussage," ZAW 117.1 (2005): 89.

43 Huber, *Menschensohn*, 227-28, for details.

44 Huber, *Menschensohn*, 228. While Dan 7:13 speaks about the "coming" of the one like a human being (ἤρχετο/ἐρχόμενος) with the clouds, its reception in Rev 14:14 has the one like a human being "sit" (καθήμενον) on the cloud. This change underscores the function of this figure: "sitting" is more appropriate for the position of a judge (see Satake, *Offenbarung des Johannes*, 323; Giesen, *Offenbarung*, 337).

45 For the structure of the chapter, see, e.g., Satake, *Offenbarung des Johannes*, 307-8.

46 See Giesen, *Offenbarung*, 337; Huber, *Menschensohn*, 242-43; Reynolds, *Apocalyptic Son of Man*, 83.

47 For details see Huber, *Menschensohn*, 231-35.

48 For details see Huber, *Menschensohn*, 246-66.

49 See Satake, *Offenbarung des Johannes*, 324-25; Huber, *Menschensohn*, 262.

50 The text of Revelation 20:4 is difficult. However, the verse probably discerns two different groups: those who had been beheaded for their testimony to Jesus (the first group) and those who had not worshiped the beast or its image (the second group). Both groups have in common that they proved themselves in their fight against the beast. The translation of the NRSV has been changed here accordingly. On this issue see Tobias Nicklas, "'Die Seelen der Geschlachteten' (Offb 6,9)? Zum Problem leiblicher Auferstehung in der Offenbarung des Johannes," in *The Human Body in Death and Resurrection* (ed. Tobias Nicklas, Friedrich V. Reiterer, and Joseph Verheyden; DCLY 2009; Berlin: de Gruyter, 2009), 343.

51 Those seated on the thrones are the same as those beheaded for their testimony to Jesus; see Christopher Tuckett, "The Son of Man and Daniel 7: Inclusive Aspects of Early Christologies," in *Christian Origins: Worship, Belief and Society* (ed. Kieran J. O'Mahony; JSNTSup 241; Sheffield: Sheffield Academic, 2003), 178.

52   For the "Millennium" as a messianic interregnum, see, e.g., the excursus in
     Satake, *Offenbarung des Johannes*, 389–92. The idea of this interregnum does
     not come from the Hebrew Bible, but originates in early Jewish literature as
     1 Enoch and *4 Ezra*.
53   See Thomas Hieke and Tobias Nicklas, *"Die Worte der Prophetie dieses Buches":
     Offenbarung 22,6-21 als Schlussstein der christlichen Bibel Alten und Neuen Testa-
     ments gelesen* (BibS[N] 62; Neukirchen-Vluyn: Neukirchener, 2003).
54   Pace Giesen, *Offenbarung*, 431.
55   For details see, e.g., Giesen, *Offenbarung*, 439–44.
56   See Satake, *Offenbarung des Johannes*, 390.
57   See Porteous, *Daniel*, 89.
58   The word ἀρνίον for "lamb" occurs mainly in the Revelation of John. The
     metaphorical use of the term within the Greek Bible underscores the notion
     of "innocence" (ὡς ἀρνίον ἄκακον: Jeremiah under persecution, see Jer 11:19;
     οἱ ὅσιοι τοῦ θεοῦ ὡς ἀρνία ἐν ἀκακίᾳ: the devout of God in *Pss. Sol.* 8:23).
     Hence, although the ἀρνίον has horns, which might suggest the translation
     "ram," the traditional rendering with "lamb" is to be preferred in order to
     display the aspects of guiltlessness and purity in the target language.
59   See Satake, *Offenbarung des Johannes*, 207.
60   Dan 7:10 has a climax (1,000/10,000), while Rev 5:11 uses the words in an
     anticlimactic sequence (10,000/1,000).
61   Compare, e.g., Jer 49:36; Ezek 37:9; Zech 2:10, 6:5; see Collins, *Daniel*, 294;
     according to Hartman, *Book of Daniel*, 211, they are a common expression in
     Babylonian literature to designate the whole world.
62   See Ernst Haag, "Zeit und Zeiten und ein Teil einer Zeit (Dan 7, 25)," *TThZ*
     101 (1992): 65–68. Hartman, *Book of Daniel*, 215, thinks that the term
     encrypts "three and a half years," i.e., half a septennium. "Half a septennium
     may be taken simply as a symbolic term for a period of evil, since it is merely
     half the 'perfect' number 'seven.'" Goldingay, *Daniel*, 181, stresses that the
     text does not read "year," but "period"; hence it does not give a chronological
     length of time, but indicates a sudden termination of a time that threatens to
     extend itself longer (a period, a double period, a quadruple period—no, just
     half a period!). See also Jürgen-Christian Lebram, *Das Buch Daniel* (Zürcher
     Bibelkommentare; Zürich: Theologischer Verlag, 1984), 92.
63   The announcement of such a truly human way of ruling implies a call to
     resistance against imperial culture. Hence the book of Revelation can be
     addressed as a "counter-imperial script"; see Greg Carey, "The Book of Rev-
     elation as Counter-Imperial Script," in *In the Shadow of Empire: Reclaiming the
     Bible as a History of Faithful Resistance* (ed. Richard A. Horsley; Louisville, Ky.:
     Westminster John Knox, 2008), 174.

Chapter 4: Hays

1   For a more comprehensive list of christological titles in Revelation, see
     Johns, *Lamb Christology*, 217–21.

2   See, e.g., Loren T. Stuckenbruck, *Angel Veneration and Christology: A Study in Early Judaism and in the Christology of the Apocalypse of John* (WUNT 2.70; Tübingen: Mohr Siebeck, 1995); Thomas B. Slater, *Christ and Community: A Socio-Historical Study of the Christology of Revelation* (JSNTSup 178; Sheffield: Sheffield University Press, 1999).

3   For example, Traugott Holtz, *Die Christologie der Apokalypse des Johannes* (TU 85; Berlin: Akademie-Verlag, 1962); Johns, *Lamb Christology*; Huber, *Menschensohn*.

4   This approach has much in common with Bauckham, *Theology of the Book of Revelation*; and Mangina, *Revelation*.

5   See Stefan Alkier, "Intertextuality and the Semiotics of Biblical Texts," in *Reading the Bible Intertextually* (ed. Richard B. Hays, Stefan Alkier, and Leroy A. Huizenga; Waco, Tex.: Baylor University Press, 2009), 3–21: "I call the external relationships of the text, in dependence upon Umberto Eco, its encyclopedic relationships. The *encyclopedia* is the cultural framework in which the text is situated and from which the gaps of the text are filled" (8).

6   See also Ps 62:12b.

7   Cf. Bauckham, *Theology of the Book of Revelation*, 63: in Revelation, "Since Christ shares the one eternal being of God, what Christ is said to do, in salvation and judgment, is no less truly and directly divine than what is said to be done by 'the One who sits on the throne.'"

8   On the complexities of the Son of Man motif in Revelation, see Huber, *Menschensohn*.

9   See N. T. Wright, *The New Testament and the People of God* (Christian Origins and the Question of God 1; Minneapolis: Fortress, 1992), 291–97. For further discussion of the various interpretations of the Son of Man's identity in Daniel 7, see Collins, *Daniel*, 304–10.

10 Interestingly, the OG text of Daniel 7:13 reads, ἐπὶ τῶν νεφελῶν τοῦ οὐρανοῦ ὡς υἱὸς ἀνθρώπου ἤρχετο καὶ ὡς παλαιὸς ἡμερῶν παρῆν, as compared to Theodotion's μετὰ τῶν νεφελῶν τοῦ οὐρανοῦ ὡς υἱὸς ἀνθρώπου ἐρχόμενος ἦν καὶ ἕως τοῦ παλαιοῦ τῶν ἡμερῶν ἔφθασεν. One wonders if such a reading influenced the Seer's conflation of the figures in Rev 1:12-16.

11 On this passage, see Huber, *Menschensohn*, 218–69; Stuckenbruck, *Angel Veneration*, 240–45.

12 Stuckenbruck, *Angel Veneration*, 241.

13 The passive verb ἐβλήθησαν in Rev 20:14 almost surely signifies divine action.

14 C. Kavin Rowe, *Early Narrative Christology: The Lord in the Gospel of Luke* (BZNW 139; Berlin: de Gruyter, 2006), 201.

15 See Bauckham, *Theology of the Book of Revelation*, 25–28, and *God Crucified: Monotheism and Christology in the New Testament* (Grand Rapids: Eerdmans, 1998), 53–54. Interestingly, while the divine title appears in the Apocalypse as ὁ πρῶτος καὶ ὁ ἔσχατος, this Greek rendering does not precisely follow the LXX, where we find ἐγὼ πρῶτος καὶ ἐγὼ μετὰ ταῦτα (Isa 44:6) and ἐγώ εἰμι πρῶτος καὶ ἐγώ εἰμι εἰς τὸν αἰῶνα (Isa 48:12). There can be no doubt that the

Apocalypse is echoing the divine self-disclosure as respresented in Isaiah; therefore, it would appear that in Revelation, we are encountering either a tradition of Greek translation independent of the LXX or a direct translation from Hebrew by the author himself.

16   In this context, it is interesting to note that when Christ appears in eschato-logical triumph as the Rider on a White Horse (Rev 19:11-16), his name is said to be a mystery: "he has a name inscribed that no one knows but himself" (19:12). In our conference at Duke, Tobias Nicklas suggested to me that the Rider's name must remain unknown because it is the ineffable divine name (cf. Exod 3:13-15). I am grateful for this interesting suggestion, which supports my line of argument in this essay.

17   For an illuminating theological analysis of the christological implications of these chapters, see C. Kavin Rowe, "For Future Generations: Worshipping Jesus and the Integration of the Theological Disciplines," *Pro Ecclesia* 17.2 (2008): 186-209, esp. 190-96. The following sketch of the passage recapitu-lates and builds upon Rowe's reading.

18   Stuckenbruck, *Angel Veneration*, 75-103, 245-61.

19   Rightly Bauckham, *Theology of the Book of Revelation*, 58-63: "the worship of Jesus must be understood as indicating the inclusion of Jesus in the being of the one God defined by monotheistic worship" (60).

20   I am not necessarily suggesting that the author of the Apocalypse is con-sciously making this point. Rather, his odd grammatical construction attests, perhaps unreflectively, to a fundamental theological intuition that the church centuries later would seek to articulate in a more systematic fash-ion. Again, Bauckham observes the grammatical issue here: John is "even prepared to defy grammar for the sake of theology" (*Theology of the Book of Revelation*, 60).

21   For discussion of this problem see Sigve K. Tonstad, *Saving God's Reputation: The Theological Function of* Pistis Iesou *in the Cosmic Narratives of Revelation* (LNTS 337; London: Continuum, 2006), 170-71, 179-82.

22   We see the same pattern in the fate of the "two witnesses" in Rev 11:3-10, who give testimony (μαρτυρία) and are therefore attacked and killed by "the beast that comes up from the bottomless pit." Although there is no specific reference here to "the testimony of Jesus," readers are surely to understand that these witnesses are carrying the same gospel message for which other witnesses in the text are said to undergo martyrdom. See also 19:10, where the angelic messenger describes himself to John as "a fellow slave with you and your brothers who hold the testimony of Jesus." Here, though presum-ably the angel is not subject to persecution by the Empire, he is declaring solidarity with those witnesses who do hold fast to the message and suffer as a result of their testimony.

23   There is an important and interesting parallel here to the account found in the Pastoral Epistles of Jesus' faithful confession before earthly power: "In the presence of God, who gives life to all things, and of Christ Jesus, who in his testimony before Pontius Pilate made the good confession (Χριστοῦ Ἰησοῦ

τοῦ μαρτυρήσαντος ἐπὶ Ποντίου Πιλάτου τὴν καλὴν ὁμολογίαν), I charge you to keep the commandment without spot or blame until the manifestation of our Lord Jesus Christ, which he will bring about at the right time—he who is the blessed and only Sovereign, the King of kings and Lord of lords" (1 Tim 6:13-15). The concluding christological title in 1 Tim 6:15 closely parallels the acclamations of Jesus in Rev 17:14 and 19:16. Thus, 1 Timothy concurs with Revelation in paradoxically describing Jesus as faithful martyr/witness who suffers at the hands of earthly powers and simultaneously as the One who rules over all such powers.

24 For that reason, the NRSV's "inclusive" translation of Rev 21:7 results in an unfortunate reduction of the christological symbolism of the text: "*Those who conquer will inherit these things, and I will be their God and they will be my children.*" But in fact the substantive participle and following pronouns in the Greek text are all singular: ὁ νικῶν κληρονομήσει ταῦτα καὶ ἔσομαι αὐτῷ θεὸς καὶ αὐτὸς ἔσται μοι υἱός (*"The One who conquers will inherit these things, and I will be God to him, and he will be a Son to me"*). I would propose that reading Rev 21:7 alongside Rev 3:21 suggests a complex but deliberate ambiguity: the primary referent of ὁ νικῶν in 21:7 is Jesus himself, God's Son, who shares the promised inheritance with those who follow his pattern of conquering through faithful endurance of death—and so ὁ νικῶν can be referred secondarily to those who follow his way and thereby show themselves to be God's sons/children (as in the NRSV).

25 For an incisive analysis of πίστις Ἰησοῦ in Revelation, see Tonstad, *Saving God's Reputation*, 157-94. On the Pauline material, see Richard B. Hays, *The Faith of Jesus Christ: The Narrative Substructure of Galatians 3:1–4:11* (2nd ed.; Grand Rapids: Eerdmans, 2002), and the literature cited there.

26 "Thus the only weapon the Rider needs, if he is to break the opposition of his enemies, and establish God's reign of justice and peace, is the proclamation of the gospel" (G. B. Caird, *The Revelation of St. John the Divine* [HNTC; New York: Harper & Row, 1966], 245). For a reading of Revelation that more fully develops this line of interpretation, see Hays, *Moral Vision*, 169-85.

27 See David S. Yeago, "The New Testament and the Nicene Dogma: A Contribution to the Recovery of Theological Exegesis," in *The Theological Interpretation of Scripture: Classic and Contemporary Readings* (ed. Stephen E. Fowl; Oxford: Blackwell, 1997), 87-100.

28 On this question, see especially the essay of N. T. Wright in this volume.

29 Once again, we see a construction in which an (implied) plural subject (the Lord and his Messiah) anomalously becomes the grammatical subject for a third-person singular verb (βασιλεύσει: "he will reign"). The grammatical irregularity may once again implicitly testify to the *Verbindungsidentität* of God and Christ.

30 See Elisabeth Schüssler Fiorenza, *The Book of Revelation: Justice and Judgment* (Philadelphia: Fortress, 1985).

31 Oliver O'Donovan, "The Political Thought of the Book of Revelation," *Tyndale Bulletin* 37.1 (1986): 90.

Chapter 5: Mangina

1   Karl Barth and Eduard Thurneysen, *Revolutionary Theology in the Making: Barth-Thurneysen Correspondence, 1914–1925* (trans. James D. Smart; Richmond, Va.: Westminster John Knox, 1964), 101.

2   Lindbeck's article first appeared in *Keeping the Faith: Essays to Mark the Centenary of Lux Mundi* (ed. Geoffrey Wainwright; Minneapolis: Fortress, 1988).

3   George Lindbeck, "The Church," in *The Church in a Postliberal Age* (ed. James J. Buckley; Grand Rapids: Eerdmans, 2004), 146.

4   At which he was an accredited Observer, representing the Lutheran World Federation. See his fascinating essay "Reminiscences of Vatican II," in *Church in a Postliberal Age.*

5   Benedict writes that, in the period leading up to Vatican II, "a eucharistic ecclesiology developed that many like to refer to also as *communio* ecclesiology. This *communio* ecclesiology actually became the centerpiece of Vatican II teaching on the Church, the new and yet thoroughly primordial thing that this . . . Council wanted to give us" (Joseph Ratzinger [Pope Benedict XVI], *Church, Ecumenism, and Politics: New Endeavors in Ecclesiology* [San Francisco: Ignatius, 2008], 17.)

6   Lindbeck, "The Church," 149.

7   Lindbeck, "The Church," 149. Of course, Hauerwas' well-known phrase "parking lots and potluck dinners" comes to mind.

8   Lindbeck, "The Church," 154.

9   Lindbeck, "The Church," 150.

10 Lindbeck, "The Church," 156–57. To be fair, Lindbeck said that other contributors in the volume (*Keeping the Faith*) where the essay was first published would be addressing these "basal dimensions."

11 Sean M. McDonough, *YHWH at Patmos: Rev. 1:4 in Its Hellenistic and Early Jewish Setting* (Tübingen: Mohr Siebeck, 1999).

12 Four of the assemblies—Ephesus, Pergamum, Thyatira, and Laodicea—are explicitly challenged to repent. But Revelation's form as a circular letter insures that the other three churches, and indeed any possible reader, will not miss the call to repentance.

13 The fact that Sardis falls outside the pattern weakens the case. Barr suggests that as a "general exhortation to wakefulness and observance," the letter to Sardis may conceivably echo the Wisdom tradition. See David L. Barr, *Tales of the End: A Narrative Commentary on the Book of Revelation* (Santa Rosa, Calif.: Polebridge, 1998), 45–46.

14 In conversation, Professor Francesca Murphy of Notre Dame suggested to me a possible parallel with Madeleine L'Engle's well-known fantasy novel, *A Wrinkle in Time*. L'Engle identifies the three supernatural beings (Mrs. Whatsit, Mrs. Which, and Mrs. Who) who aid the Murray family not just as guardian angels but also, quite literally, as stars. Whether the author had Revelation specifically in mind is doubtful. The stars–angels correlation is a natural one, given that both are located in heaven. Cf. Job 38:7.

15   Like the supernatural "princes" assigned to various nations in the book of Daniel, Michael being the particular prince assigned to Israel. See Daniel 10; Michael appears as a character in Rev 12.

16   Cf. the designation "the earthdwellers," used in Revelation to denote human reality insofar as it is *not* determined by God and the Lamb.

17   See Samuel Wells, *Transforming Fate into Destiny: The Theological Ethics of Stanley Hauerwas* (Milton Keynes, U.K.: Paternoster, 1998).

18   The very distinction is, of course, anachronistic as applied to the ancient world.

19   And of course, the fact that the worship of the Lamb is depicted as an appropriate extension (not replacement) of the worship of YHWH is significant. See Richard Hays' essay on the Christology of Revelation in this volume.

20   See Bauckham, *Theology of the Book of Revelation*, 67–70.

21   Is it an accident that it is precisely in this verse that John refers to spiritual or allegorical interpretation? He writes that the witnesses' dead bodies "will lie in the street of the great city that symbolically [*pneumatikōs*] is called Sodom and Egypt, where their Lord was crucified." This is the only direct mention of the crucifixion in the Apocalypse. Because the witnesses' story is a type of Christ's, it is drawn into the closest possible relation with Old Testament types—in this case, Sodom and Egypt. These cities typify the powers that killed Jesus and over which he triumphed. Just so, they are types of the enemies that the church must confront.

22   Col 1:24.

23   Lindbeck, "The Church," 150.

24   Robert W. Jenson, *Canon and Creed* (Louisville, Ky.: Westminster John Knox, 2010), 22 (emphasis in original).

25   It must be stressed that Lindbeck's talk of "continuation" assumes neither the faithfulness of Christians nor the unfaithfulness of Jews. Thus he goes on to say that nothing in his account "prevents us from saying that the synagogue, like remnants of ancient Israel, is at times more faithful to God's will and purposes than are unfaithful churches" ("The Church," 151).

26   Hans Urs von Balthasar, *Theodrama IV: The Action* (San Francisco: Ignatius, 1994), 15.

27   Some 24 times.

28   It is striking that the most narrative of Revelation's ecclesial visions, the story of the witnesses, occurs almost exactly halfway through the book. While I am not quite sure what to make of this, my guess is that the placement of this strange episode is no accident.

29   See Beverly Roberts Gaventa, *Our Mother Saint Paul* (Louisville, Ky.: Westminster John Knox, 2007).

30   The allusion here is to the remarkable study of Dostoevsky's apocalyptic vision by P. Travis Kroeker and Bruce Ward, *Remembering the End: Dostoevsky as Prophet to Modernity* (Boulder, Colo.: Westview Press, 2001).

Chapter 6: Wright

1   See my *Surprised by Hope* (San Francisco: HarperSanFrancisco, 2007).
2   On this point, see the important discussion in chap. 10 of my *The New Testament and the People of God*.
3   Gregory K. Beale, *The Temple and the Church's Mission: A Biblical Theology of the Dwelling Place of God* (Downers Grove, Ill.: InterVarsity, 2004).

Chapter 7: Alkier

*   My thanks go to Prof. Dr. Leroy Huizenga, who both translated my German and corrected my English.
1   Wilhelm Bousset, *Die Offenbarung Johannis* (Göttingen: Vandenhoeck & Ruprecht, 1966 [1906]), 75: "Das eigentlich Neue, das J. in die Auslegung der Apk hineinbringt, ist nun die Deutung des vierten Zeichens auf Muhamed und die 'Saracenen.' Zu vergleichen ist hier namentlich der vierte Abschnitt des vierten Hauptteils (zu Apk 13). Das erste Tier ist der Muhamedanismus, die Todeswunde des Tieres sind die Kreuzzüge. Das Tier ist seitdem trotz wiederholter Bekämpfung immer wieder aufgelebt. Seine Wunde wird ganz geheilt, wenn der elfte König (nach Daniel) kommt, das kleine Horn (vielleicht Saladin), das ´neulich´ Jerusalem genommen hat. Der Pseudoprophet aber bedeutet die Ketzerei, die neuerdings in der Kirche ihr Haupt erhebt, die Sekte der Patharener."
2   Cf. Thomas Witulski, *Die Johannesoffenbarung und Kaiser Hadrian: Studien zur Datierung der neutestamentlichen Aokalypse* (FRLANT 221; Göttingen: Vandenhoeck & Ruprecht, 2007); *Kaiserkult in Kleinasien: Die Entwicklung der kultisch-religiösen Kaiserverehrung in der römischen Provinz Asia von Augustus bis Antoninus Pius* (NTOA 63; Göttingen: Vandenhoeck & Ruprecht, 2007), 90–170.
3   Cf. Paul de Man, *Allegories of Reading: Figural Language in Rousseau, Nietzsche, Rilke, and Proust* (New Haven: Yale University Press, 1979).
4   Its inclusion in the canon was questionable well into the tenth century, especially in the eastern church. According to Martin Luther, it did not belong in the canon of Holy Scripture: kann "nicht spüren . . . , dass es von dem Heiligen Geist gestellt sei. Dazu dünkt mir das allzu viel zu sein, dass er so hart solch sein eigenes Buch mehr denn keine andern heiligen Bücher tun . . . , befiehlt und droht: Wer etwas davon tue, von dem werde Gott auch tun usw. Wiederum sollen selig werden, die da halten, was drinnen steht, so doch niemand weiß, was es ist . . . Mein Geist kann sich in das Buch nicht schicken. Und das ist mir Ursache Genug, dass ich seiner nicht hoch achte, dass Christus darin weder gelehrt noch erkannt wird" (Martin Luther, *Vorrede zu der Offenbarung Johannis*, in *Martin Luthers Werke: Kritische Gesamtausgabe* [edited by J. F. K. Knaake et al.; Weimar: Böhlau, 1883-]). It was precisely this book, however, which shaped the enduring conception of the resurrection of the dead and their destiny in heaven and hell in Christianity. Cf. Otto Böcher, "Johannes-Apokalypse," *RAC* 18 (1998): 595–646, here 596: "Bis zur Aufklärung des 18. Jh. war sie das beliebteste, meistgelesene, meistillustrierte Buch der Bibel; ihr Einfluß auf die christl. Vorstellungen

vom Jenseits (Himmel; Hölle), aber auch auf die kirchliche Kunst u. Architektur . . . kann nicht hoch genug eingeschätzt werden."

5   Cf. Bousset, *Offenbarung Johannis*.

6   Cf. Adolf von Harnack, *Geschichte der altchristlichen Literatur bis Eusebius II.1* (Leipzig: Hinrichs, 1958).

7   Indeed, Rudolf Bultmann and many of his students regarded the Gospel of John, along with the First Letter of John, as a singular theological approach among the writings of the New Testament, which next to the letters of the Apostle Paul properly drove theology. Cf. Bultmann and Otto Merk, *Theologie des Neuen Testaments* (Tübingen: Mohr, 1984), 630.

8   János S. Petöfi, "Explikative Interpretation. Explikatives Wissen," in *Von der verbalen Konstitution zur symbolischen Bedeutung From Verbal Constitution to Symbolic Meaning* (ed. J. S. Petöfi and T. Olivi; Papiere zur Textlinguistik 62; Hamburg: Buske, 1988), 184.

9   Cf. Linton, "Reading the Apocalypse as Apocalypse," 9–41.

10   Martin Karrer, *Die Johannesoffenbarung als Brief. Studien zu ihrem literarischen, historischen und theologischen Ort* (FRLANT 140; Göttingen: Vandenhoeck & Ruprecht, 1986).

11   Fiorenza, *Book of Revelation*.

12   Cf. *Semeia* 1.

13   Despite my agreement with David L. Barr, "The Story John Told: Reading Revelation for Its Plot," in *Reading the Book of Revelation: A Resource for Students* (ed. B. David L. Barr; Resources for Biblical Studies 44; Atlanta: SBL 2003), 1–23, that John tells a story, I am nevertheless convinced (unlike Barr) that the different parts of the book of Revelation interact to a very high degree.

14   I believe that the book of Revelation as a whole is better understood in light of its intertextual relationship with the Gospel of John, to which it is a sequel—a point on which there is insufficient space here to elaborate.

15   My decision to translate the Greek term *arnion* with *ram* and not with *lamb* depends on the code instruction of the text in 13:11 (cf. 5:6). A ram has horns, a lamb has no horns. This textual code instruction has more authority than any hypothetical history of terms or traditions, as interesting as they might be (see, e.g., Johns, *Lamb Christology*, 22–39). The reality of the signals in the texts should be the first criterion of any translation, exegesis, and interpretation.

16   In an instructive contribution to the language of Revelation, Traugott Holtz, "Sprache als Metapher. Erwägungen zur Sprache der Johannesapokalypse," in *Studien zur Johannesoffenbarung und ihrer Auslegung: Festschrift für Otto Böcher* (ed. Friedrich Wilhelm Horn and Michael Wolter; Neukirchen-Vluyn: Neukirchener, 2005), 10–19, presents the thesis that the injuries to the rules of grammar do not point to a lack of linguistic competence on the part of the author of the Apocalypse, but rather that the language itself is used metaphorically in a highly reflective way, thereby showing the inadequacy of human language to designate God.

17   Cf. Böcher, "Johannes-Apokalypse," 611–12; Moyise, *Old Testament in the Book of Revelation*; Sänger, ed., *Ezechielbuch*; Thomas Hieke and Tobias Nicklas, "*Worte der Prophetie.*"

18   The significance of the Spirit who works in various ways and who takes up his visionary place as the sevenfold burning torch before the throne of God is felicitously summarized by F. Hahn, "Das Geistverständnis in der Johannesoffenbarung," in *Studien zur Johannesoffenbarung und ihrer Auslegung*, 3–9.

19   The relationship between the First Witness and his followers that comes about through this is to be understood as a relationship of ruler to ruled. However, this relationship is not marked by the violent exercise of power, but rather by the love that the new ruler feels toward his own and even his making of them "kings and priests" (1:6). The new ruler loves his own and gives them a share in his power.

20   There are many more possibilities of intertextual readings. I differentiate between production-oriented, reception-oriented, and experimental intertextual readings; cf. Stefan Alkier, "New Testament Studies on the Basis of Categorical Semiotics," in *Reading the Bible Intertextually*, 223–48.

Chapter 8: Nicklas

1   Cf. Hieke and Nicklas, "*Worte der Prophetie.*"

2   For an overview of a history of the New Testament canon, Bruce M. Metzger, *The Canon of the New Testament: Its Origin, Development, and Significance* (Oxford: Clarendon, 1997) is still important. For (mainly ancient) receptions of Revelation see Georg Kretschmar, *Die Offenbarung des Johannes: Die Geschichte ihrer Auslegung im 1. Jahrtausend* (CTM 9; Stuttgart: Calwer, 1985); Kovacs and Rowland, *Revelation*; and Joseph Verheyden, Andreas Merkt and Tobias Nicklas (eds.), *Interpreting Violent Texts: Ancient Receptions of the Book of Revelation* (NTOA; Göttingen: Vandenhoeck & Ruprecht, 2011).

3   For more information see M. De Groote, "Die Johannesapokalypse und die Kanonbildung im Osten," *ZKG* 116 (2005): 147–60.

4   For more ideas about the relation between divine and human word in Revelation and its reception history see Tobias Nicklas, "Der Ewige spricht in die Zeit—Gotteswort und Menschenwort in der Offenbarung des Johannes," *Sacra Scripta* 9 (2011): 189–95.

5   For further details see Tobias Nicklas, "'The Words of the Prophecy of This Book': Playing with Scriptural Authority in the Book of Revelation," in *Authoritative Scriptures in Ancient Judaism* (ed. M. Popović; JSJSup 141; Leiden: Brill, 2010), 309–26, but see also Konrad Huber and Martin Hasitschka, "Die Offenbarung des Johannes im Kanon der Bibel: Textinterner Geltungsanspruch und Probleme der kanonischen Rezeption," in *The Biblical Canons* (eds. J.-M. Auwers and H. J. De Jonge; BETL 163; Leuven: Peeters, 2003), 607–18.

6   It is impossible to give a full overview of recent studies dealing with Revelation and its different intertextual relations to the Old Testament. I would like to mention just a few: Fekkes, *Isaiah and Prophetic Traditions*; Moyise, *Old Testament in the Book of Revelation*; Kowalski, *Rezeption des Propheten Ezechiel*;

7 See mainly Thomas Hieke's contribution on Daniel.

8 I am well aware that the question of 2 Thessalonians' authenticity is a matter of scholarly debate and many authors like, e.g., Charles A. Wanamaker, *The Epistles to the Thessalonians: A Commentary on the Greek Text* (NIGTC; Grand Rapids: Eerdmans, 1990), or A. J. Malherbe, *The Letters to the Thessalonians: A New Translation with Introduction and Commentary* (The Anchor Bible 32B; New York: Doubleday, 2000) regard 2 Thessalonians as authentic. My own position, which I am currently developing in a commentary for the German KeK-series, however, is different: because of its literary dependence on 1 Thessalonians on the one hand, but on its different eschatology, Christology, ecclesiology, and even its different idea of Paul on the other hand, I regard the text as a pseudepigraphon of the end of the first century C.E. trying to safeguard Paul's reputation in a situation of crisis.

9 Regarding the problem of the "Katechon," see Paul Metzger, *Katechon: II Thess 2,1-12 im Horizont apokalyptischen Denkens* (BZNW 135; Berlin: de Gruyter, 2005).

10 I regard 2 Peter as (probably) the latest writing of the New Testament perhaps even going back to a period in the middle of the second century C.E.

11 A similar exegesis of Psalm 90 can be found in Justin Martyr (*Dial.* 81.3), another second-century Christian writer.

12 For more information regarding the image of the Church as *Oikos* or *Polis* as it can be found in the Pastoral Epistles, cf. Korinna Zamfir, "Male and Female Roles in the Pastoral Epistles" (Diss. Habil., Regensburg, 2012).

13 Of course, I do not regard the "voices" of the Pastorals as purely derivative, but think that there can be situations within ecclesiastical life where their "voice" regarding the church *also* as part of "this world" can be of enormous importance.

14 Regarding the way the Seer of Revelation deals with his opponents within the community see, e.g., Tobias Nicklas, "Die Darstellung von innergemeindlichen Gegnern in der Offenbarung des Johannes," *Rivista di storia del Cristianesimo* 6.2 (2009): 349-61.

15 Of course, the date of Revelation is—again—a matter of debate. For an overview of different datings (from Nero to Hadrian) see, e.g., Witulski, *Johannesoffenbarung und Kaiser Hadrian*, 14-52. I regard a date at the end of the first or the first years of the second century as probable.

16 For more information on Romans 13:1-7 and its history of reception, cf. Michael Theobald, *Der Römerbrief* (EdF 294; Darmstadt: WBG, 2000), 307-10 (with references to older literature), and Ulrich Wilckens, *Der Brief an die Römer (Röm 12–16)* (EKK I.3; Neukirchen-Vluyn: Neukirchener, 2003), 43-66. Of course, the situation in the early church as a whole was much more complex than can be described here. See, e.g., the short overview by Everett Ferguson, "Tertullian," in *Early Christian Thinkers: The Lives and Legacies of Twelve Key Figures* (ed. Paul Foster; London: SPCK, 2010) 85-99, here 98.

17 The question of the impact of imperial cult for an understanding of Revelation has been a matter of several studies, among them, e.g., J. Nelson Kraybill, *Imperial Cult and Commerce in John's Apocalypse* (JSNTSup 132; Sheffield: Academic Press, 1996), and Friesen, *Imperial Cults*.

18 For a kind of "new perspective" on Marcion, his theology and his movement, see Sebastian Moll, *The Arch-Heretic Marcion* (WUNT 250; Tübingen: Mohr Siebeck, 2010), who offers a radical criticism of Harnack's image of Marcion.

19 Adolf von Harnack, *Marcion: Das Evangelium vom fremden Gott* (Leipzig: Hinrichs, 1924), 217: "Das Alte Testament im 2. Jahrhundert zu verwerfen, war ein Fehler, den die große Kirche mit Recht abgelehnt hat; es im 16. Jahrhundert beizubehalten, war ein Schicksal, dem sich die Reformation noch nicht zu entziehen vermochte; es aber im 19. Jahrhundert als kanonische Urkunde im Protestantismus noch zu konservieren, ist die Folge einer religiösen und kirchlichen Lähmung. " (The English translation in the text is by H. Räisänen, "Marcion," in *A Companion to Second-Century Christian "Heretics"* [ed. Antti Marjanen and Petri Luomanen; VCSup 76; Leiden: Brill, 2005], 100–24, esp. 120.)

20 For a discussion of Revelation's theology of creation, see Jürgen Roloff, "Neuschöpfung in der Offenbarung des Johannes," *JBTh* 5 (1990): 120–38; Ferdinand Hahn, "Die Schöpfungsthematik in der Johannesoffenbarung," in *Eschatologie und Schöpfung* (ed. M. Evang et al.; BZNW 89; Berlin: de Gruyter, 1997), 85–93; and Tobias Nicklas, "Schöpfung und Vollendung in der Offenbarung des Johannes," in *Theologies of Creation in Early Judaism and Ancient Christianity: In Honour of Hans Klein* (ed. Tobias Nicklas and Korinna Zamfir; Deuterocanonical and Cognate Literature Studies 6; Berlin: de Gruyter, 2010), 389–414.

21 For the polemical and political implications of the use of this title, see Christiane Zimmermann, *Die Namen des Vaters: Studien zu ausgewählten neutestamentlichen Gottesbezeichnungen vor ihrem frühjüdischen und paganen Hintergrund* (AJEC 69; Leiden: Brill, 2007), 233–70.

22 For more information see Thomas Hieke, "Der Seher Johannes als neuer Ezechiel," 1–30.

23 For an interpretation of Revelation, which sees Revelation 6:9-11 as a key scene, see, e.g., Tonstad, *Saving God's Reputation*.

24 I am grateful to Stefan Alkier, who reminded me of the fact that even the ongoing set of visions could be understood as a "response": God is already acting and leading the world to a good end.

25 For Isa 25:8 and its New Testament receptions, see Thomas Hieke, "'Er verschlingt den Tod für immer' (Jes 25,8): Eine unerfüllte Verheißung im Alten und Neuen Testament," *BZ* 50 (2006): 31–50.

26 Of course, other dimensions, like Revelation's Christology (see, however, Richard Hays' article in the present volume), its relation to the Johannine corpus, etc., could be added. I am grateful to Stephen Chapman's helpful and critical remarks to my paper.

27 For comparable ideas see Klaus Wengst, *Wie lange noch? Schreien nach Recht und Gerechtigkeit–eine Deutung der Apokalypse des Johannes* (Stuttgart: Kohlhammer, 2010), 272–73.

28 For a somewhat more optimistic view, see P. de Villiers, "Love in the Revelation of John," in *Seeing the Seeker: Explorations in the Discipline of Spirituality: A Festschrift for Kees Waaijman* (ed. Hein Blommestijn et al.; Studies in Spirituality 19; Leuven: Peeters, 2008), 155–68.

29 For more information, see C.-E. Bärsch, "Antijudaismus, Apokalyptik und Satanologie: Die religiösen Elemente des nationalsozialistischen Antisemitismus," *ZRGG* 40 (1988): 112–33, here 131. Another Nazi author dealing with Revelation was Carl Schneider. For information on his exegetical ideas, see Annette Merz, "Philhellenism and Antisemitism: Two Sides of One Coin in the Academic Writings of Carl Schneider," *Kirchliche Zeitgeschichte* 17 (2004): 314–30.

Chapter 9: Thompson

1 Dispensationalism is the system of interpretation that has given rise to many, if not most, of the various "futurist" systems of interpretation among popular biblical interpreters and evangelists. For a thorough and fascinating discussion of the tenets and rise of dispensationalism, see Timothy B. Weber, *On the Road to Armageddon: How Evangelicals Became Israel's Best Friend* (Grand Rapids: Baker Academic, 2004), esp. chaps. 1–3; see also Paul Boyer, *When Time Shall Be No More: Prophecy Belief in Modern American Culture* (Cambridge, Mass.: Harvard University Press, 1992).

2 Lindsey, *Late Great Planet Earth* is still in print; LaHaye and Jenkins, *Left Behind*, vols. 1–12.

3 In *On the Road to Armageddon*, Weber shows how dispensationalism gained prominence in the United States, first, during a time when tensions between conservative and liberal manifestations of Christianity were on the rise and historical criticism of the Bible often yielded negative results that threatened to undercut the authority of Scripture, and, second, because it was adopted by many of the most visible preachers and evangelists of the day.

4 See, e.g., Colin J. Hemer, *The Letters to the Seven Churches in Their Local Setting* (JSNTSup 11; Sheffield: Sheffield Academic, 1986) and Friesen, *Imperial Cults*.

5 Richard N. Soulen and R. Kendall Soulen, *Handbook of Biblical Criticism* (Louisville, Ky.: Westminster John Knox, 2001), 193.

6 So Athanasius, "For the searching and right understanding of the Scriptures there is need of a good life and a pure soul, and for Christian virtue to guide the mind to grasp, so far as human nature can, the truth concerning God the Word" (*On the Incarnation* [Crestwood, N.Y.: St. Vladmir's Seminary Press, 1953], 96).

7 See Alasdair MacIntyre, "What the reader . . . has to learn about him or herself is that it is only the self as transformed through and by the reading of the

texts which will be capable of reading the texts aright" (*Three Rival Versions of Moral Enquiry* [Notre Dame, Ind.: Notre Dame University Press, 1990], 82).

8   On the twin desires to take seriously the inalienably theological interests of the text and their status and function as Scripture for the church while simultaneously sustaining dialogue with those who do not share these presuppositions, see especially Bockmuehl, *Seeing the Word*, esp. 46–47, 64.

9   As Steve Moyise points out, while the picture of the warrior lion has been "transformed by its juxtaposition with a lamb, the lamb has also picked up many of the traits of the warrior lion" ("Intertextuality and Historical Approaches to the Use of Scripture in the New Testament," in *Reading the Bible Intertextually*, 25).

10   Robert H. Mounce, *The Book of Revelation* (NICNT; Grand Rapids: Eerdmans, 1977), 12.

11   For an overview of scholarly understanding of the (mixed) genre of Revelation, see Linton, "Reading the Apocalypse as Apocalypse," 9–41, and David L. Barr, "Beyond Genre: The Expectations of Apocalypse," 71–89, in *The Reality of Apocalypse: Rhetoric and Politics in the Book of Revelation* (ed. David L. Barr; SBLSymS 39; Atlanta: SBL, 2004).

12   See David Aune, *Revelation 17–22* (WBC 52C; Nashville: Thomas Nelson, 1998), 920–28.

13   These are among the accomplishments attributed to Augustus in *Res Gestae Divi Augusti* as reproduced in *Readings in Ancient History: Illustrative Extracts from the Sources*, vol. 2: *Rome and the West* (ed. William Stearns Davis and Willis M. West; Boston: Allyn & Bacon, 1912–13), 166–72.

14   As Craig R. Koester puts it, Revelation is a critique of "ordinary empire"; see "Revelation's Visionary Challenge to Ordinary Empire," *Interpretation* (2009): 5–18.

15   Note the title and subtitle of J. Nelson Kraybill's recent book, *Apocalyptic and Allegiance: Worship, Politics, and Devotion in the Book of Revelation* (Grand Rapids: Brazos, 2010).

16   Boxall, *Revelation of St John*, 272.

17   Caird, *Commentary on Revelation*, 178.

18   The description of the beast as having has been slain but yet now living (Rev 13:3, 12, 14) may refer to the perpetual rise of empires, but more likely it has in view the myth of Nero *redivivus*, identifying this beast with Rome.

19   One is reminded of the *Martyrdom of Polycarp*, in which Polycarp's death is dated precisely to the year, month, day, and hour; further described as, "Philip being high priest, Statius Quadratus being proconsul, but Jesus Christ being King forever" (21:1).

Works Cited

Abrams, M. H., ed. *The Norton Anthology of English Literature*. 3rd ed. 2 vols. New York: W. W. Norton, 1974.

Adam, A. K. M. "Poaching on Zion: Biblical Theology as Signifying Practice." Pages 17–34 in *Reading Scripture with the Church: Toward a Hermeneutic for Theological Interpretation*. Edited by A. K. M. Adam, Stephen E. Fowl, Kevin J. Vanhoozer, and Francis Watson. Grand Rapids: Baker Academic, 2006.

Aichele, George. "Canon as Intertext: Restraint or Liberation." Pages 139–59 in *Reading the Bible Intertextually*. Edited by Richard B. Hays, Stefan Alkier, and Leroy A. Huizenga. Waco, Tex.: Baylor University Press, 2009.

Alkier, Stefan. "Intertetuality and the Semiotics of Biblical Texts." Pages 3–21 in *Reading the Bible Intertextually*. Edited by Richard B. Hays, Stefan Alkier, and Leroy A. Huizenga. Waco, Tex.: Baylor University Press, 2009.

Alkier, Stefan, and Richard B. Hays, eds. *Die Bibel im Dialog der Schriften: Konzepte intertextueller Bibellektüre*. Tübingen: Francke, 2005.

——, eds. *Kanon und Intertextualität*. Kleine Schriften des Fachbereichs Evangelische Theologie der Goethe-Universität Frankfurt/Main. Nr. 1. Frankfurt am Main: Lembeck, 2010.

Athanasius. *On the Incarnation*. Crestwood, N.Y.: St. Vladmir's Seminary Press, 1953.

Augustus. *Res Gestae Divi Augusti*. Pages 166–72 in *Readings in Ancient History: Illustrative Extracts from the Sources*. Vol. 2, *Rome and the West*. Edited by William Stearns Davis and Willis M. West. Boston: Allyn & Bacon, 1912–1913.

Aune, David E. *Revelation 1–5*. WBC 52A. Dallas: Word Books, 1997.

——. *Revelation 6–16*. WBC 52B. Nashville: Thomas Nelson, 1998.

——. *Revelation 17–22*. WBC 52C. Nashville: Thomas Nelson, 1998.

Balthasar, Hans Urs von. *Theodrama IV: The Action*. San Francisco: Ignatius, 1994.

Barr, David L., ed. *The Reality of Apocalypse: Rhetoric and Politics in the Book of Revelation.* SBLSymS 39. Atlanta: SBL, 2006.

———. "The Story John Told: Reading Revelation for Its Plot." Pages 1–23 in *Reading the Book of Revelation: A Resource for Students.* Edited by David L. Barr. Resources for Biblical Studies 44. Atlanta: SBL, 2003.

———. *Tales of the End: A Narrative Commentary on the Book of Revelation.* Santa Rosa, Calif.: Polebridge, 1998.

Bärsch, C.-E. "Antijudaismus, Apokalyptik und Satanologie: Die religiösen Elemente des nationalsozialistischen Antisemitismus." *ZRGG* 40 (1988): 112–33.

Barth, Karl, and Eduard Thurneysen. *Revolutionary Theology in the Making: Barth-Thurneysen Correspondence, 1914–1925.* Translated by James D. Smart. Richmond, Va.: Westminster John Knox, 1964.

Bartholomew, Craig G., Scott Hahn, Robin Parry, Christopher Seitz, and Al Wolters, eds. *Canon and Biblical Interpretation.* Scripture and Hermeneutics Series 7. Grand Rapids: Zondervan, 2006.

Bauckham, Richard. *The Climax of Prophecy: Studies on the Book of Revelation.* Edinburgh: T&T Clark, 1993.

———. *God Crucified: Monotheism and Christology in the New Testament.* Grand Rapids: Eerdmans, 1998.

———. *The Theology of the Book of Revelation.* Cambridge: Cambridge University Press, 1993.

Beale, Gregory K. *The Book of Revelation: A Commentary on the Greek Text.* NIGTC. Grand Rapids: Eerdmans, 1999.

———. *John's Use of the Old Testament in Revelation.* JSNTSup 166. Sheffield: Sheffield Academic, 1998.

———. *The Temple and the Church's Mission: A Biblical Theology of the Dwelling Place of God.* Downers Grove, Ill.: InterVarsity, 2004.

———. *The Use of Daniel in Jewish Apocalyptic Literature and in the Revelation of St. John.* Lanham, Md.: University Press of America, 1984.

Beasley-Murray, G. R. "The Interpretation of Daniel 7." *CBQ* 45 (1983): 44–58.

Begbie, Jeremy. *Voicing Creation's Praise: Towards a Theology of the Arts.* London: T&T Clark, 1991.

Billings, J. Todd. *The Word of God for the People of God: An Entryway to the Theological Interpretation of Scripture.* Grand Rapids: Eerdmans, 2010.

Birch, Bruce. C., Walter Brueggemann, Terence E. Fretheim, and David L. Petersen, eds. *A Theological Introduction to the Old Testament.* Nashville: Abingdon, 1999.

Boccaccini, Gabriele, ed. *Enoch and the Messiah Son of Man: Revisiting the Book of Parables.* Grand Rapids: Eerdmans, 2007.

Böcher, Otto. "Johannes-Apokalypse." *RAC* 18 (1998): 595–646.

Bockmuehl, Markus. *Seeing the Word: Refocusing New Testament Study.* Studies in Theological Interpretation. Grand Rapids: Baker Academic, 2006.

Boesak, Allan A. *Comfort and Protest: The Apocalypse from a South African Perspective.* Philadelphia: Westminster, 1987.

Boring, M. Eugene. *Revelation.* Interpretation: A Bible Commentary for Teaching and Preaching. Louisville, Ky.: John Knox, 1989.

Bousset, Wilhelm. *Die Offenbarung Johannis.* Göttingen: Vandenhoeck & Ruprecht, 1966 (1906).

Boxall, Ian. *The Revelation of St John.* BNTC 19. Peabody, Mass.: Hendrickson; London: Continuum, 2006.

Boyer, Paul. *When Time Shall Be No More: Prophecy Belief in Modern American Culture.* Cambridge, Mass.: Harvard University Press, 1992.

Buckley, James J., ed. *The Church in a Postliberal Age.* Grand Rapids: Eerdmans, 2004.

Bultmann, Rudolf, and Otto Merk. *Theologie des Neuen Testaments.* Tübingen: Mohr Siebeck, 1984.

Caird, George B. *A Commentary on the Revelation of St John the Divine.* 2nd ed. London: A&C Black, 1984.

———. *The Revelation of St. John the Divine.* HNTC. New York: Harper & Row, 1966.

Carey, Greg. "The Book of Revelation as Counter-Imperial Script." Pages 157–76 in *In the Shadow of Empire: Reclaiming the Bible as a History of Faithful Resistance.* Edited by Richard A. Horsley. Louisville, Ky.: Westminster John Knox, 2008.

Carter, Warren. *Matthew and Empire: Initial Explorations.* Harrisburg, Pa.: Trinity Press International, 2001.

Casey, Maurice. "The Corporate Interpretation of 'One Like a Son of Man' (Dan. VII 13) at the Time of Jesus." *NovT* 18.3 (1976): 167–80.

———. *The Solution to the 'Son of Man' Problem.* LNTS 343. London: T&T Clark, 2007.

Charry, Ellen T. "'A Sharp Two-Edged Sword': Pastoral Implications of Apocalyptic." Pages 344–60 in *Character and Scripture: Moral Formation, Community, and Biblical Interpretation.* Edited by William P. Brown. Grand Rapids: Eerdmans, 2002.

Chesterton, G. K. *Orthodoxy.* Centennial edition. Nashville: Sam Torode Book Arts, 2009 (1908).

Collins, Adela Yarbro. "The Influence of Daniel on the New Testament." Pages 90–105 in *Daniel: A Commentary on the Book of Daniel.* Edited by John J. Collins. Hermeneia. Minneapolis: Augsburg Fortress, 1993.

Collins, Adela Yarbro, and John J. Collins. *King and Messiah as Son of God: Divine, Human, and Angelic Messianic Figures in Biblical and Related Literature.* Grand Rapids: Eerdmans, 2008.

Collins, John J. *Apocalypticism and the Dead Sea Scrolls.* London: Routledge, 1997.

———. *The Apocalyptic Imagination: An Introduction to the Jewish Matrix of Christianity.* New York: Crossroads, 1984.

———. *Daniel: A Commentary on the Book of Daniel.* Hermeneia. Minneapolis: Augsburg Fortress, 1993.

———. "The Son of Man in First-Century Judaism." *NTS* 38 (1992): 448–66.

De Groote, M. "Die Johannesapokalypse und die Kanonbildung im Osten." *ZKG* 116 (2005): 147–60.

de Man, Paul. *Allegories of Reading: Figural Language in Rousseau, Nietzsche, Rilke, and Proust.* New Haven: Yale University Press, 1979.

de Villiers, P. G. "Love in the Revelation of John." Pages 155–68 in *Seeing the Seeker: Explorations in the Discipline of Spirituality: A Festschrift for Kees Waaijman.* Edited by Hein Blommestijn et al. Studies in Spirituality 19. Leuven: Peeters, 2008.

Decock, Paul B. "The Scriptures in the Book of Revelation." *Neot* 33 (1999): 373–410.

Deissler, Alfons. "Der 'Menschensohn' und 'das Volk der Heiligen des Höchsten' in Dan 7." Pages 81–91 in *Jesus und der Menschensohn: Festschrift für Anton Vögtle.* Edited by Rudolf Pesch and Rudolf Schackenburg. Freiburg: Herder, 1975.

Derrida, Jacque. *Desseminations.* Chicago: Chicago University Press, 1981.

deSilva, David A. *Seeing Things John's Way: The Rhetoric of the Book of Revelation.* Louisville, Ky.: Westminster John Knox, 2009.

Di Lella, Alexander A. "The One in Human Likeness and the Holy Ones of the Most High in Daniel 7." *CBQ* 39 (1977): 1–19.

Elliott, Neil. *The Arrogance of Nations: Reading Romans in the Shadow of Empire.* Paul in Critical Contexts. Minneapolis: Fortress, 2008.

Fekkes, Jan. *Isaiah and Prophetic Traditions in the Book of Revelation: Visionary Antecedents and Their Development.* JSNTSup 93. Sheffield: Sheffield Academic, 1994.

Ferguson, Everett. "Tertullian." Pages 85–99 in *Early Christian Thinkers: The Lives and Legacies of Twelve Key Figures.* Edited by Paul Foster. London: SPCK, 2010.

Fowl, Stephen E. *Engaging Scripture: A Model for Theological Interpretation.* Malden, Mass.: Blackwell, 1998.

Frey, Jörg. "The Relevance of the Roman Imperial Cult for the Book of Revelation: Exegetical and Hermeneutical Reflections on the Relation between the Seven Letters and the Visionary Main Part of the Book." Pages 231–55 in *The New Testament and Early Christian Literature in Greco-Roman Context: Studies in Honor of David E. Aune.* Edited by John Fotopoulus. NovTSup 122. Leiden: Brill, 2006.

Friesen, Steven J. *Imperial Cults and the Apocalypse of John: Reading Revelation in the Ruins.* Oxford: Oxford University Press, 2001.

Gaventa, Beverly Roberts. *Our Mother Saint Paul.* Louisville, Ky.: Westminster John Knox, 2007.

Giesen, Heinz. *Die Offenbarung des Johannes.* Regensburg: Pustet, 1997.

Goldingay, John E. *Daniel.* Word Biblical Commentary. Dallas, Tex.: Word Books, 1989.

Gorman, Michael J. *Elements of Biblical Exegesis: A Basic Guide for Students and Ministers.* Rev. and exp. ed. Peabody, Mass.: Hendrickson, 2009.

———. *Reading Revelation Responsibly: Uncivil Worship and Witness: Following the Lamb into the New Creation.* Eugene, Ore.: Cascade Books, 2011.

Green, Joel B. *Seized by Truth: Reading the Bible as Scripture.* Nashville: Abingdon, 2007.

Greene, Thomas M. *The Light in Troy: Imitation and Discovery in Renaissance Poetry.* New Haven: Yale University Press, 1982.

Haag, Ernst. "Zeit und Zeiten und ein Teil einer Zeit (Dan 7, 25)." *TThZ* 101 (1992): 65–68.

Hahn, Ferdinand. "Das Geistverständnis in der Johannesoffenbarung." Pages 3–9 in *Studien zur Johannesoffenbarung und ihrer Auslegung. Festschrift für Otto Böcher.* Edited by Freidrich Wilhelm Horn and Michael Wolter. Neukirchen-Vluyn: Neukirchener, 2005.

———. "Die Schöpfungsthematik in der Johannesoffenbarung." Pages 85–93 in *Eschatologie und Schöpfung.* Edited by M. Evang, H. Merklein, and M. Wolter. BZNW 89. Berlin: de Gruyter, 1997.

Harink, Douglas. *Paul among the Postliberals: Pauline Theology beyond Christendom and Modernity.* Grand Rapids: Brazos, 2003.

Harnack, Adolf von. *Geschichte der altchristlichen Literatur bis Eusebius II.1.* Leipzig: Hinrichs, 1958.

———. "Marcion." Pages 100–124 in *A Companion to Second-Century Christian "Heretics."* Edited by Antti Marjanen and Petri Luomanen. Translated by H. Räisänen. VCSup 76. Leiden: Brill, 2005.

———. *Marcion: Das Evangelium vom fremden Gott.* Leipzig: Hinrichs, 1924.

Hartman, Louis F. *The Book of Daniel (Daniel 1–9).* The Anchor Bible. New York: Doubleday, 1977.

Hays, Richard B. *The Conversion of the Imagination: Paul as Interpreter of Israel's Scripture.* Grand Rapids: Eerdmans, 2005.

———. *Echoes of Scripture in the Letters of Paul.* New Haven: Yale University Press, 1989.

———. *The Faith of Jesus Christ: The Narrative Substructure of Galatians 3:1–4:11.* 2nd ed. Grand Rapids: Eerdmans, 2002.

———. *The Moral Vision of the New Testament: A Contemporary Introduction to New Testament Ethics.* San Francisco: HarperCollins, 1996.

Hays, Richard B., Stefan Alkier, and Leroy Huizenga, eds. *Reading the Bible Intertextually.* Waco, Tex.: Baylor University Press, 2009.

Hemer, Colin J. *The Letters to the Seven Churches in Their Local Setting.* JSNTSup 11. Sheffield: Sheffield Academic, 1986.

Hieke, Thomas. "'Er verschlingt den Tod für immer' (Jes 25,8): Eine unerfüllte Verheißung im Alten und Neuen Testament." *BZ* 50 (2006): 31–50.

———. "Der Seher Johannes als neuer Ezechiel. Die Offenbarung des Johannes vom Ezechielbuch her gelesen." Pages 1–30 in *Das Ezechielbuch in der Johannesoffenbarung.* Edited by Dieter Sänger et al. BTHSt 76. Neukirchen-Vluyn: Neukirchener, 2004.

Hieke, Thomas, and Tobias Nicklas. *"Die Worte der Prophetie dieses Buches": Offenbarung 22,6-21 als Schlussstein der christlichen Bibel Alten und Neuen Testaments gelesen.* BTHSt 62. Neukirchen-Vluyn: Neukirchener, 2003.

Hofius, Otfried. "Der Septuaginta-Text von Daniel 7,13-14: Erwägungen zu seiner Gestalt und seiner Aussage." *ZAW* 117.1 (2005): 73–90.

Holtz, Traugott. *Die Christologie der Apokalypse des Johannes.* TU 85. Berlin: Akademie-Verlag, 1962.

———. "Sprache als Metapher. Erwägungen zur Sprache der Johannesapokalypse." Pages 10–19 in *Studien zur Johannesoffenbarung und ihrer Auslegung: Festschrift für Otto Böcher.* Edited by Friedrich Wilnelm Horn and Michael Wolter. Neukirchen-Vluyn: Neukirchener, 2005.

Horn, Freidrich Wilhelm, and Michael Wolter, eds. *Studien zur Johannesoffenbarung und ihrer Auslegung: Festschrift für Otto Böcher.* Neukirchen-Vluyn: Neukirchener, 2005.

Horsley, Richard A. *Jesus and Empire: The Kingdom of God and the New World Disorder.* Minneapolis: Fortress, 2003.

———. *Revolt of the Scribes: Resistance and Apocalyptic Origins.* Minneapolis: Fortress, 2010.

Huber, Konrad. *Einer Gleich einem Menschensohn: Die Christusvisionen in Offb. 1,9-20 und Offb. 14,14-20 und die Christologie der Johannesoffenbarung.* NTAbh N.F. 51. Münster: Aschendorff, 2007.

Huber, Konrad, and Martin Hasitschka. "Die Offenbarung des Johannes im Kanon der Bibel: Textinterner Geltungsanspruch und Probleme der kanonischen Rezeption." Pages 607–18 in *The Biblical Canons.* Edited by J.-M. Auwers and H. J. De Jonge. BETL 163. Leuven: Peeters, 2003.

Humphrey, Edith M. "Firing the Imagination: Visions with Embedded Propositions." Pages 151–94 in *And I Turned to See the Voice: The Rhetoric of Vision in the New Testament.* Grand Rapids: Baker Academic, 2007.

Jack, Alison M. *Texts Reading Texts, Sacred and Secular: Two Postmodern Perspectives.* JSNTSup 179. Sheffield: Sheffield Academic, 1999.

Jauhiainen, Marko. *The Use of Zechariah in Revelation.* WUNT 199. Tübingen: Mohr Siebeck, 2005.

Jenson, Robert W. *Canon and Creed.* Louisville, Ky.: Westminster John Knox, 2010.

Johns, Loren L. *The Lamb Christology of the Apocalypse of John: An Investigation into Its Origin and Rhetorical Force.* WUNT 2.167. Tübingen: Mohr Siebeck, 2003.

Johnson, Luke Timothy. *The Writings of the New Testament.* 3rd ed. Minneapolis: Fortress, 2010.

Karrer, Martin. *Die Johannesoffenbarung als Brief. Studien zu ihrem literarischen, historischen und theologischen Ort.* FRLANT 140. Göttingen: Vandenhoeck & Ruprecht, 1986.

Keel, Othmar. "Die Tiere und der Mensch in Daniel 7." Pages 37–65 in *Europa, Tausendjähriges Reich und Neue Welt. Zwei Jahrtausende Geschichte und Utopie in der Rezeption des Danielbuches.* Edited by Mariano Delgado and Klaus Koch. Studien zur christlichen Religions- und Kulturgeschichte 1. Freiburg, Schweiz: Universitätsverlag; Stuttgart: Kohlhammer, 2003.

Koester, Craig R. "On the Verge of the Millennium: A History of the Interpretation of Revelation." *Word and World* 15.2 (1995): 128–36.

———. *Revelation and the End of All Things.* Grand Rapids: Eerdmans, 2001.

———. "Revelation's Visionary Challenge to Ordinary Empire." *Interpretation* (2009): 5–18.

Kovacs, Judith L. "The Revelation to John: Lessons from the History of the Book's Reception." *Word and World* 25.3 (2005): 255–63.

Kovacs, Judith, and Christopher Rowland. *Revelation: The Apocalypse of Jesus Christ.* Blackwell Bible Commentaries. Malden, Mass.: Blackwell, 2004.

Kowalski, Beate. *Die Rezeption des Propheten Ezechiel in der Offenbarung des Johannes.* SBB 52. Stuttgart: Katholisches Bibelwerk, 2004.

Kraybill, J. Nelson. *Apocalyptic and Allegiance: Worship, Politics, and Devotion in the Book of Revelation.* Grand Rapids: Brazos, 2010.

———. "Apocalypse Now." *Christianity Today,* October 25, 1999, 30–40.

———. *Imperial Cult and Commerce in John's Apocalypse.* JSNTSup 132. Sheffield: Sheffield Academic, 1996.

Kretschmar, Georg. *Die Offenbarung des Johannes: Die Geschichte ihrer Auslegung im 1. Jahrtausend.* CTM 9. Stuttgart: Calwer, 1985.

Kristeva, Julia. "Word, Dialogue and Novel." Pages in 34–61 in *The Kristeva Reader.* Edited by Toril Moi. New York: Columbia University Press, 1986.

Kroeker, P. Travis, and Bruce Ward. *Remembering the End: Dostoevsky as Prophet to Modernity.* Boulder, Colo.: Westview Press, 2001.

Kuhn, Karl A. "The 'One like a Son of Man' Becomes the 'Son of God.'" *CBQ* 69.1 (2007): 22–42.

Lacocque, André. "Allusions to Creation in Daniel 7." Pages 114–31 in *The Book of Daniel: Composition & Reception.* Vol. 2. Edited by John J. Collins and Peter W. Flint. VTSup. Leiden: Brill 2001.

LaHaye, Tim, and Jerry B. Jenkins. *Left Behind.* Vols. 1–12. Carol Stream, Ill.: Tyndale House, 1996–2004.

Lebram, Jürgen-Christian. *Das Buch Daniel.* Zürcher Bibelkommentare. Zürich: Theologischer Verlag, 1984.

Levering, Matthew. *Participator Biblical Exegesis: A Theology of Biblical Interpretation.* Notre Dame, Ind.: University of Notre Dame Press, 2008.

Lindbeck, George. "The Church." Pages 145–66 in *The Church in a Postliberal Age.* Edited by James J. Buckley. Grand Rapids: Eerdmans, 2004.

Lindsey, Hal. *The Late Great Planet Earth.* Grand Rapids: Zondervan, 1970.

Linton, Gregory L. "Reading the Apocalypse as Apocalypse: The Limits of Genre." Pages 9–41 in *The Reality of Apocalypse: Rhetoric and Politics in the Book of Revelation.* Edited by David L. Barr. Atlanta: SBL, 2006.

Lowe, Walter. "Why We Need Apocalyptic." *SJT* 63.1 (2010): 41–53.

Luther, Martin. *Luther's Works: Table Talk.* Vol. 54. Edited by Theodore G. Tappet. Philadelphia: Fortress, 1967.

———. "Preface to the Revelation of St. John [II]." Pages 399–411 in *Luther's Works: Word and Sacrament.* Vol. 35. Edited by E. Theodore Bachmann. Philadelphia: Fortress, 1960.

———. *Vorrede zu der Offenbarung Johannis*. In *Martin Luthers Werke: Kritische Gesamtausgabe*. Edited by J. F. K. Knaake et al. Weimar: Böhlau, 1883–.

Luttikhuizen, G., ed. *Paradise Interpreted: Interpretations of Biblical Paradise in Judaism and Christianity*. Leiden: Brill, 1999.

Luz, Ulrich. "The Contribution of Reception History to a Theology of the New Testament." Pages 123–34 in *The Nature of New Testament Theology: Essays in Honour of Robert Morgan*. Edited by Christopher Rowland and Christopher Tuckett. Oxford: Blackwell, 2006.

MacIntyre, Alasdair. *Three Rival Versions of Moral Enquiry*. Notre Dame, Ind.: Notre Dame University Press, 1990.

Malherbe, A. J. *The Letters to the Thessalonians: A New Translation with Introduction and Commentary*. The Anchor Bible 32B. New York: Doubleday, 2000.

Mangina, Joseph L. *Revelation*. Brazos Theological Commentary on the Bible. Grand Rapids: Brazos, 2010.

McDonough, Sean M. *YHWH at Patmos: Rev. 1:4 in Its Hellenistic and Early Jewish Setting*. Tübingen: Mohr Siebeck, 1999.

McGinn, Bernard. *Antichrist: Two Thousand Years of the Human Fascination with Evil*. San Francisco: HarperSanFrancisco, 1994.

Merz, Annette. "Philhellenism and Antisemitism: Two Sides of One Coin in the Academic Writings of Carl Schneider." *Kirchliche Zeitgeschichte* 17 (2004): 314–30.

Metzger, Bruce M. *Breaking the Code: Understanding the Book of Revelation*. Nashville: Abingdon, 1993.

———. *The Canon of the New Testament: Its Origin, Development, and Significance*. Oxford: Clarendon, 1997.

Metzger, Paul. *Katechon: II Thess 2,1-12 im Horizont apokalyptischen Denkens*. BZNW 135. Berlin: de Gruyter, 2005.

Moll, Sebastian. *The Arch-Heretic Marcion*. WUNT 250. Tübingen: Mohr Siebeck, 2010.

Mounce, Robert H. *The Book of Revelation*. NICNT. Grand Rapids: Eerdmans, 1977.

Moyise, Steve. "Intertextuality and Biblical Studies: A Review." *Verbum et Ecclesia* 23 (2002): 418–31.

———. "Intertextuality and the Study of the Old Testament in the New Testament." Pages 14–41 in *The Old Testament in the New Testament: Essays in Honour of J. L. North*. Edited by Steve Moyise. JSNTSup 189. Sheffield: Sheffield Academic, 2000.

———. "The Language of the Old Testament in the Apocalypse." *JSNT* 76 (2000): 97–113.

———. "The Psalms in the Book of Revelation." Pages 231–46 in *The Psalms in the New Testament*. Edited by Steve Moyise and Maarten J. J. Menken. London: T&T Clark, 2004.

———. *The Old Testament in the Book of Revelation*. JSNTSymS 115. Sheffield: Academic Press, 1995.

Müller, Ulrich B. "Jesus als 'der Menschensohn.'" Pages 91–129 in *Gottessohn und Menschensohn: Exegetische Studien zu zwei Paradigmen biblischer Intertextualität.* Edited by Dieter Sänger. BTHSt 67. Neukirchen-Vluyn: Neukirchener, 2004.

Murphy, Frederick J. *Fallen is Babylon: The Revelation to John.* Harrisburg, Pa.: Trinity Press International, 1998.

Neusner, Jacob. *What is Midrash?* Philadelphia: Fortress, 1987.

Nickelsburg, George W. *Jewish Literature Between the Bible and the Mishnah.* 2nd ed. Minneapolis: Fortress, 2005.

Nicklas, Tobias. "Die Darstellung von innergemeindlichen Gegnern in der Offenbarung des Johannes." *Rivista di storia del Cristianesimo* 6.2 (2009): 349–61.

———. "Der Ewige spricht in die Zeit—Gotteswort und Menschenwort in der Offenbarung des Johannes." *Sacra Scripta* 9 (2011): 189–95.

———. "Schöpfung und Vollendung in der Offenbarung des Johannes." Pages 389–414 in *Theologies of Creation in Early Judaism and Ancient Christianity: In Honour of Hans Klein.* Edited by Tobias Nicklas and Korinna Zamfir. Deuterocanonical and Cognate Literature Studies 6. Berlin: de Gruyter, 2010.

———. "'Die Seelen der Geschlachteten' (Offb 6,9)? Zum Problem leiblicher Auferstehung in der Offenbarung des Johannes." Pages 329–50 in *The Human Body in Death and Resurrection.* Edited by Tobias Nicklas, Friedrich V. Reiterer, and Joseph Verheyden. DCLY 2009. Berlin: de Gruyter, 2009.

———. "'The Words of the Prophecy of this Book': Playing with Scriptural Authority in the Book of Revelation." Pages 309–26 in *Authoritative Scriptures in Ancient Judaism.* Edited by M. Popović. JSJSup 141. Leiden: Brill: 2010 (Brill E-Books).

Nietzsche, Friedrich. *The Birth of Tragedy and the Genealogy of Morals.* Translated by Francis Golffing. Garden City, N.Y.: Doubleday, 1956.

O'Donovan, Oliver. "The Political Thought of the Book of Revelation." *Tyndale Bulletin* 37.1 (1986): 61–94.

Pattemore, Stephen. *The People of God in the Apocalypse: Discourse, Structure and Exegesis.* SNTSMS 128. Cambridge: Cambridge University Press, 2004.

Paulien, Jon. "Dreading the Whirlwind: Intertextuality and the Use of the Old Testament in Revelation." *Andrews University Seminary Studies* 39 (2001): 5–22.

Petöfi, János S. "Explikative Interpretation. Explikatives Wissen." Pages 184–95 in *Von der verbalen Konstitution zur symbolischen Bedeutung—From Verbal Constitution to Symbolic Meaning.* Edited by J. S. Petöfi and T. Olivi. Papiere zur Textlinguistik 62. Hamburg: Buske, 1988.

Porteous, Norman W. *Das Buch Daniel.* Das Alte Testament Deutsch 23. Göttingen: Vandenhoeck & Ruprecht, 1985.

Portier-Young, Anathea. *Apocalypse Against Empire: Theologies of Resistance in Early Judaism.* Grand Rapids: Eerdmans, 2011.

Raabe, Paul R. "Daniel 7: Its Structure and Role in the Book." *HAR* 9 (1986): 267–76.

Räisänen, Heikki. "Revelation, Violence, and War: Glimpses of a Dark Side." Pages 151–65 in *The Way the World Ends? The Apocalypse of John in Culture* and Ideology. Edited by William John Lyons and Jorunn Økland. Sheffield: Sheffield Phoenix, 2009.

Ratzinger, Joseph (Pope Benedict XVI). *Church, Ecumenism, & Politics: New Endeavors in Ecclesiology.* San Francisco: Ignatius, 2008 (1987).

Reynolds, Benjamin E. *The Apocalyptic Son of Man in the Gospel of John.* WUNT 2.249. Tübingen: Mohr Siebeck 2008.

Rhoads, David, ed. *From Every People and Nation: The Book of Revelation in Intercultural Perspective.* Minneapolis: Fortress, 2005.

Roloff, Jürgen. "Neuschöpfung in der Offenbarung des Johannes." *JBTh* 5 (1990): 120–38.

Rowe, C. Kavin. *Early Narrative Christology: The Lord in the Gospel of Luke.* BZNW 139. Berlin: de Gruyter, 2006.

———. "For Future Generations: Worshipping Jesus and the Integration of the Theological Disciplines." *Pro Ecclesia* 17.2 (2008): 186–209.

———. *World Upside Down: Reading Acts in the Graeco-Roman Age.* Oxford: Oxford University Press, 2009.

Rowland, Christopher C. "The Book of Revelation: Introduction, Commentary, and Reflections." Pages 501–736 in *The New Interpreter's Bible.* Vol. 12. Edited by Fred B. Craddock, Leander E. Keck, Luke Johnson, and Christopher C. Rowland. Nashville: Abingdon, 1998.

Royalty, Robert M., Jr. "The Dangers of the Apocalypse." *Word and World* 25.3 (2005): 283–93.

———. "Don't Touch *This* Book!: Revelation 22:18-19 and the Rhetoric of Reading (in) the Apocalypse of John." *BibInt* 12 (2004): 298–99.

Sänger, Dieter, ed. *Das Ezechielbuch in der Johannesoffenbarung.* BTHSt 76. Neukirchen-Vluyn: Neukirchener, 2006 (2004).

Satake, Akira. *Die Offenbarung des Johannes.* KEK 16. Göttingen: Vandenhoeck & Ruprecht, 2008.

Schnelle, Udo. *Theology of the New Testament.* Translated by M. Eugene Boring. Grand Rapids: Baker Academic, 2009.

Schüssler Fiorenza, Elisabeth. *The Book of Revelation: Justice and Judgement.* Philadelphia: Fortress, 1985.

Slater, Thomas B. *Christ and Community: A Socio-Historical Study of the Christology of Revelation.* JSNTSup 178. Sheffield: Sheffield University Press, 1999.

———. "*Homoion huion anthropou* in Rev 1.13 and 14.14." *BT* 44 (1993): 349–50.

———. "More on Revelation 1.13 and 14.14." *BT* 47 (1996): 146–49.

———. "One Like a Son of Man in First-Century CE Judaism." *NTS* 41.2 (1995): 183–98.

Soulen, Richard N. and R. Kendall Soulen. *Handbook of Biblical Criticism.* Louisville, Ky.: Westminster John Knox, 2001.

Sternberg, Meir. "Proteus in Quotation-Land: Mimesis and the Forms of Reported Discourse." *Poetics Today* 3 (1982): 107–56.

Stuckenbruck, Loren T. *Angel Veneration and Christology: A Study in Early Judaism and in the Christology of the Apocalypse of John.* WUNT 2.70. Tübingen: Mohr Siebeck, 1995.

Theobald, Michael. *Der Römerbrief.* EdF 294. Darmstadt: WBG, 2000.

Thiselton, Anthony C. *New Horizons in Hermeneutics: The Theory and Practice of Transforming Biblical Reading.* London: HarperCollins, 1992.

Tonstad, Sigve K. *Saving God's Reputation: The Theological Function of Pistis Iesou in the Cosmic Narratives of Revelation.* LNTS 337. London: Continuum, 2006.

Tuckett, Christopher. "The Son of Man and Daniel 7: Inclusive Aspects of Early Christologies." Pages 164–90 in *Christian Origins: Worship, Belief and Society.* Edited by Kieran J. O'Mahony. JSNTSup 241. Sheffield: Sheffield Academic, 2003.

VanderKam, James C. "Daniel 7 in the Similitudes of Enoch (1 Enoch 37–71)." Pages 291–307 in *Biblical Traditions in Transmission: Essays in Honour of Michael A. Knibb.* Edited by Charlotte Hempel and Judith M. Lieu. Supplements to the Journal for the Study of Judaism 111. Leiden: Brill 2006.

———. *The Dead Sea Scrolls Today.* Rev. ed. Grand Rapids: Eerdmans, 2010.

Verheyden, Joseph, Andreas Merkt, and Tobias Nicklas, eds. *Interpreting Violent Texts: Ancient Receptions of the Book of Revelation.* NTOA. Göttingen: Vandenhoeck & Ruprecht, 2011.

Vogelgesang, Jeffrey M. "The Interpretation of Ezekiel in the Book of Revelation." Ph.D. diss. Harvard University, 1985.

Von Rad, Gerhard. *Genesis: A Commentary.* OTL. London: SCM, 1972.

Vonach, Andreas. "Der Hochbetagte und sein Umfeld. Von prophetischen Theophanien zu christologischen Epiphanien." Pages 307–30 in *Im Geist und in der Wahrheit. Studien zum Johannesevangelium und zur Offenbarung des Johannes sowie andere Beiträge. Festschrift für Martin Hasitschka SJ zum 65.* Edited by Konrad Huber and Boris Repschinski Geburtstag. NTAbh 52. Münster: Aschendorff, 2008.

Wainwright, Arthur W. *Mysterious Apocalypse: Interpreting the Book of Revelation.* Nashville: Abingdon, 1993.

Wainwright, Geoffrey, ed. *Keeping the Faith: Essays to Mark the Centenary of Lux Mundi.* Minneapolis: Fortress, 1988.

Wanamaker, Charles A. *The Epistles to the Thessalonians: A Commentary on the Greek Text.* NIGTC. Grand Rapids: Eerdmans, 1990.

Weber, Timothy B. *On the Road to Armageddon: How Evangelicals Became Israel's Best Friend.* Grand Rapids: Baker Academic, 2004.

Wells, Samuel. *Transforming Fate into Destiny: The Theological Ethics of Stanley Hauerwas.* Milton Keynes, U.K.: Paternoster, 1998.

Wengst, Klaus. *"Wie lange noch?" Schreien nach Recht und Gerechtigkeit–eine Deutung der Apokalypse des Johannes.* Stuttgart: Kohlhammer, 2010.

Westermann, Claus. *Genesis 1–11: A Commentary.* London: SPCK, 1984.

Wilckens, Ulrich. *Der Brief an die Römer (Röm 12–16).* EKK I.3. Neukirchen-Vluyn: Neukirchener, 2003.

Witulski, Thomas. *Die Johannesoffenbarung und Kaiser Hadrian: Studien zur Datierung der neutestamentlichen Apokalypse.* FRLANT 221. Göttingen: Vandenhoeck & Ruprecht, 2007.

———. *Kaiserkult in Kleinasien: Die Entwicklung der kultisch-religiösen Kaiserverehrung in der römischen Provinz Asia von Augustus bis Antoninus Pius.* NTOA 63. Göttingen: Vandenhoeck & Ruprecht, 2007.

Wright, N. T. "The Fourfold Amor Dei and the Word of God." Online: http://www.ntwrightpage.com/Wright_Vatican_Amor_Dei.htm.

———. *The New Testament and the People of God.* Vol. 1. Minneapolis: Fortress, 1992.

———. *Surprised by Hope.* San Francisco: HarperSanFrancisco, 2007.

Yeago, David S. "The New Testament and the Nicene Dogma: A Contribution to the Recovery of Theological Exegesis." Pages 87–100 in *The Theological Interpretation of Scripture: Classic and Contemporary Readings.* Edited by Stephen E. Fowl. Oxford: Blackwell, 1997.

Zamfir, Korinna. "Male and Female Roles in the Pastoral Epistles." Diss. Habil., Regensburg, 2012.

Zimmermann, Christiane. *Die Namen des Vaters: Studien zu ausgewählten neutestamentlichen Gottesbezeichnungen vor ihrem frühjüdischen und paganen Hintergrund.* AJEC 69. Leiden: Brill, 2007.

Contributors

STEFAN ALKIER, Professor of New Testament and Dean of the Protestant Theological Faculty, Johann Wolfgang Goethe-Universität, Frankfurt am Main, Germany

MICHAEL J. GORMAN, Raymond E. Brown Chair in Biblical Studies and Theology, St. Mary's Seminary and University, Baltimore, Maryland, USA

RICHARD B. HAYS, George Washington Ivey Professor of New Testament and Dean of Duke Divinity School, North Carolina, USA

THOMAS HIEKE, Professor of Old Testament, Johannes Gutenberg University of Mainz, Germany

JOSEPH L. MANGINA, Associate Professor of Systematic Theology, Wycliffe College, University of Toronto, Canada

STEVE MOYISE, Professor of New Testament, University of Chichester, England

TOBIAS NICKLAS, Professor of New Testament Exegesis and Dean of the Catholic Theological Faculty, University of Regensburg, Germany

MARIANNE MEYE THOMPSON, George Eldon Ladd Professor of New Testament, Fuller Theological Seminary, Pasadena, California, USA

N. T. WRIGHT, Research Professor of New Testament and Early Christianity, University of St. Andrews, Scotland

Scripture Index

General Index